MEMORY IN BLACK AND WHITE

MEMORY IN BLACK AND WHITE

Race, Commemoration, and the Post-Bellum Landscape

PAUL A. SHACKEL

A Division of
ROWMAN & LITTLEFIELD PUBLISHERS, INC.

ALTAMIRA
PRESS

Walnut Creek • Lanham • New York • Oxford

ALTAMIRA PRESS
A Division of Rowman & Littlefield Publishers, Inc.
1630 North Main Street, #367
Walnut Creek, CA 94596
www.altamirapress.com

Rowman & Littlefield Publishers, Inc.
A Member of the Rowman & Littlefield Publishing Group
4720 Boston Way
Lanham, MD 20706

PO Box 317, Oxford, OX2 9RU, UK

British Library Cataloguing in Publication Information Available

Library of Congress Cataloging-in-Publication Data

Shackel, Paul A.
Memory in black and white : race, commemoration, and the post-bellum landscape / Paul A. Shackel.
p. cm.
Includes bibliographical references (p.) and index.
ISBN 0-7591-0262-7 (cloth : alk. paper)—ISBN 0-7591-0263-5 (pbk. : alk. paper)
1. United States—History—Civil War, 1861–1865—Influence. 2. United States—Race relations. 3. Southern States—Race relations. 4. United States—History—Civil War, 1861–1865—Monuments. 5. Memory—Social aspects—United States. 6. Memory—Social aspects—Southern States. 7. Racism—United States. 8. Racism—Southern States. 9. Political culture—United States. 10. Political culture—Southern States. I. Title.
E468.9 .S53 2003
973.8—dc21 2002013179

Printed in the United States of America

∞ ™ The paper used in this publication meets the minimum requirements of American National Standard for Information Sciences—Permanence of Paper for Printed Library Materials, ANSI/NISO Z39.48–1992.

CONTENTS

FIGURES

FOREWORD

THE MARKING OF PLACES worth remembering has a long and venerable history in the United States. From the efforts of Ann Pamela Cunningham during the 1850s in preserving the home of George Washington, the preservation/heritage industry has grown today to proportions unimagined by Cunningham and her Mount Vernon Ladies Association. As the preservation of special places has grown over the past century and a half, it has also expanded the scope of the kinds of places appropriate for preservation. For the first fifty years or so after Mount Vernon was saved, the preservation of place was limited largely to the homes of famous Americans: presidents, politicians, and patriots—all men, all white. Indeed, until the second half of the twentieth century, preserved places reflected a very limited slice of the American demographic landscape. This limited view of the American past or, more specifically, what was important to remember about the American past, was also largely in keeping with the manner in which American history was taught and studied in high schools and colleges and universities throughout the country. This dominant narrative about the creation and development of the United States was dominated by men (as historical characters and as historians) and presented as a seamless, upwardly progressive morality tale about the greatness of the country "getting better and better in every way."

Beginning in the 1960s, this country's sense of its history began to change as it became more inclusive. This expanded vision of the past added the historical voices of women, minorities, and labor to the unfolding drama of American history. With a new appreciation for alternative and complementary and sometimes conflicting views of the country's history, the role of preservation and commemoration likewise expanded, producing a richer, more representative characterization of that history on the landscape. The past forty years have been characterized by the preservation of newly recognized historic places that reflect that diversity and by reinterpretation of existing places to present historic voices and views that had been ignored or suppressed under strict adherence to the dominant narrative. Not surprisingly, the expansion of the American story prompted clashes and conflicts in how that past should be presented. In this book, Paul Shackel accurately observes, "Public memory is more a reflection of present political and social relations than a true reconstruction of the past." Arguments over history today reflect deeply felt emotions about who we are as a society, who we have been, and where we think we should be headed.

In an effort to parse out the inherent conflicts that have arisen over the remembering of history, Shackel focuses on the all-important issue of race and reminds us how race and racism have affected and continue to affect the popular presentation of the past and especially of the American Civil War. One does not have to probe very deeply to see how notions about race have shaped the memorial landscape. For example, the statue of Lady Liberty that stands atop the nation's Capitol wears feathers as a headdress instead of the intended freed-slave cap of Roman origin because then–Secretary of War Jefferson Davis thought it might send the wrong message to the four million slaves held in bondage in the antebellum United States. The base of the Iwo Jima statue near Arlington National Cemetery contains the names of all the conflicts fought by the U.S. Marine Corps. One looks in vain for the term "Civil War" because during the 1950s in congressional debate over the memorial, southern representatives insisted on the term "War between the States," invoking late nineteenth- and early twentieth-century attitudes toward the war and its causes. Custer Battlefield National Monument, established in 1946, created a shrine-like environment for the worship of George Armstrong Custer until 1991, when Congress changed the name to Little Bighorn Battlefield National Monument to honor both sides in that conflict. The dedication of the Lincoln Memorial in 1921 took place before a segregated audience.

Shackel's focus on the legacy of nineteenth-century racism at Civil War–related memorials and historic places is important, for discussions about race have been, and in places continue to be, largely absent from interpretive programs. David Blight (1989a:1176) observed over a decade ago that "slavery, the war's deepest cause, and black freedom, the war's most fundamental result, remain the most conspicuous missing elements in the American literature inspired by the Civil War." While discussions of slavery and black freedom are now very much a part of Civil War writings, these issues, so fundamental to understanding the Civil War era, often remain absent from public and popular discussions of the war. Recognizing this, the National Park Service has begun a multiyear effort to expand its interpretation of Civil War battlefields and related sites to include information on slavery as the principal cause of secession, its role in changing the course of the war, and the consequences of the war for both white and black Americans.

Memory in Black and White serves as a strong reminder of how ideas about race have influenced the preservation of places in the past and how it can affect, in both positive and negative ways, the interpretation of historic sites today. It is an important message for all of us who visit historic places, who are curious about the presentation of the past at historic sites and monuments, and who study the past and present dynamic in classrooms and public spaces. The case study approach taken here allows a detailed look at specific places where race and perceptions of race played a role in preserving and interpreting the past. By understanding how past and present generations have interpreted the past through the lens of race, practitioners of public history can better determine how historic sites should be interpreted to present and future generations. Moreover, that same understanding will allow our society to make better decisions about the kind of future we want to create for our children and grandchildren.

Dwight T. Pitcaithley
Chief Historian
National Park Service

PREFACE

SINCE 1989, I have done historical research and historical archaeology at some of the most nationally significant parks in America. Doing research at these parks, I met National Park Service (NPS) professionals who shared my enthusiasm for exploring the historical context of issues related to the social, political, and economic inequities found in the American landscape. I also encountered other professional NPS employees who believed that national parks are a stage for communicating nationally significant stories to the public only as dictated by each park's enabling legislation and that all other histories are unimportant to the park or to the national story. It became apparent that in some cases there is a clear division in both history and interpretation of a park as to what a park should tell the public about its history. After researching the development of different parks, it also became apparent that the enabling legislation for each park was created to support a particular social and/or political climate at a specific time. For instance, in the first part of the twentieth century, national parks were created by Congress to support the ideology of the greatness of our country and the heroics of certain individuals (e.g., George Washington Birthplace National Monument, Fort Raleigh National Historic Site, and Saugus Iron Works National Historic Site). By the last quarter of the century, many newly created national parks celebrated diversity (e.g., Frederick Douglass National Historic Site, Manzanar National Historic Site, and Women's Rights National Historic Park). The internal conflict at many national parks created before the 1970s is about which memory should be fostered. Should these parks continue to support a memory that bolsters nationalism, the kind that propped up the ideology of the great man myth, or should the older parks explore issues that are relevant to society, including issues of social and economic inequities and multiculturalism?

I became fascinated with the way the NPS remembers (or does not remember) some of the issues that are important to so many people today, such as slavery, racism, Reconstruction, Jim Crow, and the Civil Rights movement. How African Americans came to be represented on the American landscape after the Civil War is a complex and dynamic issue. That story is about a struggle between groups, one trying to get representation in the official public memory while the other is intentionally trying to repress it.

Collective memory is the popular notion of the past, and it tends to bolster the image of those being commemorated. Memory often presents an uncomplicated way of seeing the past through deeds and acts that are often simple, thus allowing many to remember what they want to. Histories, symbols, and commemoration ceremonies surrounding the Civil War are often filled with metaphors such as "the war of brother against brother." This "family conflict" allows for a sweeter reconciliation between the North and the South, creating a stronger bond and a more unified nation. "The metaphors transform a social and political conflict into a family saga" (Gorn 2000:B4). The memory of the Civil War that developed in the late nineteenth century and survived into much of the twentieth century created a history of reconciliation between family members and allowed for both sides to claim that they fought for a cause and that they were noble. The issues of slavery and racism were not recognized. In a recent article, James McPherson remarked that it is difficult for southern whites "to admit that the noble Cause for which their ancestors fought might have included the defense of slavery" (McPherson, quoted in Horton 1998:14). African Americans were quickly forgotten in the commemoration of the Civil War because it would be easy to question the nobility of a society when it held others in bondage and racism prevailed (Gorn 2000:B4).

While working on several NPS projects, I observed an especially dynamic relationship between the development of sacred landscapes and racism. Four examples provide the case studies that follow: the John Brown Fort, the Heyward Shepherd Memorial, the Shaw Memorial, and Manassas National Battlefield Park. All have an association with African American history, and their meanings have developed within the context of racism. While they are not necessarily related, racism and memory help shape our modern perceptions of American sacred places. Each case study shows how communities over the past century and a half treated issues of memory, racism, and landscape in different ways and how the outcome of each of these cases is local and unique. At each place, African Americans vied for representation in the official memory in different ways. A material and historical perspective of African American landscapes provides some fascinating stories related to racism and the struggle for representation in the official American memory.

All these scenarios fall within a larger context of how people and groups jockey to become part of the collective memory. While these four in-depth studies are related to the African American situation, I do not intend for them to be the only examples of how subordinate groups view their places within the collective memory. There are additional strategies, beyond the case studies, for becoming part of the public memory. In the epilogue, I provide some suggestions on how groups can do so.

There are several people who were very helpful in my research. For my work at Manassas National Battlefield Park, I am indebted to Jim Burgess and Ray Brown. At Harpers Ferry National Historical Park, I appreciate the assistance provided me by Nancy Hatcher, Bruce Noble, and Donald Campbell. Mary Johnson's article on Heyward Shepherd helped me think about the modern context of the memorial. Gregory Schwarz of Saint-Gaudens National Historic Site gave assistance. Andrea Mark of the Special Collections Division, Chicago Public Library, provided significant information on the John Brown Fort during its tenure in Chicago. I am grateful to Diane Harvey, librarian at the University of Maryland, who furnished assistance while doing research for this manuscript. Steven Pendery shared some contemporary information related to the Shaw Memorial. Susan Walters of AltaMira Press provided guidance and support during the review and rewriting of the manuscript. Paul Mullins, Jim Delle, Ed Linenthal, Dwight Pitcaithley, Erika Martin Seibert, Matthew Reeves, and Matthew Palus, as well as several anonymous reviewers, supplied helpful comments on parts of this manuscript. Barbara Little also provided valuable insights during my writing of this manuscript. I appreciate her enthusiasm and encouragement.

INTRODUCTION

Race as a Social/Historical Construct

Even though the Thirteenth Amendment abolished slavery, the Fourteenth Amendment gave those born in the United States citizenship, and the Fifteenth Amendment gave citizens (including black men) the right to vote, the conflict over racism and slavery has never really been resolved. In 1865, the Civil War was over and the issue of united states was settled. What the war did not accomplish was to change the racial ideologies that had developed in American culture over several centuries. The growth of social Darwinism in the late nineteenth century solidified ideas of race and racism—concepts that only helped to reinforce inequalities. These developments shaped how white Americans viewed and represented African Americans in the public memory and landscape.

In the case studies that follow, I provide four examples that demonstrate how memory and racism on the American landscape changed over the past century. While I show how the ideas of racism developed beginning in the sixteenth century, I also provide a context for how race relations were transformed as the memory of the Civil War changed from the late nineteenth century on. Influential institutions from the North (e.g., the National Association for the Advancement of Colored People [NAACP] and, to a minor extent, the Grand Army of the Republic) and the South (e.g., the United Confederate Veterans, the United Daughters of the Confederacy [UDC], and the Sons of Confederate Veterans [SCV]) struggled over how the Civil War should be remembered, and African Americans invariably lost out to more powerful interest groups. While African Americans continuously struggled to have their story told, it was not until the Civil Rights movement of the 1960s that they gained a more powerful voice in the social and political memory of our nation.

In particular, my examples focus on the National Park Service, keepers and purveyors of much of our national official history. At national parks, the organization uses landscapes, monuments, and structures to tell the story of nation building to millions of visitors every year. While remembering African American history on these public lands has increased significantly over the past several decades, these lands remain contested locales for the meaning of African American history. Becoming part of the national story has often been a struggle to overcome racist views of the past, and national park sites are often where this battle takes place. It is a dynamic process that is unfolding every day, and therefore it is intriguing to trace the development of the African American struggle to become part of the national collective memory at National Park Service sites and how the results of this struggle have varied in time and location.

The precedent for ignoring African Americans on the American landscape has a long history with its roots in the development of racist attitudes in Europe and the colonies in the late sixteenth century. Race is a concept that "signifies and symbolizes social conflicts and interests by referring to different types of human bodies." It is a "sociohistorical process by which racial categories are created, inhabited, transformed, and destroyed (Omi and Winant 1994:55). While people may interchange or confuse the concepts of ethnicity and race, the differences are important. Ethnic groups have always existed as clusters of people living in demarcated areas, developing lifestyles and language features that distinguish them from others. They perceive themselves as separate societies with distinct histories. However, ethnicity was never seen as "set in stone," and individuals or groups often moved to new areas, changed their identities, or acquired membership in different groups. And if outsiders (barbarians) could learn to speak the language, as in Roman and Greek societies, they could become participants in that culture and even citizens of the state. Therefore, ethnicity was fluid and malleable, and kinship connections operated as major indices of who people were. Other variables, such as occupation, beliefs, education, lifestyle, and geographic location, also determined how people were viewed and treated (Bonnett 1998; Fields 1982:144; Smedley 1998:690–95).

Domination over others depended on ethnicity rather than race, and variation among human groups was not given significant social meaning. For instance, fair-skinned Slavs (slaves) were traded down the Danube River by German tribesmen and could be sold anywhere in the Middle East. In another case, Islamic Moors from North Africa occupied part of

Iberia from A.D. 711 through 1492. They brought with them settlers and enslaved people of many nationalities, including Jews, Moors, Turks (Egyptians, Syrians, and Lebanese), white Christians (Sardinians, Greeks, and Russians), Canary Island natives (Guanches), and black Africans. The words "slave" and "African" were not synonymous. The laws that governed slavery were based on the thirteenth-century codes of the Castilian king Alfonse X. As under Islamic law, all people were born free, and enslavement was an unnatural state justified as a consequence of war or the refusal to accept a conqueror's religion. Spanish slave codes allowed enslaved people to keep family cohesion, buy their freedom, and sue their masters for mistreatment (Deagan and MacMahon 1995:6). "Only occasionally do ancient writers remark on the physical characteristics of a given person. No structuring of inequality, whether social, moral, intellectual, cultural or otherwise, was associated with people because of their skin color" (Smedley 1998:693).

Several centuries later, the creation of the concept of race changed the way people perceived human differences. It imposed social meaning on physical variations between human groups and served as a basis for structuring the total society. It became prominent in the structuring of inequalities in the American colonies, and it soon spread to other parts of the world when they too were colonized by western Europeans (Smedley 1998:693).

While race is based on physical differences, its real meaning is embedded in social and political realities. The term "race" had no clear meaning until the eighteenth century. While the English were busy conquering the world, they developed attitudes that had not appeared before in Western history. They created a new kind of understanding and interpretation of human differences. Unlike many other conquerors in the past, the English settlers in North America failed to assimilate the American Indians into their groups. They kept them at a great distance socially and called them "savages" (Smedley 1998:693).

The English also had a long history of animosity toward the Irish, creating mechanisms by which to identify them as "other." While relegating the Irish to a subordinate group, the English developed and institutionalized the concept of "savagery," a term that became very prominent in the early evolutionary theories of nineteenth-century anthropologists such as Lewis Henry Morgan and E. B. Tyler. The English expressed a hatred of both Irish culture and people, and this sentiment reached its peak during the sixteenth and seventeenth centuries when the English began their settlement of North America (Smedley 1998:694). This hatred, considered an early form of racism, provided an "other" that could be compared to the constructed identity of the "civilized" English. The concept of savagery carried with it many negative and stereotypical characteristics that contrasted with the vision and ideals that the English created of their own uniqueness (Allan 1994).

According to Richard Dyer, the British created an ideology that made the Irish an inferior group by comparing them to Africans. For example, the nineteenth-century physician John Beddoe

> invented the "index of nigrescence," a formula to identify the racial components of a given people. He concluded that the Irish were darker than the people of eastern and central England, and were closer to the aborigines of the British Isles, who in turn had traces of "negro" ancestry in their appearances. (Curtis, quoted in Dyer 1997:52)

With the rise of the Irish liberation movement in the mid-nineteenth century, British scholars increasingly compared the Irish to chimpanzees and gorillas. The Irish were seen as the missing link between apes and humans, an idea that developed in the 1840s and did not die out until the 1920s (Dyer 1997:52; Rolston 1999:95–102).

Race thus emerged as a social classification by which to create "otherness" in much the same way that the concept of savagery developed. Theodore Allan (1994) and many others (see, e.g., Breene and Innes 1980; Handlin and Handlin 1950; Jordan 1978:278; Kulikoff 1986; Morgan 1975) discuss the invention of white race and use the Chesapeake region as a good example for examining the development of racism in the New World. Racism was not codified in the first half of the seventeenth-century Chesapeake region because the demands and rewards of the tobacco economy unleashed a sense of individualism and worked against the social cohesion necessary to forge highly structured hierarchies. Breene and Innes (1980:49) claim that "the planters were, in one important respect, quite without prejudice: they were willing to employ any kind of labor, and under any institutional arrangements, as long as the labor force was politically defenseless enough for the work to be done cheaply and under discipline." It was under these circumstances that indentured servants and free whites and blacks operated in their Chesapeake communities.

Interaction between nongentry whites, such as small planters and indentured servants, and blacks occurred on a daily basis. "The two races exchanged land, traded livestock, worked for each other, sued one another, and socialized together" (Breene and Innes 1980:104). Some white servants lived with and worked for black planters (Breene and Innes 1980:105). Until the 1660s, statutes applied to enslaved blacks were similar to those for white servants. Legislators applied stiff penalties to blacks and whites equally for running away, drunkenness, and carrying arms. Over time, these regulations grew less stringent for white servants, but little changed for blacks (Handlin and Handlin 1950:244; Morgan 1975).

Differential treatment between blacks and whites created a division of interest through racial contempt. For instance, white servants who ran away with an enslaved person had their sentences doubled, for their lost time and that of the slave (Handlin and Handlin 1950:244). The division between whites and blacks in the consciousness of the freedmen appeared to be working by the 1660s. As Winthrop Jordan (1978:278) notes, "White men were loudly protesting against being made 'slaves' in terms which strongly suggest that they considered slavery not as wrong but as inappropriate to themselves." Even black servants were increasingly unable to protect themselves against this racist legislation. "White men were more clearly free because Negroes had become so clearly slave" (Jordan 1978:278).

In 1662, the Virginia legislature declared that "'if any Christian shall commit Fornication with a Negro man or woman, he or she soe offending' should pay double the usual fine" (Jordan 1978:277). The following year, the Maryland legislature declared that "Negroes were to serve 'Durante Vita,'" their entire lives (Jordan 1978:279; see also Handlin and Handlin 1950:241). By 1669, the beating of slaves was formalized by legislation (Morgan 1975:312). Within several years of Bacon's Rebellion of 1676, an insurrection of small planters, indentured servants, and enslaved blacks, a Virginian law established "an Act preventing Negroe Insurrection" and stated that negroes and slaves could not own guns (Breene and Innes 1980:27). In 1681, a Maryland act described mixed marriages as a "disgrace not only of the English butt also of many other Christian Nations" (Jordan 1978:277). After 1691, marriages between enslaved people and freemen became illegal. Consequently, by the end of the seventeenth century, legislation was couched in the terms of race, black and white. By the first decade of the 1700s, "white servants were as much the exception in the tobacco fields as slaves had been earlier" (Morgan 1975:308), reflecting the effectiveness of this codification.

The 1710s and 1720s witnessed another dramatic surge in racist legislation in Maryland, and this prohibiting legislation was masked as a naturalizing ideology. For instance, interracial marriage or copulation was prohibited because it was "unnatural or inordinate." In 1728, an act was passed "for the punishment of negro women, having bastard children by white men; and for as much as such copulation are as unnatural and inordinate as between white women and negroe men" (Kilty 1799:203). Quotas were also placed on segments of the white population. For instance, numerous laws were enacted to "prevent the importing too great a number of Irish papists into the province" (Kilty 1799:197).

The 1710s and 1720s saw more racist legislation passed than in any decade before or after. This legislation was a product of an increasing number of family dynasties elected to the Maryland assemblies in the early eighteenth century who developed political monopolies to protect their place in the hierarchy. By the 1720s, 60 percent of those elected had Maryland-born fathers. After this date, the number increased to 84 percent (Kulikoff 1986). Racist legislation was one tool that created a clear position in the hierarchy for an increasing number of enslaved people and indentured servants so that they would not threaten the established hierarchy.

> The power of whiteness depended not only on white hegemony over separate racialized groups, but also on manipulating racial outsiders to fight against one another, to compete with each other for white approval, and to seek the rewards and privileges of whiteness for themselves at the expense of other racialized populations. (Lipsitz 1998:3)

For instance, during the Stono Rebellion of 1739, colonists offered Indians a bounty for the capture or killing of escaped African Americans. At the same time, the British recruited black enslaved people to fight against Indians within the colonial militia (Nash 1974).

The new racial ideology that developed in western Europe and the Americas structured political, social, and economic inequalities as countries from these regions conquered and exploited a large part of the world. This new racial ideology contradicted the development of Renaissance ideals that promoted freedom, democracy, equality, and human rights. Europeans naturalized their new racial attitudes by focusing on physical differences and concluded that Africans and Indians were a lesser form of human beings dictated by the laws of nature, or that it was God given (Smedley 1998:694). Whites relegated blacks to a low status and constantly portrayed them as "culturally backward, primitive, intellectually stunted, prone to violence, morally corrupt, undeserving of the benefits of civilization, insensitive to the finer arts, and (in the case of Africans) aesthetically ugly and animal like" (Smedley 1998:695). Race identity took priority over all other forms of identity that once guided socialization and group interaction.

In England, Charles White observed in his 1799 treatise that

> ascending the line of gradation, we come at the last to the white European; who being most removed from the brute creation, may on that account, be considered the most beautiful of the human races. . . . Where shall we find, unless in the European, that nobly arched head . . . those rosy cheeks and coral lips? Where that erect posture and noble gait? In what other quarter of the globe shall we find the blush that overspreads the soft features of the beautiful women of Europe, that emblem of modesty, of delicate feelings, and of sense? Where that nice expression of the amiable and softer passions in the countenance; And that general elegance of features and complexion? Where, except on the bosom of the European woman, two such plump and snowy white hemispheres, tipt with vermilion. (Quoted in Dyer 1997:71)

In the early nineteenth-century United States, poor whites had little property and few economic advantages, but the concept of race was often used to divide lower groups. Theodore Allan (1994:154) quotes a person in the May 4, 1832, *Richmond Observer* who claimed that the poor whites had "little but their complexion to console them for being born into a higher caste." Richard Dyer (1997:52) remarks that color and the distinction of race were enough to quell any dissatisfaction with the established hierarchy. In the creation of race, whiteness meant that even the poor whites could have access to privilege, power, and wealth, and with the expansion of the northern industrial economy in the mid-nineteenth century and the postbellum era, it also meant that they could have access to jobs.

While the American Civil War helped reunite the United States and slavery was legally dissolved, racial ideologies remained, and the barriers that prevented blacks from integrating into American society still existed (Blight 2001). After the Civil War, a time when the United States was transforming itself into a major industrial power, a labor shortage existed in the North. Blacks had a unique opportunity to be integrated into the industrial mainstream. However, Americans continued to paint blacks as inferior and instead relied on white European immigrants to fuel late nineteenth-century industry. Whites prohibited blacks from learning new skills that would allow them to compete with whites for industrial jobs. Therefore, with the aid of northern industrialists and southern agriculturalists dependent on black labor to produce cotton, blacks returned to the fields as tenant farmers and sharecroppers (Horton 2000). Nineteenth-century sciences and social sciences also helped reinforce these racial views.

Race and Anthropology

Anthropology's roots exist within the Western natural history tradition that encouraged social observers to classify and compare human populations. By the 1830s, Samuel Morton became the authority on explaining racial differences with his book *Crania Americana* (1839). His "American School" generated some of the first theories on race developed in America that received global attention. Morton's contemporaries believed that all humans descended from Noah about 1,000 years ago. Morton, on the other hand, proposed a theory of polygenesis, and it attracted an enthusiastic following. According to Morton, blacks and Caucasians were already distinct 3,000 years ago, and Noah's sons could not account for all the racial variation. Morton scientifically "proved" that Caucasians were intellectually superior by measuring skull capacity. Caucasians had big brains with an average size of eighty-seven cubic inches, Indians fell in the middle (eighty-two cu. in.), and blacks had the smallest brain size (seventy-eight cu. in.) (Thomas 2000:38–42).

In pre–Civil War America, the country had to cope with the inconsistencies found in the dealing with the Declaration of Independence. If all men were created equal and if enslaved blacks were part of the same Caucasian stock, then this argument would support the abolitionist movement. But many whites enthusiastically supported Morton, who showed with his cranial capacity experiments and his theory of polygenesis that blacks were inferior. Multiple creations meant that blacks were created for the purpose of serving whites under the system of slavery (Thomas 2000:42).

Late nineteenth-century anthropologists, such as Lewis Henry Morgan and E. B. Tyler, proponents of unilinear evolution, worked with physical anthropologists to create a "scientific" rank of human groups that ranged from savagery to barbarism to civilization. Western societies achieved the rank of civilization, while new groups encountered through exploration and imperialism were placed in the other two categories (Mukhopadhyay and Moses 1997:517–18). According to the unievolutionists, mental development (intellectual and moral) was crucial to a group's progress and helped fuel evolutionary advancement. Facial projection and the position of the foramen magnum (the opening in the base of the skull through which the brain stem passes as it becomes the spinal cord) determined evolutionary rank. The concept of linking mental and physical traits lasted well into the twentieth century (Blakey 1987; Mukhopadhyay and Moses 1997; Smedley 1993).

Many of the unievolutionists also adhered to the ideals of social Darwinism. They argued that people struggled to survive, and therefore the rich and powerful must be the "fittest" in any evolutionary scheme. Social Darwinism became another justification for global imperialism and racism (Thomas 2000:49–50).

During the early twentieth century, psychometrics and intelligence tests were developed, first used on American military recruits during World War I and then adapted for civilian use. People interpreted results of these tests as heredity based or showing innate intelligence, and they compared scores to reinforce natural racial superiority:

> Anthropology, then, helped erect an elaborate ideological edifice—biological and racial determinism—that has deeply influenced how the world understands human variation and human behavior. This racial worldview also provided a rationale for slavery, colonialism and neocolonial domination, racial segregation, and discrimination and miscegenation movements in the United States. (Mukhopadhyay and Moses 1997:518)

While many anthropologists backed these racial typologies, some scholars tried to dismantle these constructed racial views. For instance, in 1897, Franz Boas questioned the premise behind unilinear evolution and challenged the notion that race was biologically fixed and permanent and that people could be ranked in proximity to apes (Mukhopadhyay and Moses 1997:518). Some anthropologists see Boas's *The Mind of the Primitive Man* (1911) as an important publication that placed cultural relativism and muticulturalism as important concepts in anthropological thinking. In this publication, he stressed the importance of environment over heredity in creating human populations. The work challenged the celebration of Western civilization and stressed the importance of other cultures and experiences as valid cultural expressions (Roseberry 1992:848; Visweswaran 1998:70). In *Changes in Bodily Form of Descendants of Immigrants* (1912), Boas demonstrated that morphological features, including core racial indicators such as head form, could change in a single generation because of nutritional, environmental, or cultural factors (Blakey 1987; Mukhopadhyay and Moses 1997:518). Paul Rabinow (1992:60) claims that "Boas' arguments against racial hierarchies and racial thinking have thoroughly carried the theoretical day."

Despite the efforts of Boas, a strong proponent of cultural relativism, racial typologies persisted in the mainstream culture. However, Nazism and the widespread genocide carried out in the name of creating a racially pure society caused anthropologists to reexamine racial typologies more critically. In 1938, Boas persuaded the American Anthropological Association to pass a resolution denouncing Nazi racism (Visweswaran 1998:71). After World War II, American anthropologists argued against the old classifications of racial construction and supported a socially and culturally constructed form of race. In 1952, the United Nations Educational, Scientific, and Cultural Organization (UNESCO) rejected the linkage between sociocultural capacities and biology. Carol Mukhopadhyay and Yolanda Moses (1997:519) explain:

> Evolutionary theory applied to nonhuman organisms had already produced critiques of the subspecies concept and made it easier to view hereditary variability among humans in terms of geographic gradients or clines that crosscut population boundaries. These new data and theoretical paradigms, emerging in the historical context of the American civil rights movement, stimulated the outpouring of literature on race that characterized the 1960s.

Leonard Leiberman and Fatimah Jackson (1995) show that racial thinking and the use of racial terms still exist in many of the biological sciences despite evidence derived from analyses of serogenetic, nuclear DNA, mitochondrial DNA, Y-chromosome polymorphism, and skeletal data (Keita and Kittles 1997:541). However, while racism has hardly disappeared from the American landscape, racism is no longer a scientifically credible position in much of anthropology (Rabinow 1992:60).

Meaning, Memory, and Power

I believe it is important to place the development of racism within the context of memory and power. Eric Hobsbawm (1983a:13) writes, "The history which became part of the fund of knowledge or the ideology of nation, state or movement is not what has actually been preserved in popular memory, but what has been selected, written, pictured, popularized and institutionalized by those whose function it is to do so."

Traditions, meanings, and memories are invented, and they become legitimate through repetition or a process of formalization and ritualization characterized by reference to the past. By implying continuity with the past (and sometimes that is a matter of forgetting a past) or by reinventing a collective memory, these traditions reinforce values and behavior (Hobsbawm 1983a:1–5). Some important works in archaeology that critically evaluate the production of history include those written by Mark Leone et al. (1987), Michael Shanks and Christopher Tilley (1987), and Bruce Trigger (1989). These works evaluate the management and use of prehistoric and historic resources and view the production of historical consciousness as an outcome of the struggle between competing groups.

Memory is important in creating national histories and inspiring nationalism (see, e.g., Howe 1999:222–39; Nora 1999). Nation-states tend to be rooted in tradition, and this memory of the past appears to be "so 'natural' as to require no definition other than self assertion" (Hobsbawm 1983a:14). Official histories of a nation require consensus building and the construction of a history from multiple, often conflicting memories (Anderson 1991:163–85; Kohl 1998:225; Scham 1998:301–8; Trigger 1989).

Public memory is more a reflection of present political and social relations than a true reconstruction of the past. As present conditions change socially, politically, and ideologically, the collective memory of the past will also change. The control of a group's memory is usually a question of power. Individuals and groups frequently struggle over the meaning of memory, as the official memory is often imposed by the power elite (Teski and Climo 1995:2). For instance, Richard Handler and Eric Gable's *The New History in an Old Museum: Creating the Past at Colonial Williamsburg* (1997) serves as an excellent example of deconstructing the production of history in an outdoor museum such as Colonial Williamsburg. They reveal that the museum's interpretation of the colonial era is a way to reinforce social inequalities in contemporary society. This observation has also been expressed by others (Leone 1981; Wallace 1981). Anthropologist Michel-Rolph Trouillot (1995:15) produces a compelling argument for taking a critical approach to historical narratives. Examining accounts that range from Columbus Day to the Haitian Revolution for independence, he notes that the past can be understood only in the present context. He recognizes that during the production of history, power operates in a way that silences subaltern groups.

Historians, too, often view memories as subordinated to group interests. Influential works by John Bodnar (1992), Michael Frisch (1990), David Glassberg (1990), Michael Kammen (1991), Edward Linenthal (1993), and David Lowenthal (1985) have guided public historians into addressing issues that show the connectedness between memory and power. Their work shows that we cannot assume that all groups, and all members of the same group, understand the past in the same way. The same historical and material representation may have divergent meanings for different audiences (Glassberg 1996:9–10; Lowenthal 1985), and there is often a struggle to create or subvert a past by various competing interest groups (see, e.g., Neustadt and May 1986; Peterson 1994). Different versions of the past are communicated through various institutions, including schools, amusement parks, art and literature, government ceremonies, families and friends, and landscape features designated as historical. Therefore, public memory does not rely solely on professional historical scholarship, but it takes into account the various individuals and institutions that affect and influence the versions of histories that have become part of the collective memory.

Analysis of the construction of history and public memory has taken on a renewed interest, especially when dealing with memory of the recent past and justification for the present (see, e.g., C. Blake 1999:423–35; Daynes 1997; Peri 1999:106–24). Many scholars are paying considerable attention to the memory of a generation that is coming to a close, the histories associated with World War II (Epstein 1999; La Capra 1998), and the creation of modern Europe in the post–World War II era (Markovits and Reich 1997). Remembering the Vietnam era has also occupied the scholarship of memory in recent years (see, e.g., Hass 1998).

How we remember and reinterpret a past also serves to create ethnic identities for communities, such as African Americans (Bethel 1997; Fraser 1998), native peoples in Mexico (Florescano 1994), the people of rural Australia (Goodall 1999:160–90), and those in Lesotho (Rosenberg 1999). Selective memory of the past has also been used by groups to create and justify racism and ethnic cleansing (Coslovich 1994; Larson 1999:335–62).

One of the most highly acclaimed books on the development of public memory is Michael Kammen's *Mystic Chords of Memory: The Transformation of Tradition in American Culture* (1991). He remarks that since World War II, commemoration activities in the United States have become increasingly decentralized as the federal government has played a decreasing role in the construction of public memory. The development of public memory has most recently been about consensus building that leads to social and political stability. According to Kammen (1991), the increasing interest in local events has produced depoliticized commemorations. While Kammen sees the decentralization of commemoration as a depoliticized process, others see decentralization as highly politicized. Those who are able to commemorate the past are those who have the money and political power to publicly remember a particular past. Harvey Kaye (1994:257) remarks that Kammen's work is another version of "consensus history." While Kammen sees the development of decentralizing commemoration for the sake of tradition, Kaye sees this process more as the step toward reinforcing hegemony. The governing class secures its political and social standing in society through consensus building. Kaye's criticism takes one of the most influential works on public memory and argues that power, rather than consensus, constructs public memory. The development of history and commemoration at all levels of society is not conflict free; rather, it is tied to hegemony and the powerful (see Daynes 1997:3–4).

Recognizing various types of power is valuable when examining issues related to the creation of public memory. Eric Wolf (1990) describes four modes of power: "The first is power as the capability of a person; the second is power as the ability of a person to impose upon another interpersonally; the third is tactical power which controls social settings, and the fourth is structural power, which allocates social labor" (from Little 1994:23). Contextualizing the use of power in relationship to public memory allows us to recognize the complexity of the use of power and its connections to public memory.

Public memory can be viewed as tactical power that controls social settings. Competing groups battle ceaselessly to create and control the collective national memory of revered sacred sites and objects. Different group agendas often clash, causing the established collective memories to be continuously in flux. Some subordinate groups can subvert the dominant memory, other groups compromise and become part of a multivocal history, while others fail completely to have their story remembered by the wider society. The tensions between and within groups who struggle for control over the collective public memory is ongoing since the political stakes are high.

History, Memory, and Racism

Understanding the ways histories are made and shaped by the social and political environment is important for creating a reflexive interpretation of culture. One important study that examines changing official memory of African Americans is Rebecca Kook's (1998:155) study of the changing attitudes toward racism in the United States. She shows how there has been a gradation of citizenship for African Americans, and she demonstrates the relationship between the institution of citizenship and the American collective identity. She sees the Civil Rights movement of the 1960s as the turning point of increased African American representation on the American landscape and in the public memory. Until recently, African Americans (along with women and American Indians) were seen as outside the value system that promotes American ideals. For blacks, the Emancipation Proclamation and the Reconstruction Amendments offered a chance of full citizenship and inclusiveness on the national level. But with the end of Reconstruction and the development of Jim Crow legislation in the South and the maintenance of severe informal discrimination in the North, any gains were rendered short lived.

The exclusion of blacks from the national consciousness was an active process that was reinforced through written symbols, material symbols, and commemoration. While all blacks were American citizens from the time of the Reconstruction Amendments, it was close to a hundred years before they could gain inclusion in the collective memory of the United States. For instance, textbooks from the first part of the twentieth century rarely mentioned blacks, and when they did, it was usually with racist overtones. While the racist language decreased significantly by the middle of the century, African Americans were only part of the American consciousness as slaves. They were not part of the American collective identity (Kook 1998:160; see also Kane 1970). For instance, a representative textbook of the 1950s would "beg[i]n its first section on the population of the US by saying, 'leaving aside the Negro and Indian population,' and it proceeded to do just that. The Blacks were never treated as a group at all; they were quite literally invisible" (Fitzgerald, quoted in Kook 1998:160).

Textbooks published after the mid-1960s began to tell a very different story. The amount of attention paid to African Americans increased dramatically. Before the mid-1960s, the only blacks mentioned were Booker T. Washington and Dred Scott. After this point, more personalities appear, including sports figures, artists, musicians, and politicians. Blacks were portrayed in a positive light and seen as positive role models. These changes occurred in the United States as the general collective memory began to stress concepts such as multiculturalism, ethnicity, and group and minority identity (Kook 1998:161–62).

Material culture and objects with African American representation exhibit the same pattern. A survey of postal stamps shows that until 1965, only five American stamps portrayed African Americans or represented African American issues. Between 1965 and 1990, twenty-three stamps commemorated African Americans. In 1981, the Black Heritage series was created, issuing at least one new stamp almost every year (Kook 1998:163). Other commemorative activities developed after 1965 include the creation of two national holidays. In 1976, President Ford proclaimed National Black History Month, an outgrowth of Negro History Week and the later Black History Month, established by Carter Woodson in 1926. The second commemorative holiday established was Martin Luther King Jr. Day in 1986 (Kook 1998:163–64).

In 1970, the National Park Service initiated a program to designate important sites related to African Americans as National Historic Landmarks. Initially, thirteen sites were chosen, including the church from which Martin Luther King Jr. preached during the bus boycott and the Harriet Tubman Home for the Aged in Auburn, New York. By 1977, an additional sixty-one sites had been added to the list (Mackintosh 1985).

Kook (1998:165) argues that the 1970s ushered in a new inclusion of African American representation in American culture and into the American consciousness. Black history became part of many public and academic institutions. Although Americans had institutionalized racism with Jim Crow legislation and the *Plessy v. Ferguson* decision, these institutions began to falter under the 1964 Civil Rights Act. The act covered many aspects of race relations, including voting, public accommodations, employment, education, and health care. Title 4 gave the Department of Justice the power to cut off federal funding to any state agency that engaged in discriminatory practices. "It empowered the Department of Justice to initiate suits aimed at desegregation and to intervene in voting rights cases" (Kook 1998:167). Under Title 2, which referred to public accommodations, segregation in public places, such as restaurants, hotels, and theaters, was eliminated. Thus, the symbolic displays of exclusion are slowly disappearing from the landscape. The Civil Rights Act helped change the American landscape. What was once defined solely as a white landscape is becoming more multiracial. It is now easier to incorporate African Americans into the national collective memory.

Racism and the American Landscape

Even though two peoples may share a common history, it does not mean that they shared a common experience. Material culture, be it in the form of statues, monuments, museums, artifacts, or landscapes, has some ascribed meaning (past and present) associated with it, and these meanings vary among individuals and interest groups. This material culture can be transformed into sacred objects when it serves the goals and needs of any group. Governments use objects and material culture to perpetuate a national heritage. They often present an interpretation of the past that seems authentic, but a closer contextual analysis of the meaning of national sacred objects shows how their meanings are not fixed but rather created. They are malleable and a product of an interest group trying to reinforce its power. Often, race is at the center of the struggles for creation of power and meaning.

In this book, I provide a context for the memory of African Americans and their involvement in the Civil War and how this memory changed from Reconstruction, Jim Crow, and through the civil rights era. In chapter I, I examine the development of the phenomenon known as the Lost Cause, a southern ideology justifying the Confederacy's participation in the Civil War. Controlling public memory after the Civil War and promoting the Lost Cause ideology was a highly contested issue until the death of Frederick Douglass and the *Plessy v. Ferguson* decision in the 1890s. After these events and through the Jim Crow era, African American participation in the Civil War disappeared from the American memory until the Civil Rights movement in the 1960s. Through the 1960s and into the new century, blacks have continually struggled to have their history and participation in the Civil War represented in the official memory. Their story has met resistance, especially from many southern heritage groups, although African Americans are increasingly appropriating significant landscape symbols in the effort to reclaim their history.

My first case study examines memory, racism, and the meaning of the

John Brown Fort. This structure was occupied by John Brown before his final capture in Harpers Ferry, and it became a significant abolitionist symbol for whites and blacks. John Brown captured the United States Armory on October 16, 1859, with the hope of arming enslaved and free blacks and ending the institution of slavery. Even though Brown's raid failed, his actions solidified northern abolitionist sentiment, and many historians claim that his actions helped ignite the Civil War. While the fort became an abolitionist symbol and part of the official memory, its abolitionist meaning waned dramatically in the white community from the beginning of the Jim Crow era. African American groups, however, continued to use the structure in rallying for equal rights. It served as a prominent feature during the Second Niagara movement in 1906 (the predecessor to the NAACP) and was eventually moved to the grounds of Storer College, an African American institution established for the education of newly freed slaves. It was eventually moved to the center of Harpers Ferry National Historical Park during the Civil Rights movement. Its relocation to a more visible place was a way that the federal government incorporated a symbol embraced by the minority community and made it part of the country's official memory in order to help quell civil unrest.

The second case study explores racism in the various meanings associated with the memory of the Heyward Shepherd and the Heyward Shepherd Memorial located in Lower Town Harpers Ferry. The monument was originally conceived of as the Faithful Slave Memorial by the UDC (supported also by the SCV) as a way to justify the institution of slavery. During the southern revisionist movement that accelerated during the Jim Crow era, both the UDC and the SCV believed that they should honor black slaves who did not overthrow the plantation system while most of the white Confederates were away from home fighting the war. Some southerners were appalled by the thought of honoring black slaves, while many pro-abolitionists and blacks abhorred the idea of having a monument that claimed that enslaved people were content with their situation. The monument was unveiled with great ceremony in 1931 and has remained controversial throughout its existence, especially since today it sits in a national park. This chapter traces the meaning of the monument from its planning in the early twentieth century until the present. I show how various groups, such as the National Park Service, the NAACP, and various southern heritage groups (e.g., the UDC and the SCV), continue their struggle to create and define an official meaning for the monument.

The third case study considers the context of the Robert Gould Shaw

Memorial and the issue of African American representation in statuary form after the American Civil War. Robert Gould Shaw led the first northern-raised African American troops into battle in 1863. They suffered major losses, including the death of Shaw, on their attack of Fort Wagner in South Carolina. The event became a moral victory among the abolitionist community since it demonstrated to the world that blacks could fight—and well. More than thirty years later, Augustus Saint-Gaudens created a monument to Shaw, using his black troops as a backdrop. Like any symbol, the monument can be read in many different ways. Throughout the Jim Crow era many citizens interpreted the monument as a tribute to the white colonel, while others noted that it served as a racist symbol since Shaw sits on a horse above his marching black troops. While art critics debated over its meaning, the black community co-opted the statue's meaning in the late twentieth century since it is only one of a few Civil War monuments that includes black representation. In 1997, the Robert Gould Shaw Memorial became officially known as the Augustus Saint-Gaudens Monument to Robert Gould Shaw and the Fifty-Fourth Massachusetts Regiment in a ceremony attended by Henry Louis Gates (Du Bois Institute, Harvard University), Benjamin Payton (president, Tuskegee University), and General Colin Powell.

The fourth case study explores racism and the construction of memory on the battlefield landscape at Manassas, Virginia. At the site of the First and Second Battles of Manassas (known in the North as the First and Second Battles of Bull Run), the SCV took an active role to create a commemorative landscape and make it part of the national memory. From the early Jim Crow era, the SCV held reenactments and celebrations to commemorate these two southern victories and reinforce the myth of the faithful slave. The battlefield became a national park in 1940, and even today the National Park Service has a narrow interpretive focus, and park personnel claim that its sole mission is only to interpret the battles. In the National Park Service's interpretation, the issue of slavery is not connected to the Civil War, and African American representation on the battlefield landscape is slowly being eliminated by the park. These actions come at a time when a congressional mandate requires battlefield parks to incorporate issues related to slavery when interpreting battlefields. Recently, the park removed from the landscape the remains of a structure that is important for interpreting African Americans in the Manassas community. National Park Service employees claimed that the structure did not fit within its congressional interpretive mandate. Despite this mandate and instructions from the director of the National Park Service, the official history at the battlefield park concentrates on troop movements rather than the broader social issues related to slavery. The national park has an exhibit panel that addresses the issue of slavery but does not connect slavery to the Civil War. The larger context of the war and the role of the Manassas African American community is nonexistent in the park.

All the case studies are about different and changing perceptions of race, the use of power, and the ability to use resources to control public memory. In none of these cases has a consensus been reached, but groups continue to struggle to have their history and meaning become part of public history. Today, many social scientists see race as a social construction that has nothing to do with physical differences but, rather, something to do with power, privilege, and wealth. They believe that it is far more accurate to define people by their sense of community, consciousness, and commitment rather than race. Unfortunately, racism has been very active in structuring the official history of America. Racism is a powerful tool that defines hierarchy, and it uses symbols, such as buildings, statues, landscapes, and monuments, to create and reinforce these meanings. Changes in the meanings of these symbols are closely associated with tensions between competing groups, and in this book I show the conflict within and between groups for control over meaning. As we plan the care and interpretation of our historic landscapes for the twenty-first century, it is urgent that we make ourselves aware of how these material symbols convey messages of race and power.

Contested Memories of the Civil War I

Reconstruction and the Creation of Memory

Early Memorialization and Resistance

Many scholars will agree that current social and political circumstances influence the way we view and interpret the past. Differences survive between regions, states, and ethnic groups, and confrontations exist at the local and national levels. Tensions also flare between state and national institutions, and these differences festered through the Reconstruction, Jim Crow, and civil rights eras. While the federal government has a policy of nondiscrimination mandated by the Civil Rights Act of 1964, African Americans continue to struggle for inclusion in the public memory of the Civil War. The control for the memory of the Civil War has been an ongoing struggle, and national parks have been the arena for some of this debate.

Whoever controls the public memory of the events of the Civil War controls the historical consciousness that interprets those events. Much of the memory of the war that we celebrate today developed at the beginning of the Jim Crow era and solidified through the early to mid-twentieth century. As David Blight (1989a:1159) writes,

> Historical memory . . . was not merely an entity altered by the passage of time; it was the prize in a struggle between rival versions of the past, a question of will, of power, of persuasion. The historical memory of any transforming or controversial event emerges from cultural and political competition, from the choice to confront the past and to debate and manipulate its meaning.

A struggle to control the public memory of the Civil War began immediately after the last Confederate surrender. On May 23, 1865, the victorious Union army held a grand review of its troops in Washington, D.C., and between 150,000 and 200,000 soldiers marched through its streets. This highly publicized event created an image of a grand victorious Union army. The event did not include African American soldiers since organizers did not invite them to participate in the grand review. The few African Americans who joined the parade were relegated to "pick and shovel" brigades or appeared as comic relief. For instance, tall African Americans rode Confederate mules with their feet nearly dragging on the ground. The *Inquirer* reported that the scene "created much laughter, in which the President [Johnson] and others joined in heartily" (quoted in McConnell 1992:8).

Most northerners thought that they defeated the South and dismantled the Confederacy. But immediately after the surrender, southern evangelists claimed that there would be eventual vindication and that God intended the South to be free and independent (Foster 1987:12–14). Southerners reinforced a Confederate nationalism that had developed and strengthened during the Civil War (Faust 1988).

Some of the first actions performed by newly formed Confederate organizations after the war were not necessarily about memory but rather about defiance. Confederate veteran organizations dedicated themselves to the idea of revitalizing the Confederacy. "They brooded over defeat, rallied against the North, and offered the image of the Confederacy as an antidote to postwar change" (Foster 1987:4–5). In 1869, southern generals who wanted to preserve the Confederate tradition founded the Southern Historical Society in New Orleans. The organization provided an interpretation of the Civil War that favored the Confederacy and the ideals of the Old South. When the organization began to flounder, Jubal Early moved it to Richmond (Blight 2001:158). The society published *The Southern Magazine*, which served as a vehicle to counter northern views of the war and printed "valuable contributions to the history of the Confederate War" (quoted in Kammen 1991:111). The organization continued to falter in Richmond and eventually folded.

An exodus from the South occurred by many who thought that they would be prosecuted by the federal government. In the summer of 1865, organized groups of southerners sought permanent settlement outside the United States. They fled the thought of an integrated society and hoped to reproduce the slave society that they had lost as an outcome of the Civil War. Others believed that in a short time they would be able to return and fight for secession once again. The largest emigration occurred in 1866 and 1867 (Nunn 1956; Rolle 1965). Some Confederates created colonies in Mexico and South America, and some ended up in England, France, or Canada. But many of these new settlements did not last, except for a small community in Brazil. The almost immediate collapse of these utopia-seeking communities discouraged a further exodus from the South. Unfriendly native populations and rugged pioneer life hampered any form of reconstituting the Old South in a foreign country. Jubal A. Early suggested creating a colony in New Zealand because it had "no negroes" and was "a long way from Yankeedom," although his plans never materialized (Foster 1987:16). He also proposed in 1867 colonizing Venezuela, "thinking perhaps it might be better to go and be killed off by the climate so there might be an end to my troubles in this world at last" (quoted in Foster 1987:37). Early never colonized Venezuela, and he lived for almost three more decades in the United States.

While only about 10,000 Confederates fled the country (0.2 percent of the southern population), others withdrew into a world of alcoholism and drug use. Between 1860 and 1920, southern whites exhibited a disproportionately high rate of opium addiction (Foster 1987:18). While the majority accepted the terms of defeat, they began to look for reasons to justify their cause.

Southerners immediately created a Confederate memorial movement to mourn the war dead. Communities created Confederate cemeteries, erected monuments in cemeteries, and instituted a memorial day for the dead. These activities "offered a vague hope of vindication," and the "Confederate dead became powerful cultural symbols within the New South—gave power, in other words, to the ghosts of the Confederacy" (Foster 1987:37).

During the war, some women had mobilized to provide support services, such as nursing, textile and clothing production, munitions, government office work, plantation management, and agriculture. But other southern women shared an aversion for these tasks, thinking that they displayed masculine strengths and abilities. A diarist explained that a friend who volunteered for nursing possessed such strength as to seem "almost masculine—Indeed I used to tell her I never felt easy in her society in discussing delicate subjects; I could scarcely persuade myself she was not in disguise" (quoted in Faust 1990:1216). As Drew Faust (1990:1216) notes, "Nurses were not truly women, but in some sense men in drag."

The war drained human resources and spirit from the South. About half the southern men who were of fighting age were either wounded, killed, or missing during the war. Mourning became a significant social, cultural, and spiritual duty in the old Confederacy, and women acquired the role of grieving and memorializing. Women celebrated the sanctity and martyrdom of men:

> Through rituals of public grief, personal loss could be redefined as transcendent communal gain. Women's tears consecrated the death of their men, ensuring their immortality—in Southern memory as in the arms of God—and ratifying soldiers' individual martyrdom. Such deaths not only contributed to Confederate victory but also exemplified the sacred conception of Christian sacrifice with which the South had identified its nationalist effort. (Faust 1990:1214)

This grieving role during the war led women to form local organizations to memorialize the Confederate dead after the war. While regional or state organizations did not emerge for several decades, most community organizations adopted the title Ladies' Memorial Association. Men were also actively involved in these organizations (Foster 1987:38), many of which concentrated on creating Confederate cemeteries. Prior to 1885, more than 90 percent of the confederate monuments contained some form of funerary design, and the majority of these (70 percent) stood in cemeteries (S. Davis 1982:2–21). Placed close to the entrance of the cemetery, such monuments became memorials of Confederate defeat, and dedication ceremonies reinforced the theme of bereavement (Foster 1987:41).

Southern communities, starting in Columbus, Georgia, began decorating the graves of Confederate soldiers in the spring of 1866. Many communities in the Deep South selected April 26 to decorate graves, the anniversary of the day on which General Johnston surrendered. Towns in North and South Carolina chose May 10, the anniversary of Stonewall Jackson's death. Virginians celebrated their Memorial Day anywhere from May 10 through the middle of June. By 1916, ten southern states designated June 3, Jefferson Davis's birthday, as their memorial day (Foster 1987:42; Kammen 1991:103). "Memorial activities during the first two decades after the war increased the importance of the voice of the Confederate dead—gave authority to the ghosts of the Confederacy. But the South had not yet decided who would speak for the ghosts of the Confederacy and to what large purpose" (Foster 1987:46). The town of Waterloo, New York, began the memorial commemorations in the North at about the same time, and the Grand Army of the Republic began sponsoring observances in 1868 (Kammen 1991:103).

David Blight (2001:69) provides an account of an earlier Memorial Day ceremony initiated by African Americans in 1865. During the war, the racetrack at Charleston was converted into a prison that held Union soldiers. The soldiers were kept inside the track without shelter from the elements. About 257 died from disease and exposure, and they were buried hastily in unmarked graves. After the fall of Charleston, the African American community insisted on a proper burial for the Union dead. A ten-foot-high fence was constructed around the cemetery in the racetrack. The entrance to the cemetery had the words "Martyrs of the Race Course" written on an archway built over the gateway entrance. At nine o'clock in the morning on May 1, 1865, a procession of 3,000 black schoolchildren (enrolled in the freemen's school) marched around the racetrack with roses to decorate the graves and sang "John Brown's Body" (Blight 2001:68–69). They were followed by 300 black women of the Patriotic Association, followed by men of the Mutual Aid Society. A large crowd of black and white citizens followed the procession. A *New York Tribune* correspondent described the event as "a procession of friends and mourners as South Carolina and the United States never saw before" (quoted in Blight 2001:69). When the procession ended, the entire earth was covered with flowers and petals. The black ministers of the local churches officiated the ceremony. In the afternoon, the 54th Massachusetts and the 35th and 104th U.S. Colored Troops marched around the graves and held a drill on the infield of the race course. While a Memorial Day for the Civil War dead appears to have been initiated by the African Americans of Charleston, the struggle to own the meaning of Decoration Day had only begun (Blight 2001:70).

Decoration Day became a national tradition among white Northerners and Southerners, although hate and sectionalism survived in both the North and the South, especially during early Decoration Day ceremonies. Many northerners saw the secession of the South as an act of treason and strongly adhered to this belief throughout Reconstruction. For instance, at an early 1870s Memorial Day celebration, Comrade A. B. Underwood objected to the decoration of Confederate graves. He said that he

> had none but the kindest feelings toward those who fought against us, respected their gallantry, bore them no malice, and would bury past differences and unite under one flag; but Memo-

> rial Day is the day on which we commemorate the memory of our fallen comrades, and let it be forever understood that we distinguish between loyalty and disloyalty; the latter is treason against which we fought, and the former we pay respect and tribute to. (Quoted in McConnell 1992:191)

This northern sentiment dominated throughout the 1870s and into the 1880s.

A New Southern History

Soon after Appomattox, southerners began justifying their secession from the Union. Edward Pollard's *The Lost Cause: A New Southern History of the War of the Confederates* (1866) became a very popular account of the war that justified the southern cause and helped develop and maintain the Confederate tradition. Other contemporary influential accounts included Albert Taylor Bledsoe's *Is Davis a Traitor: Or Was Secession a Constitutional Right Previous to the War of 1861?* (1866), in which he argued that the southern states had a constitutional right to secede (the North had abused the Constitution, so the South was justified in abandoning the Union); Robert Dabney's *A Defense of Virginia (and through Her, of the South) in Recent and Pending Contests against the Sectional Party* (1867), which used biblical references to justify slavery and secession; and Alexander Stephenson's *Constitutional View of the Late War between the States: Its Cause, Character, Conduct and Results Presented in a Series of Colloquies at Lake Liberty Hill* (1870), in which he argued that the South had a right to withdraw from the Union, especially after being oppressed by the North prior to the conflict. Because of Stephenson's status as former vice president of the Confederacy, his arguments carried considerable weight among southerners. Southern magazines also tried to vindicate the ways of the Old South, although these books and periodicals did not sell well. Some claim that southerners were too poor after the war to buy this literature, while others argue that southerners purchased far more northern magazines than southern. The influence of northern magazines helped prevent a strong and unified southern view and sentiment of the war. While books and magazines had some influence in contributing to the new ideology of the South, the post-Reconstruction memories of the southerners were not codified until the 1890s (Blight 2001:260–61; Foster 1987:49).

Robert E. Lee, one of the most influential postwar Confederate leaders and president of Washington College in Lexington, Virginia, preached political moderation, reunion, and rebuilding. He avoided most postwar Confederate activities and urged Confederate historians, such as Early (1867) and Dabney (1867), to tone down their secessionist rhetoric. He did subscribe to the growing southern sentiment of the Lost Cause, a public memory shaped by institutions and rituals. The Lost Cause was rooted in churches and secular institutions and shaped by journalists and fiction writers from the die-hard Confederate apologists and novelists who appealed to a national audience (Blight 1989b:228–29; 2001:263). They believed that the South fought for a just cause and lost only because it succumbed to overwhelming numbers. On Lee's death on October 12, 1870, groups formed to memorialize him and other Confederate soldiers as well as to step up the Lost Cause rhetoric (Foster 1987:51–52). Generals were deified, and Dabney (1867) suggested that Stonewall Jackson was killed at the peak of his career because he could never have been defeated or subjugated. This rhetoric strengthened by the mid-1870s, and a revitalization movement proposed the legitimacy of secession. Proponents of the Lost Cause attacked any northerner who implied that there was an equality of forces and portrayed the Confederate soldier as the best in the world. They searched for factors that would have changed the outcome of the war, such as the Confederacy's having overwhelming numbers, or if only General James Longstreet had been on time at Gettysburg (Blight 2001:160; Foster 1987:57–59; C. Wilson 1980:10–11, 24, 30).

The South began to look at the war years as a glorious and heroic era. They sought a way out of defeat, and the process became less rational "and more like other magical or millennial revitalization movements" (Foster 1987:57). Gaines Foster draws an analogy between the Confederates' revitalization movement and the Ghost Dance of the Plains Indians. The Ghost Dancers believed that the white culture would disappear only if they believed and danced:

> Similarly, the Virginians seemed to believe that if they wrote their articles and kept southerners from deserting after the war, the Yankees and all that had occurred after Appomattox would simply disappear. One can easily imagine a gathering of Early and company, wearing their grey ghost shirts and clutching a volume of the SHSP [*Southern Historical Society Papers*] that Jones thought would be impervious to the slings and arrows of northern slander. Formed in a circle about a statue of a recumbent

> Lee, the true believers dance in and back, chanting, on one foot, "overwhelmed by numbers," and on the other, "betrayed by Longstreet"—waiting for an undefeated, marble Lee to rise and lead them to victory. (Foster 1987:60)

Only a few dedicated themselves to this revitalization movement, but most, I argue, accepted it to different degrees, and the implications are still felt in our culture today.

It was not until the election of Rutherford B. Hayes as president of the United States in 1877 and the restoration of white rule in the South that the idea of reconciliation became fashionable (Blight 2001:138). Within a decade, there was a boom in written reminiscences of the Civil War (McConnell 1992). Fueling this sentiment were generals' accounts of the war, the most prominent being Ulysses S. Grant's *Personal Memoirs of U. S. Grant* (1885–1886). Four months before the publication of the first volume, wounded soldiers went door to door selling 300,000 advance copies to the American public. It became one of the most widely read books of the Gilded Age (Blight 2001:212–16). Also prominent was the series "Battles and Leaders of the Civil War," which ran in the *Century* for two years (1884–1886) and doubled the circulation of the publication; in 1888, the articles were gathered into a book. In this collection, heroism replaced the personal suffering of the war, an interpretation that developed considerably during the 1880s and 1890s (McConnell 1992:168–69). Another prominent addition to the literature was Jefferson Davis's *The Rise and Fall of the Confederate Government* (1881). The former Confederate president, charged with treason, spent two years in prison after the war and another two years awaiting trial before the federal government dropped the case. After a business failure, he retired to his home, Beauvoir, a plantation on the Mississippi Gulf coast, to write his two-volume tome. Davis provides a strong case for the southern states' right to secede. His adamant secessionist tone is an exception to the spirit of reconciliation developing in the country during this period (Blight 2001:259–60).

The Movement toward Reconciliation

In the 1880s, sectional bitterness still existed, and by the end of Reconstruction, the political importance of the war began to refocus. In the early 1880s, reunions between Union and Confederate veterans occurred despite tirades from members of both sides. Most Union veterans accepted the ex-Confederates at reunions. As long as they did not question the moral lesson of the war, they were treated cordially (Foster 1987:68–69; McConnell 1992:108). In 1881, the First Division of the Louisiana State National Guard invited the New York National Guard to New Orleans. There, many Confederate soldiers entertained their guests, "saluted the monument of the Confederate dead," and shook hands with "their brethren of the South" (quoted in Foster 1987:67). Later that same year, a New Jersey unit of the Grand Army of the Republic and a group of Knights Templars from Boston and Providence went to Richmond, where they paid their respects to the Confederate dead in Hollywood Cemetery and placed a wreath on a Stonewall Jackson statue (Foster 1987:667–68).

The following year, in 1882, Union and Confederate veterans first met at Gettysburg (see figure 1.1). Over the next five years, at least nineteen Blue–Grey reunions occurred. These reunions reinforced sectional reconciliation by allowing veterans to focus on their common wartime experiences. More important, these reunions offered explicit salutes to their honorable conduct during the war (Foster 1987:68).

Figure 1.1. Veterans Encampment, East Cemetery Hill, Gettysburg, ca. 1880 (courtesy National Park Service).

In 1887, several hundred Confederate veterans met with 1,000 veterans of the Philadelphia Brigade at Gettysburg. The Confederate veterans walked toward the Angle and stopped at the low stone wall, where the two armies had met in hand-to-hand combat. There, Confederate and Union veterans grasped each other's hands, a symbolic act that figured prominently in future reenactments (Linenthal 1993:94).

Carol Reardon (1997) notes that during this meeting in 1887, while planning commemorative ceremonies for the twenty-fifth anniversary of the battle of Gettysburg in 1888, some northern veterans believed in reconciliation, while others were appalled by the presence of Confederates at any Gettysburg reunion. One northern veteran warned southerners to "understand that the hallowed field of Gettysburg is no place to vaunt treason and glorify rebellion." Another warned any loyal Confederates to "stay home and gnaw the file of discontent in obscurity" (quoted in Reardon 1997:110). Brevet Brigadier General J. P. S. Gobin of the Grand Army of the Republic declared that he was

> tired of this gush and pretense for the glorification of the veteran simply because they wore a gray uniform with a Southern flag printed on his badge. That badge meant treason and rebellion in 1861, and what it meant then it means now. . . . I want to be distinctly understood, now and for all time, that the men who wore gray were everlastingly and eternally wrong. (Quoted in Linenthal 1993:95)

During the silver anniversary, a proposal to erect a marker to Pickett's division drew the wrath of many northerners. One man, outraged that the memorial association commissioners would consider such a monument, complained that the southern rebellion was "the most causeless and unjustifiable war that ever disturbed the peace and wasted the lives and treasure of a contented and happy people. [Virginians must] restrain themselves from extolling treason" (quoted in Reardon 1997:110). The 1888 event at Gettysburg remained a northern celebration, as only 300 Confederate veterans attended, their attendance thwarted by Congress' refusal to subsidize any veteran's travel to the reunion. James Longstreet represented the interests of the South and spoke of the heroism of Pickett's division.

Other northerners were outraged that the Philadelphia Brigade went to Richmond a few months after the Gettysburg event to dedicate the Pickett's division memorial. One critic called the Philadelphia Brigade's participation at the ceremony "another exhibition of unrepentant and blatant rebelism. [They should have refused to attend a memorial event to Pickett], a man whose only distinction was gained fighting the Government which had educated him; which supported him 20 years, and which he had solemnly sworn to defend." No true Union man should ever salute "a man conspicuous only for his efforts to make treason successful" (quoted in Reardon 1997:113–14). The following year, veterans agreed to erect a monument to "American heroism" in Gettysburg (Foster 1987:68–69; McConnell 1992:108). In 1903, Virginia and Pennsylvania sponsored a proposal to erect a monument to Robert E. Lee on the Gettysburg battlefield. The monument was not erected until 1917 because the Grand Army of the Republic protested, fearing that the act would be a horrible desecration on behalf of a treasonous "conspirator" (Kammen 1991:115).

In 1889, the United Confederate Veterans (UCV) was organized, and it stood as the most important Confederate veteran organization through the early twentieth century. The UCV succeeded in fostering a large-scale sentiment for reunion encampments. At the organization's zenith (1898–1912), one in three living veterans (160,000 men) were members. The number of encampments increased from about 36 in 1891 to 1,555 in 1898. These reunions became significant social events for many southern communities and at times drew crowds of more than 100,000 veterans and visitors (Hanley 1992:43).

The Struggle to Remember and the Cause to Forget

The 1890s is considered by many as the "decade of patriotic offensives among native-born, white members of the American middle class" (McConnell 1992:207). Americans were afraid of anarchism and foreign intervention and campaigned for immigrant restrictions. Social Darwinism and scientific racism, especially in the form of unilinear evolution, became the popular paradigm in intellectual circles.

Exclusionary groups dominated the era, and Americans created clubs and organizations at a rate never seen before or after in American history. Associations developed for group protection, and the wealthy increasingly excluded other groups. For instance, the *Social Register* was first published in the 1880s. This mechanism allowed elite groups to check social credentials and not fear that impostors would attend social events. The era saw a passion for genealogies using an aristocratic criterion of descent. Genealogy became a primarily female pursuit, and the Daughters of the American

Revolution (DAR), established in 1890, helped define a native white and overwhelmingly protestant group. The DAR became a stronghold in established wealthy areas in Connecticut, New York, and Pennsylvania, and among the millionaires of Chicago (Hobsbawm 1983b:292–93). Among many other social groups were the Society of Colonial Wars, the Order of Founders and Patriots, and the Mayflower Descendants (Harris 1970:17–19).

While the Victorian era had been a healing period between the North and the South, greater schisms developed in the country, dividing people along lines of class and ethnicity. These elite social groups consciously created explicit boundaries; the weapon used to exclude outsiders was the newly created rigid rules of behavior and household management guides that dictated the behavior of groups and classes of people.

Blue–Grey reunions from the 1880s also became a form of selective memory and exclusion. Confederates increasingly spoke about the Lost Cause and declared that they fought for what they thought was right (McConnell 1992:190). African American participation in the war became rather limited in national public memory and eventually disappeared from the American consciousness for nearly a century (Aaron 1973:332–33). "Slavery, the war's deepest cause, and black freedom, the war's most fundamental result, remain the most conspicuous missing elements in the American literature inspired by the Civil War" (Blight 1989a:1176).

Northerners became aware that they were losing the literary war as southern sentiment and the advocacy for the Lost Cause gained tremendous momentum. The *National Tribune* (1890) wrote that "a few more Confederate Histories, and it will be made to appear that all that ever confronted the Army of the Potomac was Gen. Lee, occasionally assisted by an Orderly, and a casual gentleman armed with shotguns."

African Americans faced an even more limiting situation. People such as Frederick Douglass found themselves in a growing minority when interpreting the events of the Civil War. Douglass declared in 1884 that "it is not well to forget the past. Memory was given to man for some wise purpose. The past is . . . the mirror in which we may discern the dim outlines of the future" (quoted in Blight 1989a:1160). He continually stressed that the war was about an ideological struggle over the issue of slavery and emancipation. In a speech in Washington, D.C., in 1888, Douglass proclaimed, "Well the nation may forget, it may shut its eyes to the past, and frown upon any who may do otherwise, but the colored people of this country are bound to keep the past in lively memory till justice shall be done them" (quoted in Blight 1989a:1161).

African Americans continually lost ground to a new and growing Lost Cause ideology, led by people such as Oliver Wendell Holmes Jr. and later Theodore Roosevelt. An integrated collective memory became unacceptable to the majority of white Americans. They interpreted the war as a test of a generation's valor and loyalty toward a cause. The Lost Cause mythology argued that Confederates were never defeated but rather were overwhelmed by numbers and betrayed by some key generals. For instance, Captain Bennett H. Young, commander of the UCV, claimed at a reunion that "we both fought for principles, and you won, not because we lacked courage, but because we lacked further resources" (quoted in W. Blake 1913:35).

Many black leaders denounced these veteran reunions. They believed that the meaning of emancipation was being forgotten while Americans celebrated the end of sectional tensions. The *Washington Bee,* a black newspaper, wrote about one planned reunion at Gettysburg:

> The occasion is to be called a Reunion! A Reunion of whom? Only the men who fought for the preservation of the Union and the extinction of slavery? Is it to be an assemblage of those who fought to destroy the Union and perpetuate slavery, and who are now employing every artifice and argument known to deceit and sophistry to propagate a national sentiment in favor of their nefarious contention that emancipation, reconstruction and enfranchisement are a dismal failure? (Quoted in Blight 1997b:176)

The Grand Army of the Republic's position on integrated reunion camps closely followed the Victorian northern middle class's beliefs on race. While African Americans were sometimes invited to these reunions, they were always encamped away from the main festivities. White veterans noted that they were noticed only in the evenings when they would "tune up a banjo, and they sing the old plantation melodies" (Blake 1913:184) (see figures 1.2 and 1.3).

African Americans created their own collective memory of the past as they chose to remember emancipation. A special day known as "Juneteenth" became popular in southern communities and was a day of prayer, preaching, and festivities. The particular day varied in the different regions,

Figure 1.2. African Americans were excluded from Civil War reunions. This image shows members of the Philadelphia Brigade Association and members of the Pickett's Division Association meeting at the Stone Wall and Bloody Angle, 3:15 PM, July 3, 1913, Gettysburg fiftieth reunion, July 1–4, 1913 (courtesy National Park Service).

including January 1, the day the Emancipation Proclamation became effective in 1863, and June 19, the day in 1865 when General Gordon Granger landed in Galveston, Texas, and read a government order that freed all slaves in eastern Texas. Other communities celebrated Juneteenth in early February, August, and September, depending on the day that the communities first learned of emancipation. Some regions used the date of the ratification of the Thirteenth Amendment, which made slavery illegal in the United States. Juneteenth speeches consisted of broad histories of Africans in North America, civil rights, and conditions of African Americans (Kammen 1991:122–4).

In contrast, white southerners at the turn of the twentieth century portrayed the Reconstruction era as a time of unparalleled Black violence:

> Epitomized by Thomas Dixon's books *The Leopard's Spots: A Romance of the White Man's Burden* (1902) and *The Clansmen: An Historical Romance of the Ku Klux Klan* (1906), which was later

Figure 1.3. Union and Confederate veterans meet at the Stone Wall, July 3, 1938, Gettysburg seventy-fifth reunion (courtesy National Park Service).

> made into the movie *Birth of a Nation* (1915), this version of American history declared that the African background of Afro-Americans was the reason they deserved enslavement. (Ruffins 1991:518–19)

These works, as well as many others, used Social Darwinism to justify African Americans' subordinate position in society.

W. E. B. Du Bois, in *Black Reconstruction in America* (1992), knew the significance of historical consciousness and the power of history, and he tried to resurrect the radical heritage of Reconstruction. In the last chapter, titled "The Propaganda of History," he argued that the two major centers of history, Columbia University and Johns Hopkins University, had begun a major rewrite of Reconstruction history downplaying any important role that blacks played during the era. Between 1895 and 1935, he noted that other schools of history and social investigations produced the same biased overview of Reconstruction. He described three main themes in these works: (1) "endless sympathy with the white south"; (2) "ridicule, contempt or silence for the Negro"; and (3) "a judicial attitude toward the North, which concludes that the North under great misapprehension did a grievous wrong [in Reconstruction], but eventually saw its mistake and retreated" (Du Bois 1992:718). African Americans' voices were successfully stifled, and they had few symbols that they could use to reclaim their rights as equal citizens. One symbol they embraced was John Brown, who justified the use of force in the struggle for freedom and equality. The John Brown Fort in Harpers Ferry, West Virginia, became a powerful icon that gave the African American community hope (see chapter 2).

While most members of the Grand Army of the Republic were Republicans, the Republican Party of the 1890s also became the party of big business. Gilded Age capitalists gained much from reconciliation between North and South. From the late 1890s, there was a large-scale migration of industry from the Northeast to the South. Reconciliation was necessary to allow this expansion into the South and for capitalists to exploit its cheaper, un-unionized labor (McConnell 1992:213).

Southerners experienced a tumultuous transition into industrial capitalism. They found themselves in an increasingly individualistic and competitive society, and they suffered through the economic recessions of the 1880s and the depression of the 1890s. Celebrations of the Confederacy helped southerners cope with defeat as well as the imposition of the new industrial order as nostalgia replaced bereavement (Foster 1987).

In the 1890s, southerners continually justified their remembrance of the Old South. George Moorman wrote in 1895,

> To cherish such memories and recall such a past whether crowned with success or consecrated in defeat, is to idealize principle and strengthen character, intensify love of country and convert defeat and disaster into pillars of support for future manhood and noble womanhood. Whether the Southern people under their changed conditions may ever hope to witness another civilization which shall equal that which began with their Washington and ended with their Lee, it is certainly true that devotion to their glorious past is not only the surest guarantee of future progress and holiest bond of unity, but also the strongest claim they can present to the conscience and respect of the other sections of the Union. (Quoted in Foster 1987:125)

New Memorials and the Changing Landscape

The number of Confederate monuments placed in cemeteries declined from 70 percent of all new Confederate monuments from 1865 to 1885 to just over half (55 percent) of all new Confederate monuments from 1885 to 1899. Towns increasingly chose to place monuments honoring the Confederate dead in public places, such as streets and courthouse lawns. The proportion of funerary designs also decreased dramatically, from 70 percent of all new monuments in the first period to 40 percent. The new placement of monuments out of the cemetery was a testament to southerners' changing view of the Civil War. Commemoration of the soldier was no longer about bereavement but rather was a celebration of a Confederate tradition. The typical soldiers' monument had a mass-produced soldier that stood at ease, with his rifle resting on the ground and his arms resting on it. At a distance, the Confederate monument looked much like many of the northern monuments (Foster 1987:129). And in the North, Civil War monuments almost always overlooked the involvement of African Americans in the war. Those monuments that did have African American representation often relegated them to secondary or anonymous roles (see chapter 4).

The UCV reunions of the 1890s helped intensify southern loyalties. And the Blue–Grey reunions became a place where southerners gained the admiration and respect of the Union soldiers. When southerners joined willingly to fight in the Spanish–American War (1898), it allowed them to affirm their loyalty to the Union and demonstrate their courage, as they decided that they could wear the blue uniform without too much indignity. This action received the praise of northerners and also healed many wounds, helping generate a euphoric patriotism that deepened sectional reconciliation. At the end of the Spanish–American War, President William McKinley toured the South with the express aim of promoting sectional reconciliation. He even made an offer that would allow the federal government to care for graves of Confederate soldiers. The UCV countered this offer and urged that the federal government only take care of the Confederate graves in the north since the southern graves were under the care of devoted southern women. Congress passed a bill supporting this idea in 1906. One year earlier, Congress had approved the return of captured Confederate battle flags to the South (Foster 1987:153–54).

Jefferson Davis and the Lost Cause

After the war, Jefferson Davis spent most of his time developing the Lost Cause mythology and rehabilitating his reputation. In the era of the centennial celebrations of the American Revolution, northerners vilified Davis as a modern-day Benedict Arnold, and until his death in 1889, he also served as a scapegoat for many southerners. Old Confederate enemies, such as Joseph Johnston and P. G. T. Beauregard, sharply criticized him in their postwar writings (Connelly 1977:42). In fact, the idea of creating a memorial arch to Davis in Richmond immediately after his death sharply divided the UDC. Davis's daughter, Winnie, tirelessly spoke about the heroic deeds of her father and the Lost Cause and worked to salvaged her father's reputation. The subsequent rehabilitation of Davis's reputation allowed for the erection of more monuments to him than to any American president, except for George Washington and Abraham Lincoln.

W. E. B. Du Bois, in a commencement speech to the 1890 Harvard graduating class, with the first lady of the United States in attendance, spoke about the hazards of glorifying the deeds of the South and its former president:

> I wish to consider not the man, but the type of civilization which his life represented. . . . Jefferson Davis advanced civilization by murdering Indians, now hero of a national disgrace called by courtesy, the Mexican War; and finally, as the crowning absurdity, the peculiar champion of a people fighting to be free in order that another people should not be free. . . . His life can only logically mean this: the advance of a part of the world at the expense of the whole; the overweening sense of the I, and the consequent forgetting of the Thou. This type of civilization which Jefferson Davis represented: it represents a field for stalwart manhood and heroic character, and at the same time for moral obtuseness and refined brutality. (Du Bois 1998:205)

In 1907, the Davis monument was erected in Richmond before 200,000 people, the largest crowd to celebrate any Confederate hero (Kammen 1991:105, 125–26). In 1896, Davis's house in Richmond, Virginia, became the Museum of the Confederacy with the sole purpose of commemorating the Lost Cause. It emphasized southern heritage and interpreted the events of the Civil War. Former Confederate General Bradley T. Johnston spoke at the dedication with unmitigated racism, emphasizing in his speech that "the greatest crime of the century was the emancipation of the Negro" (quoted in Blight 2001:258).

The white South felt vindicated in the early twentieth century, and this restored confidence in their worldview. Most symbolic was the unveiling of this elaborate monument to President Davis, "the vicarious sufferer of the South" (Foster 1987:145). It stands as the grandest and most ostentatious of all Confederate monuments in Richmond, and it symbolizes the righteousness of the Confederate cause:

> At its center stood an Edward Valentine statue of Davis with an arm outreached as he lectured from a history book. A 50-foot, 13 column, semicircular colonnade formed a backdrop. At both ends stood square piers, on each of which perched an eagle, and in the center directly behind the Davis figure rose a 67-foot Doric column topped by an allegorical figure of a woman. The entire monument, wrote the local newspaper, "typifies the vindication of Mr. Davis and the cause of the Confederacy for which he stood before the world. . . ." It did not appear a simple or reserved vindication. (Foster 1987:158)

After the Spanish–American War, the trend away from funerary monuments continued. About 60 percent of the Confederate monuments erected before 1913 were unveiled between 1900 and 1912, and only about 25 percent of them had any funerary design. About 80 percent of these monuments were a lone confederate soldier, and 85 percent were placed in public areas, such as courthouse lawns and downtown squares (Foster 1987:158; see also B. Emerson 1911; Widner 1982).

The Power of Southern Heritage Groups

In many southern cities, by the fiftieth anniversary of the Civil War, Confederate veterans were hailed as "conquerors" (*Atlanta Constitution* 1911). These celebrations reinforced white supremacy, and accounts told at these celebrations often described dutiful slaves. Faithful African Americans appeared at these reunions providing models of the "new Negro" born in the South, and they were used to show how loyal African Americans should behave in an increasingly segregated society. Such celebrations helped justify segregation and the increasing disfranchisement of blacks in this era (Williamson 1984:206).

The UCV and other major groups, such as the SCV and the UDC, became powerful forces in shaping a Confederate tradition beyond public celebration. They also became guardians of the southern tradition by influencing the choice of school textbooks, especially history books with a secessionist slant. In fact, some southern states had an "Endorsement of Books" committee. The UDC petitioned and won the right to examine history books before they were adopted for classroom use. These groups helped shape a southern tradition for future generations (Blight 2001:272–77; Foster 1987:6).

State chapters of the UDC often lobbied legislatures to provide them with financial support for the writing of histories of the Civil War. For instance, in 1923, the Arkansas chapter of the UDC received $2,500 to write a history of the Civil War. They hired a University of Arkansas historian, David Thomas, for the project. Although Thomas's beliefs on the war and southern tradition coincided with those of the UDC, when he submitted his manuscript to the UDC in 1925, they disagreed with some of his points. However, he made most of the requested changes and even added several points suggested by the UDC committee. "This included the contention that a majority of slave traders were New Englanders, that many slave ships were built in New England and owned by New Englanders, and that secession was first threatened in New England" (Logan 1996:E22).

Thomas's *Arkansas in War and Reconstruction, 1861–1874* (1926) acknowledged the role of slavery in sectional tensions that caused the war, but he emphasized states' rights and regional loyalty for Arkansas' secession from the Union. Thomas claimed to be a pacifist, but the examples that he provided focused on northern and African American atrocities. In one story, he noted a "negro fiend's" slaughter of two southern white women. Thomas did note, however, that Arkansas African Americans "for the most part behaved admirably throughout the war, the vast majority remaining at home and 'carrying on' for their masters . . . until the Federal army came along with the emancipation proclamation" (quoted in Logan 1996:E22). Because the Freedman's Bureau provided aid to the newly freed slaves, Thomas wrote that African Americans came to believe "freedom meant no work and plenty to eat at the hands of the government." Carpetbaggers also recruited blacks to Republican politics and turned them against their former masters. They armed them for terrorizing and plundering their former plantations. In order to confront these horrors, Thomas explains that brave Arkansans supported the Ku Klux Klan. They discouraged "the Negro from taking part in politics," and by 1875 "the nightmare of carpetbag-negro rule was over and Arkansas breathed the air of freedom once more" (quoted in Logan 1996:E22).

According to Foster (1987:48), the Ku Klux Klan dressed as ghosts and originally claimed to be the dead of Gettysburg; allegedly, this was to play on the superstitions of the local black population. The UDC became a vocal apologist for the Ku Klux Klan and their activities. Meanwhile, when the Supreme Court ruled on the desegregation of schools, students in all-white schools in Arkansas still read a UDC-approved textbook, *Living in Arkansas,* by Olin E. McKnight. McKnight's work justified the violence against blacks because they were "idle, penniless, lawless; they stole, plundered, burned houses and at times committed other crimes—often encouraged by carpet-baggers and scalawags in these acts of lawlessness." The UDC sponsored many other histories that justified the continuing myth of the Lost Cause. "Indeed, the UDC-sponsored histories would prove to be almost as enduring as the monuments of granite, stone and bronze it erected, and no doubt the textbooks had more influence on the consciousness of southerners than the lonely soldiers standing guard on the courthouse lawn" (Logan 1996:E23).

The UDC stood as a powerful and influential lobby group, and they were the most aggressive in the 1920s and 1930s for promoting the southern cause. For instance, in 1929 they persuaded mothers not to send their children to any celebrations related to Lincoln's birthday since the year before they had recited the Gettysburg Address. Lyon G. Tyler, descendant of President John Tyler, helped reopen the College of William and Mary in 1888, where he served as president until 1919. In the 1920s and 1930s, he became a major spokesperson for keeping the Confederate cause alive. He produced many pamphlets during this era, including *Propaganda in History* in 1920, *Virginia First* in 1922, and *The Confederate Catechism* in 1929. He distributed the information free, only to receive orders by the hundreds, and the demand continued for years. Tyler also bemoaned what he perceived as "educational slavery," and wrote a 106-page pamphlet that criticized history textbooks written in the North with northern biases. Not only did he emphasize the southern cause, but he also asserted the importance of Jamestown over Plymouth, Patrick Henry over James Otis, and Lee over Lincoln (Kammen 1991:382–85). In 1931, Tyler claimed that he found a collection of papers in the New York Public Library that hinted that the first Thanksgiving actually occurred in 1619 at Berkeley Hundred, a plantation near the James River. A new southern pride developed in the 1930s along with the creation of many festivals in southern cities that celebrated the Old South and antebellum life. Southern revisionist history and literature developed rapidly, and Douglas Southall Freeman's (1934–1935) four-volume biography on Robert E. Lee became a national best-seller along with *Gone with the Wind* (Woodward 1993:27–39).

A new Confederate tradition became influential throughout the first portion of the twentieth century. Pro-Confederate groups slowly changed national attitudes about the South as they gained control of the literature in grade schools and in popular culture. The resurrection of a new Confederate culture set the stage for national tensions by the mid-twentieth century.

The Civil War Centennial

In the 1950s and 1960s, Americans looked for a unifying theme that could bring some peace and tranquility to the growing antagonism between races and regions. Violence and grief marked the era as racial issues tugged at the fragile seams that held this nation together. For instance, in September 1962, more than 1,000 angry whites rampaged across the University of Mississippi campus to protest the admission of the campus's first black student. While President John F. Kennedy sent several hundred federal marshals to protect the student, the mob killed two men, more than two dozen marshals were wounded, and 120 other people were wounded amid considerable property damage (Cohodas 1997). This was not an isolated incident, and it was indicative of race relations of the time.

In the midst of this era of racial tensions, the Civil War Round Tables successfully petitioned Congress in 1957 to create a Civil War Centennial Commission. Much like the Washington birth centennial in 1931, the commission wanted to use a historic event to promote nationalism and patriotism. They fashioned memories of past conflict that attempted to transform those conflicts into symbolic struggles for unity. Abroe (1998:22) argues that the recollection of a heroic past could easily provide a diversion from the racial and political unrest sweeping through the country. "With citizens' attention fixed upon subversive threats—real or imagined—to democratic institutions, the vision of a United States tested and fortified in the crucible of civil conflict offered reassurance that the nation could meet any crisis and emerge victorious" (Abroe 1998:22).

President Dwight D. Eisenhower wrote the Civil War Centennial Commission and urged them to

> look on this great struggle not merely as a set of military operations, but as a period in our history in which the times called for extraordinary degrees of patriotism and heroism on the part of the men and women of both North and South. In this context

> we may derive inspiration from their deeds to renew our dedication to the task which yet confronts us—the furtherance, together with other free nations of the world, of the freedom and dignity of man and the building of a just and lasting peace. (Eisenhower 1960)

Eisenhower never mentioned the issue of slavery or emancipation in his letter.

Karl Betts became the first executive director of the Civil War Centennial Commission and was joined by Ulysses S. Grant III, as both men had military backgrounds.

In 1960, Grant III stated,

> The flood of popular interest is running high and cannot now be stemmed. Our children and their parents will be inspired by better knowledge of what Americans have done for the principles they held dear, and, perhaps recapture some of the enthusiasm and patriotism of that time for American institutions. We are confident that the results will lead to a better popular understanding of America's days of greatness, a more unified country. (Minutes of the Civil War Centennial Commission 1960b)

The Civil War Centennial Commission knew that such a celebration could rekindle thoughts of regionalism at the expense of the nationalist message of unity. In planning meetings, it is clear that the ideals of the Lost Cause were embedded in the national public memory of the Civil War. Grant explained that the Civil War could not be forgotten and that the Confederates were also Americans "who were heroically fighting for what they thought was right" (Minutes of the Civil War Centennial Commission 1960a). This view of heroism allowed for the common foot soldier to be recognized, but it also provided an example of how ordinary citizens followed the orders of their leaders. They fought for a larger political structure without question (Bodnar 1992:209).

The opening ceremonies of the centennial celebration occurred in New York City, where a procession gathered at the Grant Memorial. There, Major General Ulysses S. Grant III gave a speech that stressed the Civil War's importance as proof of the country's ability to reunite (*New York Times* 1961:1). That same day, opening ceremonies occurred in Lexington at Robert E. Lee's grave site and the chapel at Washington and Lee University, which Lee led after the Civil War. During his speech, Congressman William Tuck of Virginia noted that after the war, Lee urged southerners to strengthen the Union (*New York Times* 1961:1).

Despite all these efforts to emphasize unity, an incident related to the Civil War Centennial Commission did little for bettering race relations. The commission set a meeting for Charleston, South Carolina, in April 1961. However, a black member of the New Jersey Centennial Commission charged that she could not reserve a room at the meeting hotel because of her race. The hotel refused to accommodate any of the black delegation members. Several states, including New Jersey, California, Illinois, New York, and Wisconsin, threatened to "secede" from the assembly unless the commission resolved the issue. They called Major General Grant to solve the problem (Gondos 1963:64–65), and he consented to relocate the luncheon and meeting to the Charleston Naval Base. Attendance at the integrated lunch was small, however, since many of the southern delegates held their own ceremony. At this separate "Confederate States Convention," a speaker verbally attacked the New Jersey delegation for being "schizophrenic and discriminatory in its race relations" (Gondos 1963:64–65).

National criticism of the commission for allowing such divisiveness forced Karl Betts to resign. In protest, Grant also resigned. Allan Nevis, a professional historian, and James I. Robertson, former editor of *Civil War History* magazine, became the new commission leaders. Nevis declared the mission of the commission:

> Above all, our central theme will be unity, not division. When we finally reach the commemoration of Appomattox, we shall treat it not as a victory or a defeat, but as a beginning of a century of increasing concord, mutual understanding, and fraternal affection among all the sections and social groups. (Minutes of the Civil War Centennial Commission 1961)

The Civil War Centennial Commission could not, however, completely ignore the racial divisiveness within the country, and on September 22, 1962, they sponsored an event at the Lincoln Memorial to commemorate the centennial of the Emancipation Proclamation. The Kennedy administration avoided any major political stance at the event while racial tensions boiled in the country. Contemplating reelection, Kennedy most likely did not want to offend white southerners. In a recorded message played at the ceremony, Kennedy emphasized patriotic themes and commended African Americans for working on civil rights issues within the framework of the Constitution. He praised African Americans for their struggle to make life better for their people. "He thought it remarkable that despite humiliation and depravation, blacks had retained their loyalty to the nation and 'democratic institution'" (*New York Times* 1962:1, 50; Bodnar 1992:211). Adlai Stevenson, ambassador to the United Nations, represented the administration and served as a speaker. Other speeches were given at the memorial, and Mahalia Jackson, granddaughter of a slave, sang "The Battle Hymn of the Republic" (Kammen 1991:599).

On the same day, the Negro Emancipation Centennial Authority of Chicago held commemoration ceremonies at Lincoln's tomb in Springfield, Illinois. There, the speakers seemed less optimistic about conditions for African Americans. They proclaimed that racism still prevailed and that blacks were not fully integrated into society (*New York Times* 1962:50; Bodnar 1992:211; see also Branch 1988:399–400, 685; U.S. Civil War Centennial Commission 1968:18).

Reenactments during the Centennial

The Civil War centennial brought an economic boom to the South. Tourism in Mississippi doubled, and Alabama spent more than $100,000 for a five-day celebration of the centennial of Jefferson Davis's inauguration. The First Manassas Corporation spent $200,000 for a reenactment at Manassas National Battlefield Park that almost 120,000 people attended (see chapter 5). The ranks of the National Park Service (NPS) debated over the meaning of the Manassas festivities. While some believed that the reenactment would ignore the horror of one of the most tragic episodes in this country, others believed that they could not deny the American public the excitement of the event (Bodnar 1992:214). Karl Betts is reported to have said that the South may have lost the war, but it was going to win the centennial (Bodnar 1992:214).

Others were disturbed by the commercialism associated with the centennial. Ralph McGill of the *Atlanta Constitution* commented that people in the South were "wearing sleazy-imitations of Confederate uniforms, growing beards, making ancient wounds bleed again, reviving Ku Klux Klans, recreating old battles, and otherwise doing a great disservice to the memory of those who fought and died" (quoted in Bodnar 1992:214). After the Manassas reenactment, Nevis claimed that the national commission would not support these events, which he called "trashily theatrical" (U.S. Civil War Centennial Commission 1968:14). At the First Battle of Manassas, Union troops were beaten and in disorder retreated toward Washington, D.C. At the reenactment, both sides fired at each other, and at the end they joined together to sing "God Bless America." A Virginia newspaper declared that the reenactment served as a carnival that threatened to dishonor the men who actually fought there one hundred years ago. Another report claimed that the next time live ammunition should be used, allowing us to "be free of one of the sicker elements" in society (quoted in Bodnar 1992:214–15).

National Park Service Director Conrad Wirth wrote the Civil War Centennial Commission that he thought it would be unwise to sanction any further reenactments. Rather, Civil War commemorations should be limited to other forms of pageantry, such as flag presentations, infantry drills, bugle calls, and parades. Prominent Civil War historian James Robertson explained, "We feel that reenactments possess too much celebrative spirit and too little commemorative reverence. This soldier playing mocks the dead" (quoted in Bodnar 1992:215).

In early July 1963, Gettysburg celebrated the one-hundredth anniversary of the battle of Gettysburg. The event was also marked by an appeal for national unity and patriotism. Parades were carefully coordinated with the active military troops and reactivated northern and southern regiments. Despite Wirth's appeal, on the third day reenactors demonstrated Pickett's charge. More than 40,000 people came to see the charge while listening to a narration over a loudspeaker. Like the reenactment at Manassas, the battle did not end in victory for one side and defeat for the other. Instead, the reenactors joined together for a flag salute and a singing of patriotic songs (Bodnar 1992:220).

On the whole, southern participation in the centennial celebration tended to emphasize regional ideals rather than the idea of nationalism set by the Civil War Centennial Commission. Nadine Cohodas, in *The Band Played Dixie: Race and Liberal Conscience at Ole Miss* (1997), offers an explanation for why the nationalist message failed and racism prevailed in the state of Mississippi. Racism was entrenched in all the major state institutions. For instance, at the University of Mississippi, the first black students in 1962 were greeted with rock throwing and racist chants. Racism had established itself at the school several generations earlier when the university athletic team became the "Fighting Rebels" and in 1948, students filled the stadium, waving Confederate battle flags, as the Dixiecrat Party launched a campaign to maintain white supremacy. And Mississippi did not stand alone: Racism was prevalent throughout the region.

Against the backdrop of the Civil Rights movement, Alabama Governor George Wallace took the opportunity to present a countermemory of the Civil War. Addressing a crowd at Gettysburg at the dedication of a new South Carolina monument during the centennial celebration, he railed against the newly enacted federal desegregation policies. He claimed, "South Carolina and Alabama stand for constitutional government and thousands of people throughout the nation look to the South to restore constitutional rights and the rights of states and individuals" (*Newsweek* 1963:18). During the Civil War centennial celebrations, the Confederate flag was raised over many southern state capitals. And in Alabama, "the flag was raised again on the morning of April 25, 1963, the day the United States Attorney General Robert F. Kennedy traveled to Montgomery to discuss with Governor Wallace the governor's announced intention to block the admission of the first black students to the University of Alabama" (quoted in Levinson 1998:91).

An editorial in a Montgomery, Alabama, newspaper stated that the goal of the centennial was to praise the soldiers of the Confederacy "who gave their all for the right as they saw it" (Bodnar 1992:220). While citizens of Montgomery reenacted Jefferson Davis's arrival in the city, they could also read about whites restricting the political power of African Americans. The Georgia commission for the Civil War centennial also believed that the commemoration activities served to recognize the "valor and sacrifice of Georgians who fought and died for principles which they believed eternal" (quoted in Bodnar 1992:220). Mississippi encouraged the formation of the "Mississippi Greys," and communities participated in the reenactment ceremonies of Mississippi's Act of Secession in January 1861. Despite Wirth's concerns about reenactments, they were common on southern national battlefield parks. The Georgia commission justified the reenactments. "It argued that acts of bravery and courage were typical of all Americans and suggested that a willingness to die for one's beliefs was indigenous to the 'American character' and a quality that were necessary to perpetuate the nation in the future" (Bodnar 1992:222).

Virginia had some of the most elaborate Civil War celebrations, and reenactments were staged throughout the state. Commemorations began when the state celebrated the centennial of Robert E. Lee's acceptance of the commission to command Virginia's military and naval forces. Even the clash between the *Merrimack* and the *Monitor* was reenacted twenty-two times (Bodnar 1992:226). The Centennial Commission and Grant did not fully support the reenactments. They had been unwilling to encourage them since they could not be "made true to history" (Kammen 1991:605). Historian Bruce Catton also spoke about his discomfort for the events, wondering in a speech in Richmond in 1961 when the mania would end. "Is it proposed to re-enact the burning of cities, the march to the sea, the appalling bloodshed of this most sanguinary conflict?" (quoted in Kammen 1991:605). Nevertheless, reenactments served as popular events during the centennial and constitute a phenomenon that carries through to today.

The centennial ended with a ceremony at the recently reconstructed Appomattox County Court House on April 9, 1965. The NPS prohibited any reenactments, and during the ceremonies no official mentioned the actual surrender or the demise of the Confederacy. The NPS viewed the site as significant because "here a united nation [hardly!] began again to move in concert toward strength and world power" (quoted in Kammen 1991:603). In fact, the NPS promoted the idea of a moral victory for the Confederacy (Kammen 1991:603). Catton spoke about reconciliation. Lee's great grandson and Grant's grandson were both present at the ceremonies as a symbol of unity. However, the *Washington Post* (1965:3) recognized that the audience consisted mostly of Virginians and that the two biggest moments at the event occurred when the master of ceremonies introduced Lee's great grandson and the band played "Dixie."

Despite four years of commemorative events and several years of planning, the nationalist picture of unity was overpowered by regionalist interests. Vice President Hubert Humphrey closed the centennial observances with a speech at Bennett Place, the spot near Durham, North Carolina, where Joseph Johnston surrendered to William Sherman two weeks after Appomattox. In a period of mounting racial strife, Humphrey asked his southern audience for restraint, equating the "radicalism" of Reconstruction with a "senseless, revengeful extremism that even today, if left unchecked, could bring our great democracy to its knees" (quoted in Abroe 1998:24). Humphrey used the long-standing southern view of radical Reconstruction in order to cultivate in the southern audience a feeling of national solidarity at a time when the nation confronted a serious racial divide. He faced an uphill battle as the Virginia Civil War Centennial Commission wrote in its final report that the centennial celebration provided a "sympathetic appreciation everywhere of the Southern position" (Virginia Civil War Centennial Commission 1965).

The Lost Cause Today

Many historians of southern cultural relations will agree that the verdict of Appomattox is still contested today. The Lost Cause became the dominant ideology in southern culture and had transformed itself into American public memory—North and South—by the 1890s. The proponents of the Lost Cause saw their crusade justified as the federal government abandoned the Freedman's Bureau and Jim Crow legislation was championed in the Supreme Court's *Plessy v. Ferguson* decision, which legitimized segregation. African Americans increasingly lost rights in the post-Reconstruction era, while the Lost Cause celebrated southern heritage, manly sacrifice, states rights, and the defeat of Reconstruction. One late nineteenth-century citizen noted that "the South surrendered at Appomattox, and the North has been surrendering ever since" (quoted in Blight 1997a).

Some of these ideals are still being reinforced by many Civil War groups. For instance, Dennis Frye, former president of the Association for the Preservation of Civil War Sites, recently explained the meaning of battlefields:

> "Battlefields are the heart and soul of who we are. If we lose this history, we are lost as a nation." Members of the Rotary Club stared as Frye pounded the podium to illustrate the men in battle moving toward certain death. "The men never wavered. . . . Each man, leading himself. No man can falter, everyone must move forward. On the site where these men fought, people can touch history. The battlefields are some of the most effective classrooms in America. On the battlefield you can learn much. The battlefield is not a place to study death, destruction and how to kill, it teaches moral courage, the value of commitment to a cause and the ultimate sacrifice." (Sacharnoski 1998:A-7)

Saying that battlefields are not a place to "study death" and "destruction" but rather are about learning "moral courage" and "the value of commitment" is a way to depoliticize the meaning of war. It does not allow for the American public to address the tough questions related to the Civil War, such as slavery and racism.

Many Civil War historians continue to talk about how battlefields and battlefield preservation are about remembering courage and dedication to a cause and the connection of slavery and the Civil War is sometimes missing. However, a number of national battlefield parks are beginning to address issues related to slavery and include African Americans in their interpretations. Fort Sumter, Richmond, and Chickamauga/Chattanooga have just installed exhibits on slavery as a cause of the war.

How African Americans and southern heritage groups have struggled with each other to influence American public memory is what this book is about. African Americans were present and visible on the American landscape, but the selective sight and memory of those in control of the state and national story forced African Americans out of the American consciousness. In many cases, racism is entrenched in local and state institutions and helps explain why nationalism has failed to overcome the Lost Cause. Up to this point, I have offered a national context for the development of race and race relations with events surrounding the American Civil War, and I showed the changing representation of the African American memory during Reconstruction, Jim Crow, and the civil rights eras. Following are several instances where the meanings of African American symbols have changed as the role of African Americans in American society and in history has transformed.

The John Brown Fort: Unwanted Symbol, Coveted Icon

2

THE JOHN BROWN FORT is a well-maintained structure that sits at the heart of Harpers Ferry National Historical Park. It is prominently situated on the landscape and can be seen easily by the park's 400,000 annual visitors. Its placement seems natural, as it is positioned in the midst of a monumental landscape. Without knowing the fort's physical history, one can easily believe that its appearance and symbolic meaning are timeless, rooted in the abolitionist cause for equal rights. But appearances can be deceiving. The fort was not always revered by the majority of Americans, and much like the Ark of the Covenant, it moved from place to place, often honored only by a small and select group of people. It has taken refuge at several oases during its 150-year existence—displayed and revered only to be moved again. At the beginning of the Jim Crow era, it lay dismantled in Chicago, where several citizens worked toward one goal: to bring the fort back from obscurity. They provided a haven where it could be protected from those who despised its symbolic meaning and preserved for those few who revered its meaning. During the Civil Rights movement, the fort was returned to a spot close to its original location where it became, once again, part of the national public memory. The powerful meaning and memory associated with John Brown and the John Brown Fort continue today (Shackel 1995) (see figure 2.1).

The Martyrdom of John Brown

John Brown, born in 1800, is considered by many to be one of the most controversial abolitionists in American history. During his adult life, he guided fifteen businesses into failure, and by the age of fifty-two he found himself enticed by promotional literature to the Kansas territory. Arriving there in 1855, he and part of his family found themselves in the midst of

Figure 2.1. Image of the John Brown Fort in Lower Town Harpers Ferry, 1995 (courtesy Paul A. Shackel).

a debate over whether Kansas should be a slave or a free territory. A civil war erupted in Kansas, and Brown's family joined the skirmish against the pro-slavery factions (Malin 1942:492–97; Oates 1970:33–77; Sanborn 1885:191 ff.; Villard 1910:36 ff.). Brown became known for his participation in several battles and was also linked to the killing in cold blood of five pro-slavery men in the presence of their families in Pottawatomie. East Coast newspaper correspondents glorified Brown's abolitionist role in Kansas, and one reporter wrote, "I left this sacred spot [Camp Brown] with a far higher respect for the Great Struggle. . . . And I said, also, and thought, that I had seen the predestined leader of the second and the holier American Revolution" (Redpath 1860:112–14). Brown's reputation as a great abolitionist grew tremendously, and he sought council with other major abolitionist figures, such as Frederick Douglass and Franklin Sanborn.

Brown revealed to them his secret plan to attack the South, believing that once he attacked, enslaved African Americans in the area would revolt and join his cause. He planned to first attack the queen of the slave states, Virginia, and capture the arsenal at Harpers Ferry, which contained tens of thousands of guns that could be used to arm newly freed slaves. Brown created a provisional constitution that would establish a new state in the southern mountains. Even if his plans failed, he believed it would serve to consolidate northern emotions and the hatred for slavery and thus promote a crisis (Douglass 1881; Oates 1970:224–79; Sanborn 1885:440 ff.).

Brown eventually rented the Kennedy farm on the Maryland side of the Potomac River several miles from Harpers Ferry. On the night of October 16, 1859, Brown and his party of twenty-one men captured the federal arsenal with relative ease, taking several hostages. Ironically, the first casualty of the raid, shot by one of Brown's men, was an African American baggage handler for the railroad, Hayward Shepherd. As the town filled with panic, many of the town's families fled from the Lower Town area. The church bells tolled, and townspeople and farmers were warned of an insurrection. The next day, Brown was on the armory grounds but refused to escape when he had the chance. By 11:00 AM, a small battle raged in Harpers Ferry. Some of Brown's men found themselves at the rifle works waiting for orders to withdraw, but Brown, stationed on the armory grounds, mysteriously delayed. The Jefferson Guard from Charlestown arrived and secured control of both bridges. An angry, crowd, growing intoxicated, surrounded the armory. Brown no longer had the opportunity to flee with hostages and weapons, and, under fire, he and his men took refuge in the armory engine house. Those stationed at the rifle works were killed as they tried to flee (Oates 1970:279–300; Shackel 1995).

A group of Marines under the command of Colonel Robert E. Lee arrived at Harpers Ferry on the night of October 17. The following morning, Lee sent J. E. B. Stuart to the engine house under a flag of truce and handed Brown a note from Lee, asking for his unconditional surrender. Brown refused. Then Stuart jumped away from the door and waved his cap, and a party of Marines stormed the fort and overpowered Brown (see figure 2.2). Brown's war for slave insurrection lasted only thirty-six hours, and not a single slave had come to Harpers Ferry. Some of the slaves Brown forcibly liberated during his raid refused to fight with him; others escaped and returned to their owners (O. Anderson 1972:36; Hinton 1894:311 ff., 709 ff.; Oates 1970:293–300; Shackel 1995; Villard 1910:440).

Northerners received news of John Brown's raid with varying degrees of condemnation and approval. Wendell Philips wrote that Harpers Ferry

Figure 2.2. U.S. Marines, led by Colonel Robert E. Lee, storm the engine house to capture John Brown. The engine house later became known as the John Brown Fort (courtesy Harpers Ferry National Historical Park).

"is the Lexington of to-day. . . . Virginia is a pirate ship, and John Brown sails the sea as Lord High Admiral of the Almighty" (Oates 1970:318). Ralph Waldo Emerson claimed "that new saint, than whom none purer or more brave was ever led by love of men into conflict and death, the new saint awaiting his martyrdom, and who, if he shall suffer, will make the gallows glorious like the cross" (quoted in Redpath 1860:40). Henry David Thoreau wrote, "I almost fear to hear of his deliverance, doubting if a prolonged life, if any life, can do as much good as his death" (quoted in Oates 1970:318). James Redpath (1860:42) wrote that "history will place John Brown, in her American Pantheon, not among Virginia's culprits, but as high, at least, as Virginia's greatest chiefs."

While northerner abolitionists praised Brown's deeds, Brown himself was content on becoming a martyr. During his imprisonment, Brown composed some of the most important abolitionist prose. Tried by the state of Virginia, the jury found him guilty of treason, and he was sentenced to hang. On the day of his execution, December 2, 1859, he wrote, "I John Brown am now quite certain that the crimes of this guilty land: will never be purged away; but with blood. I had as I now think: vainly flattered myself that without very much bloodshed; it might be done" (quoted in Oates 1970:351). In his death, Brown became a symbol for the abolitionist movement. The engine house where he took refuge became known as the John Brown Fort, and it has become one of America's most provocative symbolic statements of abolitionist history (Shackel 1995).

The Making of the John Brown Fort

The John Brown Fort was constructed in 1847 as the U.S. Armory's "Engine and Guard House." The one-story brick building with slate roof and copper gutters stood near the armory entrance. It contained two fire engines and served as quarters for a night watchman (Fairbairn 1961). It was one of the only armory buildings to escape destruction during the Civil War. The condition of the engine house during the Union's early occupation was described by Robert Gould Shaw, known for leading the Massachusetts 54th Volunteer Infantry, the first northern organized African American regiment, in a letter to his sister Susie:

> There are three or four loopholes which he made to fire through, and marks of musket balls on the walls inside. It seems the worst place he could have chosen to defend against an attack; for when the doors are shut, it is like a brick box, as all the windows are high up, and the loopholes are so small that they give no range at all to the men firing through them. (Quoted in Duncan 1992:119; see also Gould, in Burchard 1965:41–42)

The engine house became a rallying point for northern troops, and several accounts chronicle the singing of the familiar tune "John Brown's Body Lies a-Moldering in the Grave" as troops marched passed the fort (Hearn 1996).

Immediately after the Civil War, the John Brown Fort stood neglected and was vandalized by many visitors who took souvenirs of the famous 1859 raid. The U.S. government sold the fort along with the rest of the armory grounds at an 1869 auction to a group of investors from Washington, D.C., headed by Captain Francis C. Adams. Adams told the local population that he intended to reuse the water power developed by the armory and build industry on the banks of the Shenandoah River. Adams schemed to acquire the lands that contained the Baltimore & Ohio Railroad and file suit against the railroad since it ran through his newly acquired property. Adams's suit failed, and since he had never paid for the land he successfully bid on, the land reverted to the U.S. government (Shackel 1995).

Contested Memories of the Fort

Harpers Ferry: Creating an Icon

After the Civil War, visiting battlefield sites became a popular recreational activity for many middle-class citizens. Railroads also built attractions and promoted destinations for families to visit. The John Brown Fort and the Civil War ruins became a central part of Harpers Ferry's tourist attractions, along with an amusement park developed on an island in the Potomac River by the Baltimore & Ohio Railroad. Harpers Ferry became a mecca for the middle class; the town's population swelled during the summer months, and summer homes sprang up. Advertisements ran in Washington and Baltimore newspapers for special excursions to Harpers Ferry on both the Chesapeake and Ohio Canal and the Baltimore & Ohio Railroad (Fairbairn 1961:13, 20). For several decades after the Civil War, the abolitionist movement became part of the official history of the United States, and John Brown was often recognized as a hero and martyr in much of the northern published literature (Hinton 1894; Redpath 1860; Von Holst 1888; Webb 1861).

During the town's economic revitalization in the early 1880s, Thomas Savery purchased the armory grounds, including the former armory, arsenal, rifle works, and the John Brown Fort. The fort received little care during Savery's ownership, although the words "John Brown's Fort" were painted on the engine house for easy tourist identification (see figure 2.3).

Savery capitalized on owning the John Brown Fort, scavenging bricks from the structure and giving them to people as souvenirs. One of Savery's children wrote,

> Not everything father did was perfect, of course, and one thing which pulled the average down a little, was his making souvenirs of bricks taken from John Brown's Fort. On each brick was pasted a steel engraving of the fort, then the brick was placed in a black-leather-covered box, the lining which was SATIN,—of all things some were lined with red, some with light blue satin. And these were given around to favored friends and relatives. He

Figure 2.3. John Brown Fort on the armory grounds in Harpers Ferry, 1882–1886 (courtesy Harpers Ferry National Historical Park).

> also sent them to people of note who would appreciate their historical value,—Harriet Beecher Stowe, J. G. Whittier, William Cullen Bryant, and several others. (Savery, n.d.) (see figure 2.4)

While many tourists came to Savery's property and visited the John Brown Fort, some local townspeople disapproved of having the structure in town. Community discontent already existed over having Storer College, an institution for the education of African Americans, within Harpers Ferry. The school's goal was to provide technical skills and an education for African Americans so that they could provide for themselves in a segregated society. Racial tensions flared during the college's early years, and the Ku Klux Klan sometimes threatened those associated with the college. One teacher was "hooted at" when she went to the local post office, and some local residents stoned her in the streets on several occasions. It became necessary for armed militiamen to escort women associated with Storer College when they ventured into town (Anthony 1891:10–11).

Figure 2.4. Brick from the John Brown Fort with a stylized image of the fort. The brick was distributed by Savery to friends (brick in possession of Harpers Ferry National Historical Park; image, courtesy Paul A. Shackel).

Townspeople also felt threatened by the possibility of an influx of African Americans coming into town to visit the fort. Solomon Brown, a longtime employee of the Smithsonian Institution, was a leading preservationist in the Washington, D.C., black community, especially in the Anacostia section. Active in African American literature and historical societies, he was "renowned in the 1880s and 1890s for organizing annual trips to Harpers Ferry on the anniversary of John Brown's 1859 raid" (Ruffins 1991:526). Because of this interest in the John Brown Fort within the African American community, some Harpers Ferry residents became excited about ridding the town of the fort. When a rumor in 1888 claimed that the John Brown Fort would be relocated to a New York park, the local newspaper's editor wrote in favor of this idea and exclaimed, "& joy go with it" (*Spirit of Jefferson* [*SoJ*] 1888:1).

Racial tensions flared with these rumors. For instance, on October 21, 1890, a *Spirit of Jefferson* supplement ran an article titled "To Africanize West Virginia." The title spread fear among working-class families, and the subtitle of the story claimed, "To colonize the state with the blacks of the south. West Virginia working men to be turned out of the mines and the shops, to give place for the Negro of the south" (*SoJ* 1890).

The following year, Savery sold the fort to the John Brown Fort Company, a group founded by A. J. Holmes, a former congressman from Iowa. He wished to exhibit the structure at the World's Columbian Exposition of 1893 in Chicago, and the company formed an act of incorporation for the "owning, controlling and exhibition of the building known as the John Brown Fort as well as other historical relics." The sale had become necessary when the Baltimore & Ohio Railroad made plans to move the railroad track 250 feet west from the banks of the Potomac River and the right-of-way was to cut through the John Brown Fort (*SoJ* 1889:3; Fairbairn 1961:22a).

During these transactions in the 1890s, the public memory of the Civil War was being transformed from that of a conflict about abolitionist ideals to that of a war of bravery and loyalty to a cause. The story of reconciliation that developed included white northerners and southerners, and blacks were omitted from the picture. During this time, a published confession by James Townsley, a friend of Brown, remarked that John Brown instigated the Pottawatomie murders, and soon after John Brown Jr. admitted that his father participated in the event. It became more difficult to justify the abolitionist actions of John Brown in the official history, and many writers began to interpret his deeds as vicious and fanatic (Karsner 1934; Malin 1942; Masters 1922, 1926; H. Wilson 1913).

Chicago: An Icon in Trouble

The John Brown Fort Company had dismantled the structure by November 1892, having commissioned George O. Garnsey, architect and editor of the *National Builder,* to supervise the work (*Graphic* 1892). While it has been commonly believed that the company erected the fort on the fairgrounds at the Columbian Exposition, no records exist to confirm this assumption. It certainly did not appear with any West Virginia exhibits (see Handy 1893:101, 573–76, 750–52, 1111). Rather, the structure was shipped to Chicago by rail and erected at 1341 Wabash Avenue with the intent of capitalizing on its proximity to the fairgrounds (Flinn 1893:132). On Wabash Street, the structure stood close to another attraction, the Libby Prison Museum. The fort sat in a square building with a conical roof that looked something like a haystack. "Rising from each side of the entrance are towers that reach nearly the height of the main building" (*Chicago Tribune* 1892:25). At the time of the *Chicago Tribune*'s article, the exhibit building was completed, although apparently the fort had yet to be reassembled.

After considerable delay, the fort opened for public visitation ten days before the Columbian Exposition closed, and it was said to have been reconstructed carefully and that the "slightest differences can not be found in the construction of the building" (Flinn 1893:132) (see figure 2.5). The fort contained curios related to Brown, and a public lecture was delivered by Colonel S. K. Donavin, an eyewitness to the raid, trial, and execution. The company attempted to persuade relatives of Brown to speak during the Columbian Exposition, but a daughter replied, "I may be a relic of John Brown's raid of Harpers Ferry, but I do not want to be placed on exhibition with other relics and curios, and such" (Gee 1958:94). Because the fort opened in the waning days of the fair and temperatures became increasingly cold in Chicago's chilly autumn days, the company collected

Figure 2.5. Building that held the John Brown Fort in Chicago on Wabash Street, 1892 (from John Brown's Old Fort, *Graphic,* January 9, 1892).

only eleven paid admissions. At fifty cents each, the John Brown Fort Company had lost close to $60,000—the cost of moving and rebuilding the structure in Chicago (Shackel 1995).

Buena Vista: Saving the Fort from Its "Ignoble Use"

The John Brown Fort Company abandoned the structure in Chicago. In 1895, the *Chicago Tribune* published an article titled "Ignoble Use of John Brown's Fort," stating that the fort was being moved so that it could become part of a stable for delivery wagons for a new department store. Since the John Brown Fort Company could not pay the rent specified in the lease, the improvements on the property, including the fort, reverted to the owner, Charles L. Hutchinson, president of the Corn Exchange Bank. Hutchinson, according to the *Chicago Tribune,* understood the historical importance of the structure and offered it as a free gift to any Chicago public park that would accept and care for it. At the time of the article (April 1, 1895), the fort was sitting on house movers' blocks in preparation for its move to become a department store stable (*Chicago Tribune* 1895a; Fairbairn 1961:14, 26, 33, 34; Gee 1958:94).

Mary Katherine Keemle Field, a publisher and reporter from Washington, D.C., seized this opportunity. At the time, she was known for *Kate Field's Washington,* a weekly editorial column that ran for about five years. In her column, she documented the theater and arts and heckled Congress on social reform issues: "From time to time she engaged in battles for such causes as international copyright, Hawaiian annexation, temperance, prohibition of Mormon polygamy, . . . [and] gained considerable vogue as a correspondent from London and elsewhere of the N.Y. *Herald* the N.Y. *Tribune* and other newspapers" (Whiting, in Fairbairn 1961:31).

Field also was actively involved with issues concerning post–Civil War African Americans. One of her missions included a fund-raiser to purchase the John Brown farm and grave at North Elba, near Lake Placid, New York, in the late 1860s, in order to save the site from ruin and decay. Field successfully used her column as a vehicle to solicit funds for the restoration.

Field heavily promoted the Columbian Exposition, and she knew that the John Brown Fort sat in the city. She stayed in Chicago from May to November to promote the fair, and in gratitude for her support, members of the Columbian Exposition awarded her a medal and diploma (Fairbairn 1961:31). Field established an agreement with the department store owner, who allowed her to search for an appropriate home for the fort. In 1895, she campaigned for donations to move the fort from Chicago back to Harpers Ferry (Fairbairn 1961:14, 31) to be close to Storer College, although these plans agitated many Harpers Ferry townspeople. At the same time, members of the African American community held meetings at Storer College to discuss a monument for John Brown and the Baltimore & Ohio Railroad's plans to provide a site (*SoJ* 1894:2). The railroad offered to have the fort relocated to an area near the original site, which would have encouraged tourism on the railroad line (Gee 1958:97).

At the same time, rumors developed about reburying John Brown's remains at Harpers Ferry. The *Spirit of Jefferson*'s editorial proclaimed that it was against disinterring John Brown's remains and erecting a monument, although the paper favored the return of the fort "where Robert E. Lee captured the old villain" (*SoJ* 1895b:2). Harpers Ferrians were also displeased about the idea of moving the bodies of the raiders, buried in a common grave on the Shenandoah across from Harpers Ferry, and to reinter them with a marker at the restored fort (*SoJ* 1895c:2).

Field contacted Alexander Murphy of Jefferson County, West Virginia, about the possibility of deeding five acres of his farm, Buena Vista, for the placement of the fort. The five-acre spot was over a mile from the fort's original location and railroad line, but Murphy convinced Field that his farm would be a suitable place for the fort. He wrote,

> I hope you will explain to the Committee the advantage of my place. Being close to the railroad Station on the Valley Road it is only a short walk to my place—no bother with carriages, etc.—Then another advantage is that whenever you wish more ground for the park, etc., you can get as much as you wish at a reasonable price. I am not one to extortion on strangers. If you will enquire around I think you will find that I have that name. Hoping you will decide to settle on my place. (Quoted in Fairbairn 1961:appendix)

On July 23, 1895, Kate Field signed a contract with Murphy and his wife, who deeded five acres of their farm for one dollar, a parcel that overlooked the Shenandoah River. The agreement stated that if the John Brown Fort was not moved from Chicago to the parcel of land, the agreement would be null and void, and the land would revert to the Murphys (Jefferson County Deed Book 1895:473–74). Field had envisioned an avenue of houses that would approach a park that encompassed the fort (Gee 1958:97).

In 1895, Kate Field was a weary fifty-seven-year-old and ready to pass the torch on to others. She discontinued publication of *Kate Field's Washington* and took a position as a roving correspondent in Hawaii. Before she left Chicago, she addressed an African American congregation at Quinn Chapel on Wabash Ave and 24th Street, about ten blocks north of where the fort stood in Chicago. Attendees pledged $100 for restoring the John Brown Fort at its original home in Harpers Ferry. Members of the congregation established the John Brown Fort Association at the meeting, and they were its founding members.

There is a strong likelihood that the fort had already been dismantled and that its bricks were sitting in Hutchinson's yard. Hutchinson had given Field permission to move and rebuild the structure wherever she chose. Since the original location of the fort in Harpers Ferry was now under fourteen feet of railroad fill, Field "settled to place the old building on the historic Bolivar Heights [Murphy's farm], which overlook the Shenandoah and Potomac valleys" (*Chicago Tribune* 1895b:9; Fairbairn 1961:34).

Many of Field's arrangements to move the fort to the Murphy farm remained unfinished when she departed Chicago. She wrote,

> So much was accomplished before I reached Chicago a few days ago. Then the real tug began. For although that public-spirited citizen Charles L. Hutchinson who fell heir to the Fort turns it over to me as a gift and although the site and transportation are arranged without cost, $1500 are needed for removal, reconstruction and other expenses. This is a big sum to raise. Still it is now or never with me. I am en route to Hawaii where I ought to have been a month ago, and the Fort must be dealt with at once or the winter storms and perennial hoodlums will not leave a rack behind. It is packed in a back yard exposed to the hoi polloi. (Letter from Kate Field to *Chicago Daily News,* n.d.; Fairbairn 1961:32)

Field left final arrangements for the fort's transportation to Harpers Ferry and its rebuilding to C. T. Cummins, who wrote her that he considered his task "a labor of which any man may be justly proud" (Letter, C. T. Cummins to Kate Field, August 11, 1895). The Baltimore & Ohio Railroad agreed to transport the building back to Harpers Ferry for no charge (*SoJ* 1895a:2).

Once the fort arrived at his farm, Alexander Murphy played a role in the construction of the fort on the five-acre parcel. In an oral history with Murphy's daughter-in-law, Mrs. Will Murphy, she noted that Murphy had to drain a spring on the property in order to make a decent location for the building's construction (Mrs. Will Murphy 1961). Cummins arrived at the five-acre parcel during the last week of September with three masons.

Reconstruction did not go as smoothly. On November 4, 1895, E. B. Chambers, a friend of Field, wrote her that the construction of the fort on Murphy's farm proceeded very slowly and that Cummins took very little interest in his work. Cummins was paid $300 when he loaded the fort on a train in Chicago and $300 more when he completed the foundation. While all the bricks from the fort sat on the grounds, an additional 8,000 bricks needed to be purchased in order to complete the building, which meant an unexpected expense:

> This leaves very little to complete the job and his hands are dissatisfied with his management. You should know beyond a doubt that all bills for labor and materials are settled before settling with Mr. Cummins otherwise there will be mechanics Liens on the property. I have no money on hand as parties who subscribed would not pay because it was placed on Bolivar heights instead of the old site at Harpers Ferry. (Letter, Chambers to Field, November 4, 1895)

The masons working on the John Brown Fort project also wrote to Kate Field and pleaded that they needed to get paid since they owed five weeks of board in Harpers Ferry and their families in Chicago needed the money. They asked that Field send the money to Chambers since Cummins never came to the job site and was "fishing and drunk all the time" (Letter, Stuckwain, Stuckwain, and Neeser to Field, November 4, 1895). In another letter dated the same day, the masons remarked that they thought the whole project existed to "swindle the Poor Working." While Mr. Cummins wanted to build the fort on top of the ground with a minimal foundation, Mr. Chambers insisted on constructing a cellar eight feet deep. Four African Americans constructed the cellar in four weeks, and the masons wrote that Mr. Cummins tried to cheat them of their wages (Letter, Stuckwain, Stuckwain, and Neeser, November 4, 1895).

Mr. McCabe, a contractor from Baltimore, was placed in charge of the project by Field, and on November 12 he discharged Cummins. He reported to Kate Field that since the firing of Cummins, the work progressed rapidly (Letter, McCabe to Field, November 12, 1895).

At the completion of the reconstruction on the Murphy farm, it is uncertain how many bricks of the John Brown Fort were actually part of the original structure. Souvenir hunters took bricks from the fort from the outbreak of the Civil War, and while it lay dismantled in Hutchinson's yard in Chicago it fell prey to scavengers again. With an order for 8,000 bricks, one can speculate that with a fieldstone foundation many of the bricks were used in the reconstruction of the walls of the fort. If they were all used in the fort, as much as three and a half to four vertical feet of the fort's walls consisted of newly purchased bricks (Shackel 1995).

Many expenses were incurred by Murphy. He had to hire a caretaker to maintain the building, receive visitors, and fend off the souvenir hunters. Visitors sometimes climbed over fences and littered the fields, and carriages trampled Murphy's crops (according to an undated newspaper article in possession of Murphy family). Kate Field had verbally agreed to reimburse Murphy for these expenses; however, she died suddenly in 1896 in Hawaii (*Chicago Tribune* 1896:6, in Fairbairn 1961:34), leaving no estate to provide money necessary for the upkeep of the John Brown Fort. The John Brown Association ceased to function without her support (*Martinsburg Journal* 1964:8).

While the fort had served as a rallying point for federal troops during the war and many middle-class tourists visited the building throughout the Reconstruction era, the structure's meaning was transformed during the beginning of the Jim Crow era. Although African Americans may have always implicitly revered the John Brown Fort as a symbol of their abolitionist struggle, the structure became an explicit and prominent symbol among African Americans from this point on. For instance, in July 1896, the first national convention of the National League of Colored Women met in Washington, D.C., and took a day trip to the John Brown Fort at the Murphy farm. This meeting, led by Mary Church Terrell, is the first known occurrence of African Americans explicitly embracing the fort as a symbol of their struggle for freedom and equality (Shackel 1995).

Still burdened with the expense of upkeep, Murphy in 1901 filed a bill against the administrator and the unknown heirs of Kate Field's will. Murphy's suit included $1,116 for the upkeep of the fort and property; his bill was also filed against the five-acre parcel and the John Brown Fort owned by Kate Field's estate (according to an undated newspaper article in possession of Murphy family).

The property was advertised for sale, and Murphy purchased the property for $800 after bidding against two other competitors. Murphy paid $100 in court costs and took title to the five acres and the John Brown Fort (*Farmers Advocate* 1902:3; Jefferson County Court Records 1901, 1902a, 1902b; *SoJ* 1902:3). He dismissed the caretaker, curtailed access to the fort, and planted the surrounding fields with crops (Mrs. Will Murphy 1961). Murphy used the fort as a grain barracks (*SoJ* 1903), and Field's dreams of a park and an avenue of houses surrounding the John Brown Fort never came to fruition.

Many local histories often conveyed the message that the fort was closed to visitors, although this was not necessarily true. In August 1906, the Second Niagara Movement Convention was held in Harpers Ferry, and members visited the John Brown Fort on the Murphy farm. The Niagara Movement was founded in Fort Erie, Ontario, Canada, in July 1905 with fifty-four members from eighteen states. Its principal guidelines (quoted in P. Foner 1970:144–49) included the following:

1. Freedom of speech and criticism
2. An unfettered and unsubsidized press
3. Manhood suffrage
4. The abolition of all caste distinctions based simply on race and color
5. The recognition of the principle of human brotherhood as a practical present creed
6. The recognition of the highest and best training as the monopoly of no class or race
7. A belief in the dignity of labor
8. United effort to realize these ideals under wise and courageous leadership

Nearly one hundred visitors came to Harpers Ferry for the second meeting of the Niagara movement. While in town, they celebrated John Brown's Day and came to the fort on August 17, 1906, to commemorate John Brown's one-hundredth birthday and the fiftieth anniversary of the Battle of Osawatomie. (In actuality, John Brown's one-hundredth birthday would have been in 1900.) At 6:00 in the morning, the conference participants left the convention site, Storer College, and started their journey to the fort, about a mile away. As they approached the fort, they formed a procession, single file, "took off their shoes and socks, and walked barefoot as if treading on holy ground" (Quarles 1974:4) (see figure 2.6). Following a speech, the group marched around the fort and sang "The Battle Hymn of the Republic," with supplemental verses of the John Brown song. They then entered the fort and climbed the wooden bell tower to view the Shenandoah Valley (Quarles 1974:4).

The participants listened to a prayer led by Richard T. Greener. He offered remarks and personal recollections of John Brown and told the crowd that when he served as consul at Vladivostok, he heard Russian troops burst into song: "John Brown's body lies a-mouldering in the grave" (Quarles 1974:4).

Max Barber (1906:404), one of the founders of the Niagara movement, wrote in *The Voice of the Negro* about his experience at Harpers Ferry and the John Brown Fort:

> I have heard men speak of the peculiar sensation, the thrill which comes to one as he stands in the shadow of some mighty structure or on a spot where some great deed was wrought that

Figure 2.6. Marching to a monument for freedom: The 1906 Niagara movement procession to John Brown's Fort, by Richard Fitzhugh (courtesy Richard Fitzhugh).

> perceptibly advanced the world. Men have journeyed to the other side of the world to drink a draught of air that played around a Calvary, Trafalgar, or a Runnymede, and they have felt well paid for their trouble. I too have known what it meant to meditate at Valley Forge, Queenstown, and Gettysburg. But I must confess that I had never yet felt as I felt at Harpers Ferry.

Later that day, W. E. B. Du Bois read the Niagara Address to the delegation, and Max Barber (1906:408) remarked that the address "was profound and scholarly and claimed the intellectual admiration of the entire convention." Du Bois's tone allowed others in the press to label him a militant and agitator. He told the congregation of African Americans' increasing loss of political and social rights. "We claim for ourselves every single right that belongs to a freeborn American, political, civil, and social; and until we get these rights we will never cease to protest and assail the ears of America" (Du Bois, quoted in P. Foner 1970:170–71). He continued:

> The battle we wage is not for ourselves alone but for all true Americans. It is a fight for ideals, lest this, our common fatherland, false in founding, become in truth the land of the thief and the home of the slave—a byword and a hissing among the nations for its sounding pretensions and pitiful accomplishments. (Du Bois, quoted in P. Foner 1970:170–71)

He claimed that he did not believe in obtaining equal rights through violence, but

> we do believe in John Brown, in that incarnate spirit of justice, that hatred of a lie, the willingness to sacrifice money, reputation, and life itself on the altar of right. And here on the scene of John Brown's martyrdom we reconsecrate ourselves, our honor, our property to final emancipation of the race which John Brown died to make free. . . . Thank God for John Brown! Thank God for Garrison and Douglas! Sumner and Philips, Nat Turner and Robert Gould Shaw. (Du Bois, quoted in P. Foner 1970: 172–73)

Du Bois remarked on five points that were later incorporated into a resolution passed at Harpers Ferry. They included the following:

> First, we want full manhood suffrage and we want it now. Second, we want discrimination in public accommodations to cease. Third, we claim the right of freemen to walk, talk, and be with them that wish to be with us. Fourth, we want the laws enforced against rich as well as poor, against capitalist as well as laborer, against white as well as black. Fifth, we want our children educated. They have a right to know, to think, to aspire. We do not believe in violence. Our enemies, triumphant for the present, are fighting the stars in their courses. Justice and humanity must prevail. We are men, we will be treated as men. And we shall win. (Quoted in Hughes et al. 1973:259)

The Reverend Reverdy C. Ransom followed Du Bois. Barber described his speech on "The Spirit of John Brown" as spiritually uplifting. "Women wept, men shouted and waved hats and handkerchiefs and everybody was moved" (Barber 1906:408). Another major outcome of the Niagara movement meeting at Harpers Ferry was the passing of the resolution to admit women to full membership on an equal footing with men.

Storer College: African Americans Embracing the Fort

In 1909, the college trustees of Storer College voted to buy the John Brown Fort. Members of Storer College had begun negotiating with Murphy shortly after his 1903 purchase, and in 1909 the college agreed to pay $900, which covered Murphy's purchase price and court costs. Dismantled in 1910, the fort again fell prey to souvenir hunters. The college rebuilt the structure near Lincoln Hall on campus grounds, and it remained an important symbol of the African American community while the official national history increasingly denigrated John Brown and his actions (see figure 2.7). Robert Penn Warren (1929) once called John Brown a courageous common thief, and James Malin (1942:22) remarked that Brown was "a hypocritical fiend more vile than anything his worst enemies have pictured him." Historian C. Vann Woodward (1952) offered evidence from nineteen affidavits that Brown was insane and had inherited this condition from his mother's family. He later wrote that "unheroic millions could now sing 'John Brown's Body' in naive identification with the demented old hero" (Woodward 1993:74). Lee Edgar Masters (1926), in his *Lee: A Dramatic Poem*, has John Brown play a spectator and vengeful

Figure 2.7. Students and faculty of Storer College gather in front of the John Brown Fort when it was located on the Storer College campus, ca. 1940s (courtesy Harpers Ferry National Historical Park).

instigator of the downfall of General Lee, who had commanded the troops that captured Brown in October 1859.

During this southern revisionist movement, blacks continued to view the fort as a symbol of their cause for social justice (Fairbairn 1961:14). W. E. B. Du Bois wrote a major biography of John Brown in 1909 that recaptured and reinforced the sympathy for John Brown that was prevalent in the literature of the Reconstruction era. Du Bois's work countered the southern sentiment that denigrated the methods and cause of John Brown and the abolitionist movement. Calling John Brown a prophet, Du Bois (1962:339) remarked that Brown justifiably used militant actions at Harpers Ferry. Du Bois, along with many others, allowed the legacy of John Brown and the abolitionist movement to be remembered, and the John Brown Fort served as a rallying point for these ideas.

In 1943, U.S. Congressman Jennings Randolph of West Virginia introduced legislation to create a national park at Harpers Ferry. The *Baltimore Sun* reported that Randolph proposed to commemorate "the Harpers

Ferry campaigns of the War Between the States and the great cause of human freedom." Matthew Page Andrews of the Sons of Confederate Veterans protested the legislation and wrote the senator that he perceived this action as a "backdoor entrance into the original plan to honor John Brown and his ersatz brand of freedom" (Letter, Andrews to Randolph, 1943:1). Andrews remarked,

> He was a small-scale edition of a Trotsky or perhaps an awkward prototype of Schicklgruber, without either's gift for rabble-rousing. . . . Brown engaged in secretly sowing sedition in the U.S. Army and for a time seized a U.S. arsenal while proclaiming a "Provisional Government" with himself as President or Fuhrer. . . . Public opinion sometimes condones murder on a grand scale, but it should at least be impossible to make a hero out of a masquerader guilty of forgery and other felonies, just because he alleged he had in mind a noble purpose. (Letter, Andrews to Randolph, 1943:1)

Andrews evoked the Lost Cause and claimed that a depoliticized monument that conjures the feeling of heroism would be more suitable at Harpers Ferry:

> That phrase about "human freedom" will be interpreted in its context as pointing to a war waged by one side with such a purpose in view and by the other in opposition thereto. . . . Such a "Monument" could well be set apart in memory of heroism on either side; or, as it should be, heroism on both sides. If this should be announced purport of the bill, the monument would rest on a solid foundation rather than the sands of variant opinions. (Letter, Andrews to Randolph, 1943:1)

The United Daughters of the Confederacy (UDC) simultaneously protested the legislation to create a monument at Harpers Ferry just as an earlier attempt by Randolph to establish "The John Brown Park" had been met by a storm of protests. The president of the UDC wrote in 1943, "Now, by a different wording 'The Harpers Ferry National Monument,' you are again trying to accomplish the same thing in a new covering, but underneath is the same old skeleton" (Letter, Powell to Randolph, 1943:1). Despite these protests, President Franklin Roosevelt signed legislation in 1944 to establish Harpers Ferry National Monument.

Lower Town Harpers Ferry: Remaking a National Symbol

The fort remained on the grounds of Storer College after it closed in 1955 until 1968, when the National Park Service moved the fort to its present location. Unable to place the fort on its original foundations, now under fourteen feet of fill on railroad property, the National Park Service relocated the fort to the former Arsenal Yard that Brown had briefly captured more than one hundred years before.

The movement of the fort occurred during an important episode in American history: the Civil Rights movement. This movement and the passing of the Civil Rights Act allowed for alternative histories to become part of the official memory. The 1960s witnessed the development of the new social history—a new paradigm that encouraged a focus on the histories of those who have been traditionally forgotten. African American history developed as a viable intellectual pursuit, and the southern revisionist histories of John Brown were challenged. Novelist John Oliver Killian (in Sandage 1993:161) wrote, "You give us moody Abraham Lincoln, but many of us prefer John Brown, whom most of you hold in contempt and regard as fanatic." Many of the original, sympathetic accounts of John Brown's raid were reprinted in the 1960s and 1970s (American Anti-Slavery Society 1969; O. Anderson 1972; Quarles 1974). Benjamin Quarles (1974) created an edited volume of letters written by African Americans about John Brown. The 1861 story of Osborne Anderson, an African American who collaborated with John Brown and one of only three members of the raiding party that escaped Harpers Ferry, was reprinted in 1979 (Libby 1979). W. E. B. Du Bois's 1909 biography of John Brown was reprinted in 1962. Louis Ruchames developed a collection of readings that resurrected the favorable prose of John Brown by including authors such as Henry David Thoreau, Oswald Villard, and Stephen Vincent Benet. Ruchames (1959:15) remarked that the goal of his compiled book was to educate the American public to the evils of slavery and to "help our own generation . . . toward a greater appreciation of those very ideals which motivated Brown and his friends."

The fort's move occurred during the height of social upheaval and racial strife in the 1960s. It happened in the same year that Detroit and Newark burned and brought international attention to racial inequalities in the United States. That same year, Robert Kennedy and Martin Luther King Jr., two social reformers, were assassinated, and President Johnson's New Society, based on the social reform policies of John F. Kennedy, was initiated. During this era, the National Park Service began to pay more attention to urban areas and began to address issues that were important to the urban population, including racism. By moving the John Brown Fort, the National Park Service took a symbol of radical rebellion and co-opted it, placing it within the center of a national park. It not only became a symbol of African American identity but once again became part of the national official memory. The federal government incorporated a fringe symbol into its main ideology—a symbolic action to help quell some of the dissatisfaction found among a large segment of the African American population (Shackel 1995).

Today, Harpers Ferry is one of the most visited national historical parks in the United States, and John Brown and the John Brown Fort contribute significantly to the visitor's recognition of the place. The fort is surrounded by a nicely manicured lawn, which contributes to the creation of a monumental landscape commemorating the deeds of the abolitionist and his men.

The John Brown Fort is a monument that has physically changed many times during its 150-year existence. What has not changed significantly is how the fort has been embraced by a large portion of the African American community. The John Brown Fort serves as one of only a few Civil War shrines or monuments claimed by that community. After the Civil War, the nation began constructing monuments, a testimony to moral reformation and the justification of the most violent epoch in American history. Vernacular monuments were placed throughout the American landscape with uncontroversial inscriptions. They do not mention slavery or African Americans, and they generally justify the war as "the cause" or an issue of "state sovereignty." The common soldier portrayed in these monuments is always understood to be a white Anglo-Saxon (Savage 1994:135).

Among the thousands of Civil War monuments, only a few have African American representation, even though blacks played a major role in the balance of power. Two monuments show a single black surrounded by other white soldiers; a third is a single black soldier in a cemetery in Norfolk, Virginia; a fourth is the African American soldiers' monument recently erected in Washington, D.C.; and a fifth is the Robert Gould Shaw Memorial in Boston, Shaw being a local white hero who led the first northern black troops, the 54th Massachusetts Volunteer Infantry, into battle. This memorial shows Shaw on horseback adjacent to his marching African American troops, and the monument can be interpreted as more of a monument to Shaw than to the infantry (Savage 1994:136). The introduction of African American troops into the Civil War was influential in changing the tide of the war, yet the lack of African American representation among Civil War monuments is noticeable and shocking. Savage (1994:135) writes, "Public monuments do not arise as if by natural law to celebrate the deserving; they are built by people with sufficient power to marshal (or impose) public consent for their erection."

There are few memorials that the African American community can embrace that relate to the moral struggles of the Civil War. The John Brown Fort is one such memorial that symbolizes the fight against inequality, and it has been embraced by whites and blacks in varying degrees. The histories of John Brown have changed among whites along with the political climate of this country, although John Brown has always been revered by the black community. Many leading African American citizens visited the John Brown Fort while it stood on the Murphy farm for fifteen years, and the structure even found a home on an African American college campus for more than fifty years.

Recently, the West Virginia Chapter of the National Association for the Advancement of Colored People (NAACP) held its fiftieth-anniversary celebration at the fort in 1994. In 1996, the National Park Service sponsored a celebration of the ninetieth anniversary of the Niagara movement meeting at Harpers Ferry with a symposium and ceremonies. The two-day celebration was titled "The Call for Justice and the Struggle for Equality: The Niagara Movement, A Ninety-Year Retrospective." About one hundred people came to a sunrise service held at the remaining foundations of the John Brown Fort on the Murphy farm. Much like the original participants, at the end of the ceremony the attendees marched around the perimeter of the fort's foundation and sang "The Battle Hymn of the Republic" (see figure 2.8). Unlike the original ceremony, a bus awaited the participants to take them back to the park.

Today the John Brown Fort stands about 150 feet from its original location, which is under railroad fill. It is a bit smaller than its original size, and many new bricks were added when it was placed on Buena Vista, the Murphy farm. Several plaques were also placed in the fort when it was subsequently rebuilt. The structure contains mementos that recognize the 1895 rebuilding sponsored by Kate Field, the 1910 rebuilding on the Storer College campus, and the stone placed on the fort's exterior wall by the college's alumni in 1918 to acknowledge the "heroism" of John Brown and his twenty-one men. Several times in the fort's history it has almost

Figure 2.8. The ninetieth-anniversary celebration of the meeting of the Niagara movement at Harpers Ferry in August 1996. Participants marched around the foundations of where the John Brown Fort was located, on the Murphy farm, in 1906 (courtesy Paul A. Shackel).

vanished completely in landscapes of violence and tragedy (see Foote 1997:274–77). But like the phoenix, it rose from obscurity through the help of many ordinary citizens performing extraordinary feats to save and preserve the fort and help transform it into a symbol of freedom in the national public memory.

Today, the staff of the National Park Service uses the fort as a prop to help tell the story of Harpers Ferry. Each National Park Service interpreter has a slightly different spin on how John Brown and the John Brown Fort should be seen in American history. While standing inside the structure, some interpreters will only tell the story of John Brown, and others will interpret his act as a form of civil disobedience, comparing his deed to the Vietnam protests. The National Park Service interpreter leaves the visitor with the notion that determining the difference between civil disobedience and a criminal act can vary between people and groups and that opinions may change through time.

Southern Heritage and the Faithful-Slave Monuments: The Heyward Shepherd Memorial

3

SOUTHERNERS CLAIMED that the Confederacy was not formed to protect the institution of slavery but rather to protect states' rights. Conversely, historian Drew Gilpin Faust (1988) points out that the leaders of the secession movement cited slavery as the reason for southern independence, a reason often repeated in press, pulpit, and schools until the end of the war. She notes that editorials often claimed, "Negro slavery is the South, and the South is Negro Slavery" (quoted in Faust 1988:60). After the war, both northerners and southerners built monuments to commemorate the events of the war. Northerners celebrated their victory and paid tribute to the dead, while southerners used monument building to remember a cause and mourn their losses. They used monuments to praise the deeds of their soldiers and to revere the ideals of the Lost Cause. During Reconstruction, the monument movement served as a vehicle for southerners to distance themselves from their association with slavery.

During the Jim Crow era, blacks were increasingly subordinated to white control, and southerners gained more political power in the United States. Southern heritage groups realized that statues could be used to validate the continued subordination of blacks and justify their role in maintaining and fighting for slavery during the war. One type of monument that has received little attention among historians is the "faithful-slave monument." While several were built in the South—the most notable erected in 1896 in Fort Mills, South Carolina, by a former plantation owner (Blight 2001:288; Savage 1997b:155–61)—little is known about the coordinated national effort of southern heritage groups to place one in Harpers Ferry. Its meaning and location in a national park continue to stir emotions today, involving the United Daughters of the Confederacy

(UDC), the Sons of Confederate Veterans (SCV), the National Association for the Advancement of Colored People (NAACP), and the National Park Service (NPS).

The "faithful-slave" myth became a vehicle for southerners to justify the institution of slavery. Southern heritage groups paid homage to slaves and servants who did not rebel against their masters during the Civil War. This phenomenon allowed twentieth-century southern heritage groups to declare that African Americans were content as slaves. From the mid-1890s through the end of the 1930s, the *Confederate Veteran* published hundreds of stories about faithful slaves. David Blight (2001:287) writes,

> In this flood of testimony about faithful blacks at the heart of the Civil War memory, history gives way completely to mythology. The thousands of slaves who escaped to contraband camps, joined the Union army or navy, or fled when opportunities came while working in Confederate hospitals or on railroads and fortifications—as well as the daily revolution that occurred in the master-slave relationship during the war—had been steadfastly repressed in Southern memory.

The development of the faithful-slave monument is best understood in the context of the development of memorial building after the Civil War.

Memorial Building in the Former Confederacy

Southerners created more monuments to their defeat than any other civilization in history. It was their dedication to the Lost Cause and justifying their actions during the Civil War that encouraged the proliferation of these markers (McPherson 1982:488). The idea of the Lost Cause, kept alive by southern patriotic groups such as the UDC and SCV, survived through the twentieth century and into the twenty-first. These southern heritage groups were, and still are, engaged in cultural warfare to establish a "Confederate tradition." This tradition focuses on the white South's view of history, appreciation for rule by the white elite, a fear of the enfranchisement of African Americans, and a reverence for the Confederate cause (Blight 2001; Foster 1987:5). The paradigm preaches racial separation and the virtues of an aristocratic South.

Historian Michael Kammen (1991:117) notes that the erection of monuments after the Civil War replaced religious civic culture with nationalism and political ideology. Southerners erected the earliest Civil War monuments in cemeteries. The Victorian cemetery served as a quiet place for family picnics, and many community members could learn about and contemplate patriotism and heroic deeds from these places. Northerners broke from this tradition and erected monuments in town squares and parks beginning in the late 1860s (Kammen 1991:116).

Southerners continued to erect monuments in cemeteries for several decades after the Civil War. They were swept with bereavement over the lost war, the end of the plantation system, and the loss of a large proportion of the male population. During Reconstruction, southerners feared reprisal from the occupying federal army if they brought their commemoration of the Confederate cause to town centers. They created new cemeteries for the dead soldiers, and memorialization became a way for southerners to extract meaning from the war. The dead became a powerful cultural symbol of southern ideals (Foster 1987:42–47). This becomes obvious when examining early southern postwar monuments. The Confederate monuments erected before 1885 reflect themes of bereavement, and 90 percent had a funereal aspect in placement or design (Foster 1987:40–41; Kammen 1991:117).

It was not until the mid-1880s that southerners broke from this Victorian tradition. The tone of bereavement at commemorative events and at Decoration Day celebrations had changed drastically. For instance, at a Decoration Day service in Augusta, Georgia, in 1889, a man read,

> Yes, soon with the tolling
> Of Funeral Knells
> Will Mingle the rolling
> Of famed "Rebel Yells."
>
> Be ready to meet it—
> This Great Day so near,—
> And zealously greet it,
> Ye citizens dear. (From Foster 1987:121)

In another instance, more than 100,000 people attended the unveiling of Robert E. Lee's memorial in Richmond, Virginia, in the late 1880s. As participants pulled the canvas from the sculpture, the crowd cheered wildly and tossed their hats in the air. It was a far cry from the mournful ceremonies that had dominated Confederate memorialization less than a decade earlier. In fact, after the 1880s, only about 40 percent of monuments had funerary designs, and the majority of new monuments had an anonymous Confederate soldier on a pedestal. The emphasis in commemoration began to change to nostalgia and the celebration of heroicism. "The memory of the war was no longer relegated to the city of the dead" (Foster 1987:129).

About 60 percent of the markers unveiled before 1913 were erected between 1900 and 1912. About 80 percent featured the lone Confederate soldier, and 85 percent of these stood in public places, such as courthouse lawns. Only 25 percent had some funerary symbols. These new markers in downtown southern cities became a form of vindication. In fact, some southern memorial groups moved their monuments from cemeteries to more visible places in downtown areas (Foster 1987:168–69). Lizzie Pollard, the first president of the Southern Memorial Association, wrote in 1897 about a bronze Confederate monument. She remarked,

> These monuments we build will speak their message to generations. These voiceless marbles in their majesty will stand as vindicators of the Confederate soldier. They will lift from these brave men the opprobrium of rebel, and stand them in the line of patriots. This is not alone a labor of love, it is a work of duty as well. We are correcting history. (Confederated Southern Memorial Association 1904:66–68)

The large number of monument unveilings after 1900 is a reflection of the growing strength of the various Confederate organizations, especially the UDC. Northern organizations never showed the same enthusiasm as these southern groups, even though they erected more monuments than their southern counterparts. The Grand Army of the Republic believed that they were destined to win the war. Their victory was preordained, and the greatness of their forefathers was unquestioned. On the other hand, the southern organization had put a different spin on the outcome of the war. They "looked back nostalgically to the supposed greatness of their forefathers' civilization. The South would have to rise again to achieve a modicum of its previous glory. They celebrated a lost empire by trying to preserve it in writing the past anew" (National Register of Historic Places 1996:E18).

The struggle over what memory to celebrate was settled by the end of Reconstruction. As David Blight (1989a:1159) writes,

> Historical memory . . . was not merely an entity altered by the passage of time; it was the prize in a struggle between rival ver-

> sions of the past, a question of will, of power, of persuasion. The historical memory of any transforming or controversial event emerges from cultural and political competition, from the choice to confront the past and to debate and manipulate its meaning.

Whoever could control the events and the creation of public memory of the events of the Civil War would eventually control historical consciousness of the interpretations of the war. African Americans, such as Frederick Douglass, found themselves in a growing minority when interpreting the events of the Civil War. Douglass continually stressed that the Federals fought the war over an ideological struggle about the issue of slavery, emancipation, and Reconstruction. Like many other contemporaneous African American leaders, they lost ground to a new and increasingly popular memory that viewed the war as a test of a generation's valor and loyalty to a cause. Veteran groups led by Jefferson Davis and Jubal Early created the Lost Cause and wrote partisan Confederate histories. They argued that they were never defeated but rather that they were overwhelmed by numbers and betrayed by some key generals. They dreamed of a return to "an undefeated confederacy" (Blight 2001; C. Wilson 1980). As their movement gained momentum, the Lost Cause mythology won in the battle to control the memories of the Civil War, and the idea of reconciliation dominated the meaning of the Civil War throughout the twentieth century (Blight 1989a:1162–63, 2001; Connelly and Bellows 1982).

From the late nineteenth century through most of the twentieth, African American participation in the war received limited attention in American literature, and this omission effectively removed them from the American consciousness (Aaron 1973:332–33). "Slavery, the war's deepest cause, and black freedom, the war's most fundamental result, remain the most conspicuous missing elements in the American literature inspired by the Civil War" (Blight 1989a:1176). W. E. B. Du Bois also noted this discrepancy with historical accounts in 1935 when he wrote *Black Reconstruction in America 1860–1880.* Du Bois remarked that the Jim Crow histories of the Civil War "paints perfect men and noble nations, but it does not tell the truth" (Du Bois 1992:722).

The Heyward Shepherd Memorial in Harpers Ferry

The Making of a Martyr

A faithful-slave monument to Heyward Shepherd in Harpers Ferry is reflective of the Lost Cause ideology. The monument recalls the John

Brown raid, one of the most controversial events in American history. Brown, who had gained a national reputation as an abolitionist, planned to capture the U.S. Armory at Harpers Ferry. He believed that his actions would encourage a slave rebellion and that together they would march south to free other slaves.

On the night of October 16, 1859, Brown and his party of twenty-one men captured the federal arsenal with relative ease. A group of Marines under the command of Colonel Robert E. Lee eventually overthrew Brown, and not a single slave had come to Brown's aid (O. Anderson 1972:36; Hinton 1894:311 ff., 709 ff.; Oates 1970:293–300; Villard 1910:440). Brown was found guilty and hanged for treason on December 2, 1859. Many northern abolitionists immediately made Brown a martyr, while southerners claimed that his attack on the U.S. Armory amounted to treason and that death was a just penalty for the act. Many historians claim that his acts ignited a smoldering fire that developed into the Civil War.

One of the great ironies of the raid is that the first person killed was Heyward Shepherd, a free African American working for the Baltimore & Ohio Railroad. Shepherd served as a baggage handler and sometimes tended the office (Barry 1979:84).

By about 1:00 AM on the night of the raid, the raiders had cut the telegraph lines and also stopped the Baltimore & Ohio express train that had just arrived from Wheeling, West Virginia. Curious about the commotion, Shepherd walked to the Potomac River bridge, where two of Brown's raiders posted at the bridge confronted him. In a report to the U.S. Congress, John Starry testified that

> he had been ordered to halt by some men who were there, and, instead of doing that, he turned to go back to the office, and as he turned they shot him in the back. . . . He was in the employment of the Baltimore and Ohio Railroad Company, and . . . he was a free negro. (Mason Report 1860:23; see also Barry 1979:49–50)

Shepherd died the next afternoon.

Shepherd lived in Winchester, Virginia, about thirty miles south of Harpers Ferry, and was well regarded by the Harpers Ferry community (M. Johnson 1997:3). The accounts of Shepherd's role in the attack have varied over the years. The editor of the *Virginia Free Press* (hereafter *VFP;*

1859a), a local newspaper sympathetic to secession, initially reported that the raiders told Shepherd about the purpose of the raid, but he refused to join them and fled. An account published in the same paper, but thirty-seven years later during the Jim Crow era, suggested that Shepherd initially helped the raiders but changed his mind when it became clear that the capture of Harpers Ferry would eventually fail (*VFP* 1896:2). The memory of Shepherd, controlled by the white press, became an important tool in the late nineteenth and early twentieth centuries for aiding and justifying the Lost Cause.

The use of the image of Shepherd to justify the existing social system and to demonize John Brown began almost immediately after his death. The *VFP* (1859b:2) reported, "He was shot down like a dog. A humble negro as he was, his life was worth more than all of the desperadoes of the party, and his memory will be revered, when theirs will only be thought of with execution." The editorial described Shepherd as "an unoffending trust worthy free Negro man."

Several militia groups and white citizens accompanied Shepherd's body back to his hometown as testimony to their high regard for him. The procession honored an African American in a slave society for his commitment and loyalty to his job and his station in life. The newspaper highlighted the irony of the raid—Shepherd, a black man, was Brown's first victim in the raid (*VFP* 1859b). The editors of the *VFP*, including William Gallaher, continually reminded their readers of this irony for many years to come (*VFP* 1867, 1879, 1884b; M. Johnson 1997:5). In fact, near the twentieth anniversary of Brown's execution, the editors continued the demonization of Brown and reinforced the martyrdom of a faithful African American who worked diligently in a white-dominated society. The paper reminded its audience that

> John Brown's first act toward the forcible liberation was the emancipation of Heyward, a peaceable, industrious colored man, from honest toil and a contented life by a bullet in his back. His worshipers may sing to their heart's content "John Brown's body lies mould'ring in the ground" and his "soul goes marching on," but the blood of poor Heyward is on his saintly robe all the same; and we imagine it will be an indefinite "marching on" before his soul finds a saint's rest. The killing of Heyward, the inoffensive colored railroad porter at Harper's Ferry, was a brute murder—without an occasion or provocation. (*VFP* 1879:2)

When Frederick Douglass came to Harpers Ferry in 1881 to deliver a speech on Brown at Storer College, the editors of the newspaper remarked they would not let the "negro-worshippers" forget that "the first victim of the old murderer was an inoffensive, industrious and respected colored man, brutally shot down without provocation or excuse" (*VFP* 1881:2). And in 1884, when African Americans voted overwhelmingly for the Republican Party, the *VFP* (1884a) reminded the public about the irony of Shepherd. When an editor of a local Harpers Ferry newspaper, the *Sentinel,* suggested that Shepherd was accidentally killed in the raid, the *VFP* editor (1887b:2) replied,

> John Brown who has been canonized as a saint—who came into a happy and peaceful community making professions of regard for colored people, . . . fatally shot an industrious, inoffensive colored man. Why did he shoot him? Not "accidentally," but because Heyward could not be used by him. Heyward's immediate refusal to join John Brown is a refutation of the statement, by a paper that ought to be jealous of the fair name and fame of Harper's Ferrians, that he was "oppressed," "harassed,"—"hardly permitted to stay at Harper's Ferry." Harpers Ferrians regarded Heyward for his personal worth and treated him kindly, and the persuasive power of a Sharpe's rifle could not induce him to enter upon a murderous midnight assault upon them as they slept peacefully.

In the next issue, the editors remarked, "Don't stultify the *Sentinel* by proclaiming the industrious, inoffensive colored man was 'accidently' killed" (*VFP* 1887c:2).

Reinforcing the "faithful African American" myth and the demonization of Brown, the *VFP* (1888b:2) continually harped on the subject. In 1888, the editors remarked,

> He was deliberately, cruelly, and mercilessly murdered without warning and without giving the slightest provocation. Yet there are . . . friends of the negro who worship John Brown as a Saint on Glory; and several newspaper men who tear passion into tatters because we state, occasionally, the historic fact that John Brown's first victim at Harper's Ferry was an industrious, inoffensive colored man!

The term "inoffensive colored railroad porter" (or something similar), first used in the newspaper's October 27, 1859, account of the raid, was often used to describe Shepherd in subsequent accounts. This phrase reappears during the next several decades, although it angered many African American groups (*Farmers Advocate* 1920:2; *VFP* 1879:2, 1887a:3, 1888a:2, 1894:2, 1895:2, 1896:2, 1899:2, 1902:2).

African American presses grew in strength in the late nineteenth century, and one, located in the nearby community of Martinsburg, West Virginia, tuned in to the rhetoric of the *VFP*. The *Pioneer Press*'s editor, J. R. Clifford, found the phrase offensive. In response, he wrote that if Shepherd was "'an industrious, inoffensive colored man' we rather take sides with John Brown, i.e., if Brown considered him inoffensive enough to be killed, we have no fault to find" (*Pioneer Press,* quoted in *VFP* 1893:2). The editors of the *VFP* responded,

> It is rather unsafe to say that any man may arrogate to himself the right to kill because he has it in his mind that a man is "offensive enough to be killed." His killing of Heyward Shepherd was an unprovoked murder, and Editor Clifford is the only man to our knowledge, who has had the temerity to publicly approve it. (*VFP* 1893:2)

That same year, the editor of the *VFP* (1892:2) insisted that when an artist came to town to paint Harpers Ferry as it appeared during the John Brown raid, he offered to get an accurate likeness of Heyward Shepherd, the "first victim of John Brown's raid," especially since he was an "inoffensive, industrious colored man." A "picture of the raid with Shepherd left out would be like Hamlet play without the Dane."

Later, in 1902, when the *Pioneer Press* protested the use of segregated railroad cars in the South, the editors of the *VFP* suggested that "Shepherd, like other 'respectable colored people,' would have made such accommodations unnecessary because he never would have 'obtruded himself' on the white passengers" (M. Johnson 1997:5).

These newspaper accounts show the transformation of the image of Shepherd. The white press continually reminded its readers that Shepherd, an innocent black man, was murdered by John Brown's raiders. They point out that while Brown attempted to free all enslaved black people, his first victim in the raid was an African American. By the beginning of the Jim Crow era, Shepherd's image changed. The press now highlighted that

Shepherd was a respectable citizen who was faithful to the existing system and was satisfied with his subordinate role in society—a second-class citizen. This new memory of Shepherd helped lay the foundation for a faithful-slave memorial.

Planning a Monument to Heyward Shepherd

In 1894, rumors stirred around town that African Americans, led by Frederick Douglass, wanted to erect an obelisk in Harpers Ferry to commemorate the deeds of John Brown. The *VFP* (1894:2) immediately responded by calling Heyward Shepherd "the industrious, inoffensive colored man. . . . By the way, it is suggested that the white people erect a monument to the memory of Brown's first victim at Harper's Ferry." The following year, an obelisk commemorating Brown was erected at the site of the engine house on Baltimore & Ohio Railroad property. It seemed as though the voice of the editor had fallen on deaf ears, since it took years before any groups began to talk about a monument to Shepherd. Whether the newspaper had any influence in creating momentum for the monument is uncertain (M. Johnson 1997:5).

The UDC was created in 1895, and within a decade the organization was debating the erection of a faithful-slave monument (*Confederate Veteran* 1905:123–24). Some UDC members believed that a faithful-slave monument was a vehicle to counter the memory created by northerners about the South and the institution of slavery. Not only could southerners tell future generations about the "self sacrifice and devotion" of slaves, but they could also show "the traditions, romance, poetry, and picturesqueness of the South" (*Confederate Veteran* 1905:123).

Members of the UDC also campaigned from at least 1905 and through the 1920s to erect a national mammy memorial in Washington, D.C. Many women of the UDC believed that they "must remember the best friend of their childhood" (quoted in Blight 2001:288). Meanwhile, interviews with ex-slaves done in the early twentieth century relay stories of personal pain, hardship, family breakups, poor labor conditions, and the lack of progress toward property ownership (Blight 2001:369).

Some UDC women opposed the creation of a faithful-slave monument, or a "national mammy memorial," remarking that they could not honor former slaves (*Confederate Veteran* 1904:525). A letter to the *Confederate Veteran* (1904:525) called African Americans a "black fiend." The "old faithful mammy and uncle of slave times . . . were fully rewarded for faithful trust," but only 10 percent remained to work for their former masters after the Civil War. She also noted that the "negro of this generation would not appreciate any monument not smacking of social equality."

Other members of the UDC from the J. Harvey Matthews Chapter of Memphis, Tennessee, countered this sentiment. They believed that it was important to erect a monument "to the faithful old slaves who remained loyal and true to their owners in the dark days of the sixties and on through the infamous reconstruction period" (*Confederate Veteran* 1905:123). The monument would be dedicated to

> the loyal slaves to whose care the women and children were intrusted during the entire period of the War between the States. To those slaves who watched the fireside, tilled the soil, helped spin, weave, and make raiment for the master and sons on the battlefield—to those slaves who protected and provided for the families at home is due a monument. (*Confederate Veteran* 1905:123)

A faithful-slave monument would be a way to show that southerners "respected the good qualities as no one else ever did or will do. It would bespeak the real conception of the affection of the owner toward the slave and refute the slanders and falsehoods published in 'Uncle Tom's Cabin.'" The monument would "have great effect as a proof of the feelings of gratitude that centers the hearts of Southern people from the sixties to the present day." The monument would tell future generations "that the white men of the South were the negro's best friend then and that the men of the South are the negro's best friend to-day" (*Confederate Veteran* 1905:123–24).

The national meeting of the UDC in 1907 could not agree on the creation of a monument, so they postponed any consideration until a later meeting (Poppenheim et al. 1938:77). The idea of a faithful-slave monument lay dormant for over a decade until Matthew Page Andrews, a member and strong supporter of the SCV, believed it was appropriate to erect a faithful-slave monument at Harpers Ferry to honor a faithful slave killed during the John Brown raid.

Andrews lived in Shepherdstown, West Virginia, about thirteen miles outside Harpers Ferry. His views were probably influenced by those family and neighbors who continually told stories about the raid. He went to college at Washington and Lee, considered a bastion of Confederate ideals.

Andrews dedicated much of his life to celebrating the views of the South, and as a member of the SCV, he served on its Grey Book Committee, its textbook committee. He "was 'always on the alert for anything . . . detrimental to the cause for which the Sons' stood and 'ever ready to combat false propaganda' being spread throughout the south in textbooks written by Northerners" (M. Johnson 1997:7). The *Confederate Veteran* (1932:236) described Andrews as

> always on the alert for anything that would be detrimental to the cause for which the Sons stand, and is ever ready to combat false propaganda that is being disseminated throughout the South by textbooks written by men of the North out of sympathy and misinformed of the real conditions prior to and subsequent to the War between the States.

Andrews also received an award from the UDC that made him an honorary associate member for his work "guarding our Southern history" (M. Johnson 1997:7).

Andrews was dedicated to countering any pro–John Brown sentiment in this country. At one point, he even engaged in a debate with West Virginia's congressman (and later senator) Jennings Randolph as Andrews campaigned against the creation of Harpers Ferry National Monument (see chapter 2; see also Shackel 1995, 1996, 2000).

Andrews's anti–Brown campaign reached the halls of the UDC annual meeting at Asheville, North Carolina, in 1920. President General Mary McKinney recommended to the membership that they follow Andrews's anti-Brown lead so that "future generations may be impressed with the real truth [about Brown]." McKinney told the group that Brown killed a faithful slave "because he held too dear the lives of 'Ole Massa' and 'Ole Mis-s'us,' to fulfill Brown's orders of rapine and murder." McKinney remarked, "The hero of Harpers Ferry was not the Soldier of Fortune, but a black man who gave his life for his friends. Honor his memory. With a thrill of appreciation tell to future listeners the story of this faithful slave, who stood between Southern womanhood and a renegade adventurer " (UDC 1920:40). The convention applauded and elected to work with the SCV to erect a monument at Harpers Ferry "to the faithful slave who gave his life in defense of his master during the John Brown raid" (*Confederate Veteran* 1921a:117). Both the UDC and the SCV agreed to contribute $500 toward the monument with the cost not exceeding $1,000 (*Confederate Vet-*

eran 1920:436; M. Johnson 1997:7). The SCV suggested that the boulder should be 6 feet 2 inches high, 3 feet 6 inches wide, and 2 feet thick (UDC 1921:208–9).

The president of the UDC asked Andrews to write an inscription for the faithful-slave memorial. Andrews initially proposed to include the commemoration of James, a hired slave of Colonel Lewis Washington who drowned during the raid. Apparently, the monument intended to honor these "humble, innocent victims of a proposed servile insurrection" and of all blacks who had refrained from violence against whites (*Confederate Veteran* 1921b:237).

Andrew's initial draft inscription to be placed on the faithful-slave memorial stated,

> Here early in the morning of October 17, 1859, Heyward Shepherd, an industrious and respected negro man, fell mortally wounded by John Browns [*sic*] raiders. Near here also died James, faithful servant of Col. Lewis W. Washington, who was drowned while endeavoring to escape from those who offered him pikes and staves for bloody massacre.
>
> In the name of these humble, innocent victims of a proposed servile insurrection this bowlder [*sic*] is set up by the Sons and Daughters of the South in loving memory of all those faithful negroes who, under this temptation and through subsequent years of a war of invasion, so conducted themselves that no stain of violence was left upon their record as long as the old relationship remained.
>
> May this memorial be an inspiration to all alike to prove themselves worthy of a past that produced such characters as George Washington, Robert Edward Lee, and a noble host of their compatriots of European origin, together with the descendants of tens of thousands of once heathen Africans faithfully instructed in the principles of Christianity and, though less known to fame, equally deserving of the eternal reward which is theirs. (*Confederate Veteran* 1921b:237–38)

The inclusion of James's name on the memorial became problematic with the faithful-slave memorial committee when they received various accounts surrounding the circumstances that led to James's drowning. Joseph Barry (1979:83), a local Harpers Ferry historian, claimed that

James was shot by one of Brown's raiders while trying to flee Brown. In the biography *John Brown, 1800–1850; a Biography Fifty Years After,* Oswald Villard (1910) remarked that James did not drown while escaping Brown's raiders but rather died of gunshot wounds while running from townspeople. Because of this controversy, the faithful-slave memorial committee decided to delete any inscription to James on the memorial. Between the 1920 and the 1921 conventions, Andrews made nearly two dozen draft inscriptions for the memorial (UDC 1921:208–9).

The committee struggled to find an appropriate site for the memorial. Initially, they contacted the Baltimore & Ohio Railroad and asked for permission to erect the monument on its property. The proposed location was on "a vacant triangle lot at the intersection of streets opposite the B. & O. Railroad Station" (quoted in M. Johnson 1997:8). A committee member wrote to the president of the Baltimore & Ohio Railroad that a boulder commemorated "the memory of the faithful slave, Hayward [*sic*] Shepherd, a negro who was the first victim of the John Brown Raid on Harper's Ferry" (Letter, Carr to Willard, May 12, 1922). The proposed location is significant since nearby stands the John Brown Fort obelisk, erected in 1895. Both monuments would have stood in direct sight of each other. The railroad asked the town council how they felt about the proposed monument and forwarded the proposed revised inscription to the town council:

> Here in the night of October 16, 1859, Heyward Shepherd, an industrious and respected colored man, was mortally wounded by John Brown's raiders. In pursuance of his duties as watchman, he became the first victim of the attempted insurrection.
>
> The Negroes of the neighborhood, true to their Christian training, would have no part with those who offered pikes and staves for bloody massacre.
>
> This boulder is set up by the Sons of Confederate veterans and the United Daughters of the Confederacy as a memorial to Heyward Shepherd exemplifying the character and faithfulness of thousands of Negroes who, under many temptations throughout subsequent years of war, so conducted themselves that no stain was left upon a record which is the peculiar heritage of the American people, and an everlasting tribute to the best in both races. (Letter, proposed inscription, Heyward Shepherd Memorial, June 2, 1922; UDC 1921:209)

Henry McDonald, town recorder for Harpers Ferry and president of Storer College, wrote on the request that he "saw to it that the offer was rejected" (Letter, Julian S. Carr to Daniel Willard, May 12, 1922; Letter, Daniel Willard to Henry McDonald, June 27, 1922). McDonald then wrote the Baltimore & Ohio Railroad remarking that the council opposed the erection of the monument. He noted that the town council "look[s] with disfavor upon the placing in our midst such a monument as proposed with the inscription thereon suggested, as being likely to occassion [*sic*] unpleasant racial feelings in a community where we are so entirely free from it. We see no good purpose that can be served in this case and believe that harm would result to our community" (Letter, Recorder to Willard, June 2, 1922). The railroad agreed, believing that the monument "might disturb the existing pleasant relations" (Letter, Campbell to McDonald, June 23, 1922; UDC 1922:216–18; see also M. Johnson 1997:9–11).

Therefore, the UDC searched for an alternative place for their faithful-slave memorial. One of these places was Capital Square in Richmond, where the monument could be erected near monuments to George Washington and Robert E. Lee and "other excellent citizens and heroes who knew and appreciated the Southern negro and often tested the faithfulness of such men as Heyward Shepherd and the dear 'Black Mammy' " (UDC-WV 1923:20). Two months later, the faithful-slave memorial committee reported at the national convention that the town council would accept the monument if the committee changed part of the inscription from "The negroes in the neighborhood, true to their Christian training, would have no part with those who offered pikes and staves for bloody massacre" to "The negroes of this neighborhood, true to their Christian training, would have no part in this terrible raid" (UDC–WV 1923:217–19). Andrews agreed to changing "bloody massacre" to "terrible raid," but he did not want to change any other words. However, the word changes would have been costly since they had already inscribed the text onto the stone. The convention voted not to accept the changes and to continue to pursue the matter (UDC–WV 1923:218–19).

The work of the faithful-slave memorial committee slowed considerably after this point (UDC 1924:227–28) as the strength of the Ku Klux Klan grew in the South. By 1924, the Klan had more than two million members and a strong presence in Harpers Ferry. They caused a deep division between the town residents, and some students left Storer College because they feared for their lives. Many residents feared that the promotion of southern heritage would further ignite racial strife in town (*Farmers Advocate* 1923; Letter, Taylor to McDonald, November 16, 1922).

During this era, a member of the inactive faithful-slave memorial committee visited Harpers Ferry and found the John Brown Fort on the Storer College campus and realized why considerable opposition to the faithful-slave monument existed. First, there was a tablet on the fort, mounted in 1918, dedicated to the heroism of John Brown and his men. The college also used the fort as a museum containing artifacts related to the enslavement of African Americans. She told the committee about what she saw when she went to the John Brown Fort—"iron collars with spikes, described as a thing the slaves were compelled to wear around their necks, next was a pair of hand-cuffs said to be placed upon slaves while plowing in the fields." Exasperated, she exclaimed that "the relics were such libelous canards" (UDC 1925:225–27).

The faithful-slave memorial committee floundered for another five years until Elizabeth Bashinsky became the president general of the UDC in 1930. She committed the organization to erecting the monument at Harpers Ferry, "but not until the inscription should be changed omitting every word of bitterness, since we wished it to perpetuate loyalty & truth rather than any word that might suggest any bitterness or reflect upon the cruelty of others" (*Confederate Veteran* 1930:4). With this new spirit, Matthew Page Andrews agreed to change the wording on the boulder to accommodate the phrases that the council had requested years earlier. He also inserted the word "freeman" and made a reference to Shepherd's employment with the Baltimore & Ohio Railroad (M. Johnson 1997:12–13).

After a decade of work to locate a place for the monument, the UDC and SCV finally succeeded. At the beginning of the Great Depression, African Americans found themselves further segregated by Jim Crow legislation. In 1930, Harpers Ferrians elected James Ranson, the son of a Confederate veteran, as mayor, and within a year the town council had unanimously agreed to allow the faithful-slave monument to be erected in Harpers Ferry. A local druggist and member of the local committee, Dr. Walter E. Dittmeyer, allowed the committee to place the monument on his property on the sidewalk on Potomac Street. It faced the John Brown Fort obelisk, close to where the raiders shot Heyward Shepherd. It was easily visible from the train tracks, and visitors could readily see it when they disembarked from the train (Andrews, n.d.).

A date was set for the dedication, and the speakers included Henry McDonald, the white president of Storer College, as well as members from southern heritage groups. Prior to the dedication, many people inquired about McDonald's participation in the unveiling of the memorial. A friend, Boyd Sutler, wrote McDonald and remarked about his concerns over having McDonald speak at the ceremony since Andrews had made several undesirable comments about the marker "in the *Confederate Veteran* and other 'unreconstructed' publications." Sutler remembered Andrews saying that the marker would act "as an antidote to John Brownism of the period" in front of McDonald. Therefore, McDonald's participation in the ceremonies puzzled Sutler (Letter, Sutler to McDonald, October 4, 1931). The *Afro-American,* a Baltimore newspaper, telegraphed McDonald and asked whether he planned to make an address "at unveiling Uncle Tom, anti John Brown monument, October Fifteenth (*Afro-American* 1931a). The secretary of the NAACP, Walter White, also wrote McDonald four days before the ceremonies and asked him to consider the implications of his participation. He suggested that the participation of the president of Storer College could only legitimize the Lost Cause:

> This attempt to destroy the truth and to perpetuate a story that Negroes did not participate of their own free will in the struggle for their emancipation, and the effort to vilify the name of John Brown, will be heartily condemned by all individuals, North and South and of both races, whatever may be their opinion of the wisdom of the action of John Brown. (Letter, White to McDonald, October 6, 1931)

McDonald responded to the *Afro-American* and reassured them that he was not participating in any ceremonies that celebrated an "Uncle Tom anti John Brown monument." He claimed that the gathering "will voice the spirit of fellowship and enduring good will. It is an expression of a new era of inter-racial understanding" (Letter, McDonald to *Afro-American,* October 6, 1931). McDonald also responded to White's letter, reassuring him that the event coordinators informed him that these ceremonies would not vilify John Brown. "If it had, I would be the last man to be identified therewith" (Letter, McDonald to White, October 8, 1931). Not knowing the full extent of the speeches to be delivered by Andrews and the president general of the UDC, McDonald added,

> I have no reason for disbelieving the plain language of the leaders in this event. Their simple and repeated statement is, that it is intended to be a recognition of the fidelity of Heyward Shepherd

> and all the colored people, who like him were faithful to trust. That certainly will find a sympathetic response in the hearts of all fair-minded men and women North and South. (Letter, McDonald to White, October 8, 1931)

McDonald believed that the ceremonies would create goodwill between the races.

Members of the college staff also registered their apprehension over participation in the ceremonies. Several days before the ceremonies, Pearl Tatum, a music teacher at Storer College, wrote McDonald that she thought it was unwise for the college to participate. She questioned, "Do you think we should appear on such a program when we honor John Brown and feel that while he may have used the wrong methods, his motive was just? I feel now that should we take part we should be most inconsistent" (Letter, Tatum to McDonald, September 22, 1931).

Unveiling of the Heyward Shepherd Memorial

On October 10, 1931, about 300 whites and 100 blacks came to the dedication of the Heyward Shepherd Memorial. The honored guests included members of the UDC and SCV as well as two descendants of Union soldiers. Three black men also ranked among honored guests: Dr. George F. Bragg, a preacher from Baltimore, Maryland; Jimmie Moten, the current baggage handler for the Baltimore & Ohio Railroad; and James Walker, a descendant of Heyward Shepherd (Andrews, n.d.:6, 19, 32). Also present was Mayor Ranson, the local committee chairman, and his father, B. B. Ranson, a Confederate veteran who had been part of the military company present at Brown's execution. A choral group from Storer College and the school's president, Henry McDonald, also participated in the ceremonies. While he had opposed the placement of the memorial in Harpers Ferry nearly a decade earlier, McDonald introduced the new resolution to the town council in 1931 in favor of the memorial (M. Johnson 1997:13) (see figure 3.1).

The granite boulder monument stood against a building along Potomac Street, covered with a Confederate flag and surrounded by green ivy. Across the street, a speaker's stand, draped in Confederate red and white bunting, stood along the Baltimore & Ohio Railroad embankment. The invocation was delivered by Reverend Richard E. Washington, a near rela-

Figure 3.1. Unveiling ceremony for the Heyward Shepherd Memorial, October 10, 1931 (courtesy Harpers Ferry National Historical Park).

tive of Colonel Lewis Washington, one of the first hostages of the John Brown raid. Dr. Henry McDonald provided the introductory remarks. He proclaimed that the event should not be a day to "remember discord and a past, however memorable and glorious," but we should look into the future with "the spirit of peace" inspired by the memorial. He believed that African Americans would see "this truth," that whites would share their advantages with all races who were faithful (McDonald 1931).

Then, Matthew Page Andrews offered the historical address for the dedication. Andrews's speech criticized John Brown and justified slavery rather than memorializing Heyward Shepherd. He noted that Brown was mentally ill and suffered from "some kind of warped psychosis or paranoia" and was a crazed man who attempted to overthrow the U.S. government (Andrews, n.d.:25). Andrews argued that changes in the economy would have gradually emancipated all the slaves, and he also tried to reason the necessity of slavery. He remarked,

> When we stop to think of the Dark Continent in the seventeenth and eighteenth centuries, are we not justified in wondering if the bondage of the body in America, which, however, freed the soul of the captive, was not preferable to the bondage of both soul and body which enveloped the life of the majority of those captured on the Congo. (Andrews, n.d.:20)

For a good part of his speech, Andrews claimed that the Africans had a better life in this country and that those who went back to Africa to settle in Liberia saw the continent as uncivilized. Taking a paternalistic tone, Andrews quoted letters of former slaves begging their white sponsors for money, food, and clothing. He noted that the conditions there were too unfriendly to survive (Andrews, n.d.:20–23). He praised southerners for nurturing and caring for their slaves. "Should not some measure of praise be granted by public opinion to the Southern white people who raised another race up from the lowest known scale more rapidly, perhaps, than any people had ever risen before?" (Andrews, n.d.:23).

The president general of the UDC, Elizabeth Bashinsky, told of her love of country and also of her devotion to the Confederate flag. She stated that the slaves in the United States did not violently rise against their masters, like they did in Haiti, because they were well clothed, fed, housed, treated kindly, and taught Christianity. Bashinsky remarked that Heyward Shepherd "gave his life in defense of his employer's property, and in memory of many others of his race who were loyal and true during a period that tried men's souls . . . Heyward Shepherd's conduct was honorable, just, and true, and merits the praise we bring him" (*Confederate Veteran* 1931:411). She proceeded to demonize Brown and then spent the majority of her time talking about the loyalty of many slaves during the war. She noted that they were treated kindly and trained in Christianity:

> A feeling of such trust and confidence existed between the white and colored that when the war began, the soldiers shouldered arms and went to the front with full confidence that the women and children were safe under the protection of the Negroes who would protect their defenseless homes and families. The negroes knew that a bitter war was being fought which would vitally affect their destinies, yet even this did not blind them to their sense of duty, and they served and protected the women and chil-

> dren of the South with unwavering loyalty and devotion, qualities which we memorialize today. (*Confederate Veteran* 1931:412)

In her closing remarks, Bashinsky returned to Heyward Shepherd and noted that the boulder was dedicated to Shepherd and other African Americans who remained faithful to the system. "It commemorates the loyalty, courage, and self-sacrifice of Heyward Shepherd and thousands of others of his race who would, like him, have suffered death rather than betray their masters or to be false to a trust" (*Confederate Veteran* 1931:413–14). The *Shepherdstown Register* (1931) noted that Bashinsky's remarks received were "loudly applauded, for every word that she uttered could be distinctly heard and was heartily approved."

After Bashinsky's speech, several local women including Mary Loretta Kern, granddaughter of a confederate soldier, unveiled the monument. The memorial's inscription is shown in figure 3.2 (UDC 1931:58–59). The chairman of the memorial committee, Mary Dowling Bond, placed a wreath on the monument.

Then the Storer College Singers were scheduled to sing. Taking exception to the tone of the event, the musical director, Pearl Tatum, stood and turned to the crowd. She did not speak about the music but rather protested the tone of the event. She remarked to the crowd,

> I am the daughter of a Connecticut volunteer, who wore the blue, who fought for the freedom of my people, for which John Brown struck the first blow. Today we are looking forward to the future, forgetting those things of the past. We are pushing forward to a larger freedom, not in the spirit of the black mammy but in the spirit of the new freedom and rising youth. (*Pittsburgh Courier* 1931)

The choir group then sang their schedule of songs.

The Reverend Dr. George F. Bragg, a distinguished African American clergyman, gave the benediction. He later wrote the president of the Heyward Shepherd Memorial Foundation and praised Andrews for his speech at the ceremonies. Bragg wrote (in Andrews, n.d.:5),

> As a missionary effort, in the interest of increasing good will and the very best of feeling between the white and colored races, I ardently wish that the way can be found whereby this able and

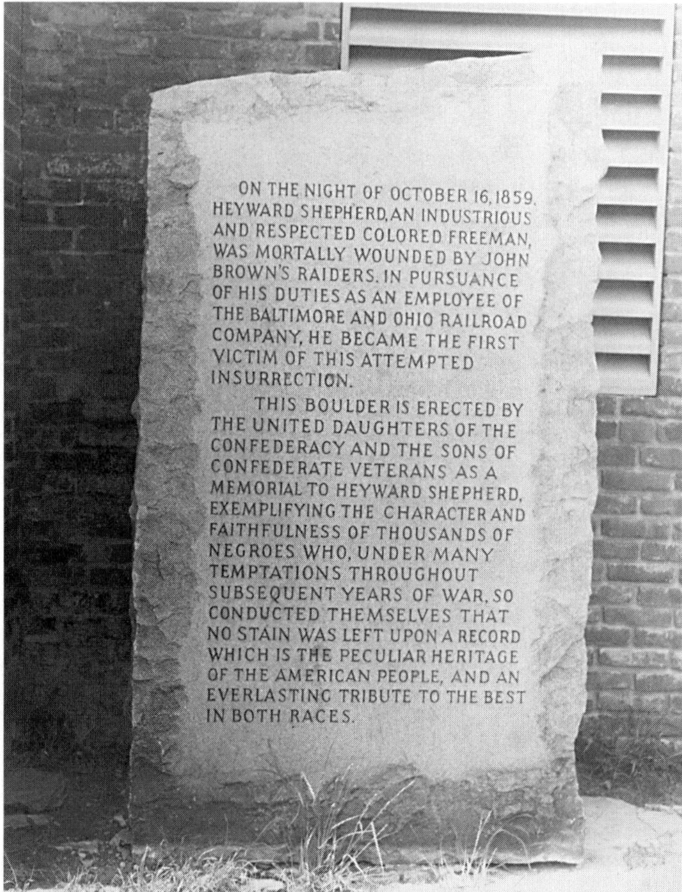

Figure 3.2. Heyward Shepherd Memorial in Harpers Ferry National Historical Park prior to the 1970s renovation project (courtesy Harpers Ferry National Historical Park).

informing treatise could be published and sent to all the colored leaders of thought throughout the country.

The Aftermath

The editor of the *Afro-American* attacked both McDonald and the Reverend Bragg for their participation in the ceremonies (Letter, Andrews to McDonald, October 12, 1931). Many African American groups praised Pearl Tatum for her "fortitude in defense of that much maligned champion of human rights, John Brown . . . and your repudiation of the 'Black mammy' and 'Uncle Tom' servility that certain agencies seek to glorify and perpetuate" (Letter, Winters to Tatum, October 16, 1931). The *Afro-American* (1931b) wrote about Tatum's action: "Yankee Woman Steals Rebel Girls' Show: Confederate Daughters Gape as She Lauds John Brown." The national pilgrimage chairman of the John Brown Memorial Association, Inc., asked McDonald why Pearl Tatum was the "only one who could feel the dynamic presence of the old Martyr and dared translate it into words and action" (Letter, Winters to McDonald, October 16, 1931).

Max Barber, president of the John Brown Memorial Association, Inc., remarked that the association, of which McDonald was a member, wanted to put him on record. Barber asked, "Were you aware of the objects of the daughters in coming to Harpers Ferry? If so, what was your object in participating in the program" (Letter, Barber to McDonald, February 21, 1932). In an editorial, Barber suggested that McDonald should have been "shocked and disgusted" at the statements made at the ceremony and that he erred in participating in an event coordinated by "a bunch of unregenerated rebels" (*Pittsburgh Courier* 1931). W. E. B. Du Bois wrote in *Crisis* (1932:467) that the dedication was a "pro-slavery celebration" and called McDonald's and Bragg's participation in the event "disgraceful" (see also M. Johnson 1997:15–16).

McDonald replied to Barber and acknowledged that he knew the inscription on the marker. He claimed that he was proud that he influenced the change of the original tone of the inscription and that the inscription does not contain any malice toward John Brown and his men:

> In everything of which I had any knowledge, the event was known as the Heyward Shepherd memorial—and in no sense any attempt at belittling the man [Brown], whom I include in the list of the three or four real American Reformers. Nor is there anything about this Memorial to alter that fact. (Letter, McDonald to Barber, February 23, 1932)

McDonald did not appear upset by Andrews's tone at the ceremonies since he wrote Andrews and expressed his delight with the ceremonies. McDonald remarked that the Heyward Shepherd Memorial was one of the most significant memorials erected in the past decade. "There was such a fine and understanding spirit manifested. The new and best South was in action. I was glad to be identified therewith." He then proceeded to invite Andrews to give a speech at Storer College on the topic of Liberia, a colony for African Americans who wanted to return to Africa (Letter, McDonald to Andrews, October 15, 1931; Letter, McDonald to Andrews, October 19, 1931).

Andrews did speak at Storer College in early November, only to the outrage of the *Afro-American.* The president of the weekly newspaper referred to Andrews as a representative of the UDC and the True Slave Organization (Letter, Murphy to McDonald, November 12, 1931). McDonald defended his actions to allow Andrews to speak at Storer College and remarked that Andrews was "a man of letters." Andrews's grandfather was one of the founders of the Liberian Republic, and McDonald believed that Andrews was sympathetic to the problems of the people of that country (Letter, McDonald to Murphy, November 13, 1931).

McDonald participated in the ceremony because he believed that it was an "expression of good will and better inter-racial feelings" (Letter, McDonald to White, October 19, 1931). McDonald further remarked that people would soon forget what had been said at the memorial services, although the inscription would remain. "Certainly one cannot agree that its sentiment and phrasing is peaceful and wholly praiseworthy in what it says. No one pays attention to it" (Letter, McDonald to Barber, February 23, 1932). A letter written by McDonald more than a decade later may provide some clues as to why he supported the monument in the first place. While contemplating retirement in 1943, he provided a paternalistic view and subscribed to a form of social Darwinism. He wrote,

> I am one who firmly agrees believes that white people and colored people should cooperate in such institutions for the benefit of colored men and women. I still think our ancestry, training and larger fitness enable us—white people—to do something for colored students, which they can get in no other way. (Letter, McDonald to Ford, November 11, 1943:2)

But many African Americans believed otherwise. They interpreted McDonald's participation in the event as catering to the agendas of the UDC and the SCV. Charles Hill, a Storer College graduate, remarked,

> The Daughters of the Confederacy and the Sons of Confederate Veterans merely used Heyward Shepherd and his admirable qualities as a camouflage to cloak their real motives, which are to

> counteract the memory and influence of John Brown's raid and also to place a premium on "Uncle Toms and Black Mammies," as is evidenced by the fact that this monument was erected under the auspices of the "Faithful Slave Memorial Committee," and the general glorification of the "Black Mammy" by Mrs. Leopold Bashinsky, who also condemned the Haitians, because they rebelled against their masters and fought for liberty—that God-given right of all men.
>
> The two above named organizations do not stand for the broadest progress and advancement of colored people, and this fact is evidenced in the southern states by "Jim Crow" cars, denial of the right to vote, segregation, lynchings, peonage and limited public school facilities. The reaction of this, and similar monuments, is an insult to intelligent, progressive colored men and women throughout the country. (Letter, Hill to McDonald, November 15, 1931)

Hill summed up his thoughts by telling McDonald that his participation was "a colossal blunder" (Letter, Hill to McDonald, November 15, 1931).

Some African Americans, however, took an opposite view. James Walker, a descendant of Heyward Shepherd, sat on the platform during the ceremonies. He wrote Pearl Tatum and expressed his displeasure with her remarks and noted that the ceremonies attempted to bridge sectionalism. Citizens from the North and South came to honor a loyal and trustworthy man. He stated, "Your untimely blow-out might have wrecked the car of racial progress" (Letter, Walker to Tatum, undated typescript). The Reverend Bragg also remarked that the ceremonies promoted good interracial relations and noted that Andrews's speech was "simply magnificent" (quoted in Andrews, n.d.). Members of the Charlestown, West Virginia, UDC also reported that African Americans found Andrews's speech inspiring, and they requested that it be published in pamphlet form (M. Johnson 1995:30).

In response to these events, the NAACP asked to have a meeting on the Storer College campus in the spring of 1932 in order to honor John Brown and to dedicate the new inscription on the John Brown Fort. McDonald granted permission for the meeting but also requested a place on the program "because some have misunderstood my attitude in respect to the Heyward Shepherd Memorial (Letter, McDonald to Clifford,

March 17, 1932). McDonald replied favorably to the NAACP's request for a new plaque on the fort, although he asked that the Storer College Board approve the inscription (Letter, White to McDonald, March 23, 1932; Letter, McDonald to White, March 25, 1932). The proposed inscription, written by W. E. B. Du Bois, read,

> Here / John Brown / Aimed at human slavery / A Blow / That woke a guilty nation. / With him fought / Seven slaves and sons of slaves. / Over his crucified corpse / Marched 200,000 black soldiers / And 4,000,000 freedmen / Singing / "John Brown's body lies a mouldering in the grave / But his Soul goes marching on!"
>
> In gratitude this Tablet is erected / The National Association for the Advancement of Colored People / May 21, 1932. (Letter, White to McDonald, April 16, 1932)

McDonald did not approve of the wording, and on consultation with the trustees, they proposed another inscription: "John Brown 1800–1859 "His soul goes marching on" (Letter, McDonald to White, April 25, 1932). Walter White was outraged by the trustees' response and remarked,

> Inasmuch as there is in the immediate vicinity a nationally publicized tablet giving the Confederate point of view and, far more important, because there has been a growing tendency within recent years towards a new copperheadism so far as the historians treat the Civil War and the reconstruction period, it was our wish to place permanently a statement of the point of view of the Negro and his friends. (Letter, White to McDonald, May 2, 1932)

The NAACP gathered for the dedication of the new plaque at Storer College on May 21, 1932, and included such dignitaries as McDonald, Oswald Garrison Villard (a famous John Brown biographer), J. Max Barber, and Du Bois, along with several hundred others in attendance. Not until the meeting did they hear that the college and its trustees refused to place the inscription on the John Brown Fort walls. Villard's and Barber's speeches praised the deeds of Brown (*Washington Tribune* 1932), while Du Bois defended his inscription. He claimed that the UDC influenced the college's decision and noted the college's lack of courage for not allowing his proposed inscription on the building.

After the meeting, McDonald once again came under heavy criticism for his participation in the Heyward Shepherd Memorial ceremonies. The *Washington Tribune* (1932) called McDonald and the trustees the "white Judases" of Storer College. They noted that they were the men who refused the NAACP permission to place a tablet on the John Brown Fort and who assisted the UDC in erecting a memorial to "glorify human slavery." The *Washington Tribune* remarked that the college was "a failure" and "a detriment to Negro freedom and manhood," and it urged African Americans to blacklist the college. The *Afro-American* (1932a) described McDonald as the kind of white leader who was more dangerous than racist demagogues—"the Bleases, Tillmans, or Heflins"—southern senators who championed African American disenfranchisement and who fueled white hatred of blacks for political gains. The newspaper remarked that "it was written in every facial expression that Dr. McDonald, apologist for those Southern whites, who would desecrate John Brown's memory while glorifying the slave regime, must go" (*Afro-American* 1932a). The *Afro-American* (1932b) also called for McDonald's resignation. McDonald weathered the immediate storm and retired twelve years later, replaced by an African American.

The Memorial in a National Park

In the 1950s, the NPS acquired all the land in Lower Town Harpers Ferry, including the Heyward Shepherd Memorial and the building it stood against. Apparently, the NPS did not know what to do with the monument, so they turned it around so the inscription faced the building. It remained in that position for a while until a congressman applied pressure on the NPS to turn the monument around so that it once again faced the street and could be viewed by the public (Layman 1970). Writing in 1970, Joseph Prentice, superintendent of Harpers Ferry, wrote that he had wished he could remove the monument by dropping it into the deepest part of the river. He did not know

> how much of a stink this might stir up, so I took the more discretionary move of turning the text to the wall. I had hoped that those of the UDC and the SCV who had participated in the original erection would not be around or would have forgotten and that, after a reasonable interval of time, I could consign it to the basement of the building next to which it stands by the sim-

> ple expedient of letting it fall backwards during the reconstruction of the brick wall. (Letter, Prentice to Ben, August 28, 1970)

The superintendent also remarked how amused he was when town drunks, "in their daily perambulations, were wont to use the space between the granite stone and the brick wall as their private urinal. I felt that it was near poetic justice to such text to receive its daily bath of urine from these drunken outcasts of the white race" (Letter, Prentice to Ben, August 28, 1970). Prentice continued by stating that he believed that it "is not only twisted rhetoric which purports to glorify the negro slave, it exemplifies the warped thinking of the descendants of some white Southerners to the present day, they who delude themselves with the idea that the negro slave was delighted with his servitude" (Letter, Prentice to Ben, August 28, 1970). Prentice believed that the monument should not be displayed in a national park.

Funding became available for building renovations in the park in the mid-1970s, and in 1976 the buildings adjacent to the Heyward Shepherd Memorial underwent renovations. The NPS removed the memorial to its maintenance yard. Workers placed it in a horizontal position on wooden rails and wrapped it in canvas. Delegates of the UDC met with the park superintendent and were initially satisfied since the monument would be protected from construction activities (*Martinsburg Journal* 1976:7; *Spirit of Jefferson* 1976). Members of the UDC and the SCV visited the monument again in 1980 and found it still in storage four years after the initial visit. They wanted to see it on display again in Lower Town Harpers Ferry, where hundreds of visitors could view it every day. In a letter to Lucille Bush of the UDC, the park superintendent maintained that the "4 ton boulder was in the maintenance yard for its protection due to historic building restoration as authorized by Congress and which is not complete. . . . Any future disposition of the Heyward Shepherd Monument should be the decision of the N.P.S. planning team for this park" (Draft letter, reply to Lucille Bush, February 1, 1980).

In 1981, the NPS moved the Heyward Shepherd Memorial back to its original location in Lower Town Harpers Ferry against a three-story building on Potomac Street. When the park received reports of possible plans to deface the monument, the park superintendent ordered that it be covered with a plywood box (Meyer 1995:C2) (see figure 3.3). The Park Superintendent, Donald Campbell, justified this action as necessary to protect the monument as an important resource at Harpers Ferry National

Figure 3.3. Heyward Shepherd Memorial covered with a plywood box in Harpers Ferry National Historical Park, 1995 (courtesy Paul A. Shackel).

Historical Park (Campbell 1996). The park intended to redisplay the monument with an interpretive sign. The proposed text read,

> John Brown's raid on the armory at Harpers Ferry caused the death of four townspeople. One of those who died in the fighting was Heyward Shepherd, a railroad baggagemaster and a free black.
>
> Although the true identity of his assailant is uncertain, Shepherd soon became a symbol of the "faithful servant" among those who deplored Brown's action against the traditional southern way of life.
>
> This monument, placed here in 1931, reflects these traditional views. (Anonymous 1981)

The NPS found itself between two opposing organizations. The NAACP saw the monument as offensive, and one of its members wrote Secretary of the Interior James Watt that the "marker is an insult to all black Americans. It insults our intelligence and it speaks an 'untruth.' We urge you to direct the National Park Service to leave the marker covered" (Letter, Headen to Watt, October 5, 1981). Meanwhile, the UDC and SCV struggled to have the monument uncovered and displayed to the public.

The president of the West Virginia Chapter of the NAACP saw the monument as a statement that claimed "all slaves were satisfied to be whipped, raped, tortured, torn away from their families and sold." He remarked that it is "terrible to have one of these organizations imply that these people, my ancestors, were satisfied. That is down right ridiculous" (Tolbert, quoted in R. White 1989:4). If the NPS removed the box covering, it would tell visitors that African Americans were "satisfied and had no desire for freedom. No one can come around here and tell me that was so" (Tolbert, quoted in R. White 1989:4).

Mrs. Dewey Wood of the UDC did not want to see an interpretive sign next to the Heyward Shepherd Memorial. She believed that the message was clear in its meaning. She remarked,

> Why should the NAACP be opposed to this? It is a monument to one of their people. . . . There were 40,000 slaves in Maryland, and none of them came to [John Brown's] support. They were loyal to their people. . . . I really don't know what they find offensive about it. (Wood, quoted in R. White 1989:4)

Apparently, the park superintendent tried to get all interested parties together in order to write an interpretive plaque to be placed next to the monument, but no common ground could be reached. The local NAACP executive committee was not supportive of placing the monument in its former location with an interpretive plaque. Nor did they support placing the monument in an interpretive exhibit in one of the buildings in Lower Town. Mr. Rutherford, president of the local chapter of the NAACP, requested that two representatives of the NAACP and the UDC meet to discuss the matter. Mrs. Wood of the UDC thought that it would be inappropriate to meet directly with the NAACP, as the decision on the monument rested with the NPS (Letter, Campbell to Johns, July 15, 1980).

Efforts to have all groups reach a compromise failed. Campbell saw the monument as a historic artifact, and since the UDC and the NAACP could not reach a compromise, he was reluctant to make any decision to move or uncover the boulder. "Until we get some agreement, we must keep it in safe keeping" (Campbell, quoted in R. White 1989:11). Interest in redisplaying the monument waned in the late 1980s, and the box that covered the monument remained unnoticed by the many people who came to the national park.

On January 13, 1994, Elliot Cummings, commander of the Maryland Division of the Sons of the Confederate Veterans, wrote Superintendent Campbell and remarked that the covering of the Heyward Shepherd Memorial was a "serious and disturbing situation" (Letter, Cummings to Campbell, January 13, 1994). When the NPS told him that the monument would be uncovered only when an interpretive display was created, Cummings demanded that the monument be returned to the SCV, and they would find a suitable place for its display on private property (Letter, Cummings to Kennedy, September 23, 1994). The NPS was flooded with letters from SCV and UDC members asking that the monument be placed on display immediately and without any additional interpretation. For instance, Virginia H. Sollers-Hoffmaster of the UDC wrote,

> As a member of The United Daughters of the Confederacy, I find it intolerable and unconscionable, that such a move (placing an interpretive placard next to the monument) has occurred. I cannot imagine how long it will take to educate so-called historians that one cannot, I repeat, cannot re-write or alter history. (Letter, Sollers-Hoffmaster to Campbell, June 15, 1994)

Others wrote that the NPS not displaying the monument "has caused those of Confederate heritage to be greatly offended!" (Letter, Grabows to Campbell, March 17, 1994). One year later, Senator Jesse Helms (R-N.C.) received a letter from Cummings. He complained that the monument, a form of southern heritage, remained covered "for reason of political correctness" and that the NPS did not respond to his inquiries. Cummings remarked that he did not know why the NPS sees the unveiling of the monument as controversial. "The original 1931 program shows that blacks from the local 'negro' college even actively and willingly participated in the dedication ceremony and provided the chorus for the event." He argued against an interpretive sign next to the monument to explain its historical context. "This is the exact same line used by the perverters of history at the Smithsonian to justify a distorted story line about the Enola Gay. . . . This kind of thinking jeopardizes the heritage of all of us" (Letter, Cummings to Helms, January 30, 1995). The park received a congressional inquiry from Helms (Letter, Helms to Merrill, April 3, 1995). Within a month, Helms received a letter from the regional director of the

National Capital Region of the NPS that stated, "In 1995, the park plans to remove the Heyward Shepherd Monument from storage and display it" (quoted in Bailes 1995:A2; Meyer 1995:C1–C2). Secretary of the Interior Bruce Babbitt received hundreds of preprinted form cards requesting that the monument be returned to the SCV if it could not be restored to public view and that it should be displayed without an interpretive display (Letter, Fafarman to Noble, September 20, 1995).

Cummings also had the notion that the NPS only owned the buildings in the national park but not the sidewalk and, therefore, not the monument (see Eckhardt 1995). He again requested that the Department of the Interior return the monument to the UDC and SCV. The chief historian of the NPS responded that the monument did convey to the federal government when the NPS acquired the lands in Harpers Ferry (Letter, Pitcaithley to Cummings, July 17, 1995).

On June 9, 1995, the park removed the plywood crate without telling any of the concerned groups and again placed the monument on display to the public. Beside the monument stands a wayside that creates a context for the monument (see figure 3.4). It reads,

> On October 17, 1859, abolitionist John Brown attacked Harpers Ferry to launch a war against slavery. Heyward Shepherd, a free African-American railroad baggage master, was shot and killed by Brown's men shortly after midnight.
>
> Seventy-two years later, on October 10, 1931, a crowd estimated to include 300 whites and 100 blacks gathered to unveil and dedicate the Shepherd Monument.
>
> During the ceremony, voices raised to praise and denounce the monument. Conceived around the turn of the century, the monument endured controversy. In 1905, the United Daughters of the Confederacy stated that "erecting the monument would influence for good the present and coming generations, and prove that the people of the South who owned slaves valued and respected their good qualities as no one else ever did or will do."

Also on the wayside is a section titled "Another Perspective." It is the same response to the Shepherd Memorial that Du Bois wrote in 1932 and hoped to have inscribed on the John Brown Fort. While the Storer College trustees did not allow these words to be placed on the fort, they now appear next to the Shepherd Memorial.

Figure 3.4. Heyward Shepherd Memorial with National Park Service wayside, 1997 (courtesy Paul A. Shackel).

In 1932, Du Bois, founder of the Niagara movement and the NAACP, responded to the Shepherd Memorial by penning these words:

> Here / John Brown / Aimed at Human History / A Blow / That woke a guilty nation / With him fought / Seven Slaves and sons of slaves. / Over his crucified corpse / Marched 200,000 black soldiers / and 4,000,000 freedmen / Singing / "John Brown's Body lies a mouldering in the grave / But his Soul Goes marching on."

In response to the new interpretive wayside, Harriett Elizabeth Nichols Binkley, honorary president of the West Virginia Division of the UDC remarked, "They put there just what they wanted. It still isn't the true history" (quoted in Meyer 1995:C2). The SCV was also outraged that an interpretive sign stands adjacent to the monument. The commander of the Maryland Division, Elliot Cummings, demanded that the national park give the monument back to those who paid for it (the UDC and the SCV) or else remove the interpretive wayside sign. He issued a "heritage violation" to those on his division's mailing list, asking Civil War reenactment groups to boycott events at the park unless they removed the sign:

> My position is that the monument should not be interpreted. They should be allowed to exist as they are and people should be allowed to make whatever interpretation they want. . . . Do I get to put an interpretive plaque on the Lincoln Memorial saying this man was responsible for the deaths of 250,000 Southerners and usurped the Constitution. (Quoted in Bailey 1995:22)

Campbell responded by saying that the wayside does not interpret the monument. "Everything on the wayside exhibit is history—what happened here at Harpers Ferry and the African-American perspective on the monument. . . . It's a minimum amount of contextual information necessary to explain the story" (quoted in Bailey 1995:22). Cummings fumed, "Contextual labeling—that's just a buzzword. It's the park service trying to develop a politically correct line" (quoted in Bailey 1995:23). "It is history," replied Campbell. "It's minimum, it's neutral, and we invite visitors to come see it and make up their own minds" (quoted in Bailey 1995:23).

The president of the West Virginia Chapter of the NAACP never wanted the monument to be unveiled in 1995. James Tolbert remarked, "I don't think it's history. I think it is a misrepresentation of the life and role of Heyward Shepherd. We don't think that the Daughters of the Confederacy and the Sons of the Confederacy had that much love for Negroes" (quoted in Deutsch 1995:1A). During its August meeting, the NAACP chapter passed a resolution that condemned the monument (Bailes 1995:A1). Tolbert later added, "I believe it should be taken by crane to the Potomac River and dropped at the river's deepest point (quoted in Deutsch 1995:9A; *Jet Magazine* 1995:22–23).

The *Winchester Star* (1995:E1) responded, "Activists who would revise, alter, or ignore history simply because the record does not satisfy or accommodate their specific ends, are at it again. This time, it's the membership of the West Virginia chapter of the National Association for the Advancement of Colored People."

Other voices took a middle road. Amidst the controversy over the unveiling of the boulder, the *Spirit of Jefferson* (1995) suggested that the monument remain so that it could be a reminder to people about the prejudices that existed in 1931 and the conflict that persists today.

The president general of the UDC wrote park historian Bruce Noble thanking him for his efforts to uncover the monument. She also noted that several members of her organization viewed the plaque "and in general find nothing offensive as to the wording of the plaque as presented" (Letter, Palmer to Noble, November 8, 1995).

Conclusion

The acts of John Brown at Harpers Ferry will always be debated, and the memorial to Heyward Shepherd sparked considerable controversy during its planning and unveiling. It has also triggered many emotions while incorporated and interpreted in Harpers Ferry National Historical Park. The inscription on the boulder was perceived as racist by many people in the 1930s, and it remains a controversial memorial today. The memorial explicitly justifies the conditions of slavery and claims that African Americans willingly existed within the racist system. The memorial also implicitly defends legalized segregation during the Jim Crow era.

After the Civil War, many southerners reminisced about the goodwill and loyalty between master and slaves. By the late nineteenth century, many of the advancements made by African Americans in the South were eliminated under Jim Crow legislation. Many southerners believed that African Americans could play only a subservient role in a new and segregated South. They claimed that African Americans under Reconstruction were inept in handling their newfound freedom. This notion became part of popular culture during the Jim Crow era with the release of such films as D. W. Griffith's *The Birth of a Nation* (1915) (Ayers 1992:136–58; Blight 2001:111, 263; E. Foner 1988:xix–xxi).

In 1896, in the small manufacturing town of Fort Mill, South Carolina, a former slaveholder and Confederate veteran erected a modest obelisk on the town green near a Confederate soldier monument. Captain Samuel White, who also owned the local cotton mill, had the following words inscribed onto the monument:

> Dedicated to the faithful slaves who, loyal to a sacred trust, toiled for support of the army, with matchless devotion; and with sterling fidelity guarded our defenseless homes, women and children, during the struggle for the principles of our "Confederated States of America." (From Savage 1997b:156–57)

The monument, according to Savage (1997b:157), muses nostalgically over the former institution of slavery.

At the time of the erection of the Fort Mill faithful-slave monument, a few plaques and shafts began to appear in public to memorialize slaves. One Confederate soldier monument, erected in Columbia, North Carolina, in 1912, has an inscription that states, "In appreciation of our faithful slaves" (Savage 1997b:158). These monuments "transform this extreme institution of domination into the nostalgic fiction of a lost love. Dear as this fiction was to many white southerners, it had to be banished from their more official program of memory because the institution of slavery . . . was no longer 'American'" (Savage 1997b:161).

The creation of the Heyward Shepherd Memorial became part of this larger campaign by southern heritage groups such as the UDC and SCV to remember a Lost Cause and to justify the system of the plantation South. These southern heritage groups believed that Shepherd was true to the existing system, and therefore the monument became a vehicle to show the world that African Americans did not take up arms against the South or revolt against the institution of slavery because they were content with the status quo. They were too inept to govern themselves or to take a much larger role in society.

The decision to erect the memorial in Harpers Ferry occurred in 1920, an era that saw the development and the strengthening of the NAACP and the resurgence of the Ku Klux Klan. The controversial nature of the project was clear from the beginning. While the UDC and SCV pressed to have the monument erected in Harpers Ferry, both the Baltimore & Ohio Railroad and the town of Harpers Ferry refused to have the monument erected on its lands. Finally, a private citizen allowed it to be erected outside his building. Ironically, the monument stands outside and adjacent to the building that now contains the NPS's John Brown exhibit. Across the street is the John Brown obelisk, erected in 1895.

The erection of the Heyward Shepherd Memorial in 1931 displeased many African Americans, and they are still battling with the UDC and the SCV over the meaning of the monument. While the two southern heritage groups fought to have the monument restored to its original location, the NAACP is bitter over the fact that the memorial is once again on view to the American public. As long as the monument stands in Lower Town Harpers Ferry, its meaning will be contested and its place within the national public memory challenged.

Saint-Gaudens's Shaw Memorial: Redefining the Role of the 54th Massachusetts Volunteer Infantry

4

Critics have described Augustus Saint-Gaudens, a well-known American sculptor during the Victorian era, as "an American Michelangelo, a superb craftsman, a poet and philosopher" (Dryfhout 1982:25). Saint-Gaudens is probably best known for his memorial to Robert Gould Shaw, which sits on the Boston Common opposite the statehouse (see figure 4.1). Shaw led the first volunteer regiment consisting solely of free African Americans. The 54th Massachusetts Volunteer Infantry left Boston in late May 1863 and joined the assault on the forts that surrounded Charleston, South Carolina. Shaw was killed, along with nearly half his troops, in an attempt to capture Fort Wagner. Attempts to memorialize Shaw began immediately, but a monument to commemorate his deeds was not erected for three decades. The monument, unveiled in 1897, displays Shaw in the foreground, riding elevated on horseback. The African American troops march in stride and are a background to Shaw, who occupies the central portion of the monument.

White artists and art critics have often claimed that Saint-Gaudens's Shaw Memorial demonstrates shows how he was "one vastly gifted, socially responsible white artist, operating on intractable material with an objective eye, and absolute control over hand and eye" (Benson and Kirstein 1973:n.p.). While a century of critics have hailed Saint-Gaudens's sculpture as a magnificent piece of art, his portrayal of the troops and the work's full meaning have been contested by others. In the more than one hundred years since its unveiling, there have been various and conflicting meanings associated with the Shaw Memorial.

Robert Gould Shaw

Born on October 10, 1837, Robert Gould Shaw came from a Unitarian background with strong abolitionist sentiments. He spent part of his

Figure 4.1. The Shaw Memorial (courtesy Paul A. Shackel).

childhood on a large estate next to the utopian community of Brook Farm in Massachusetts, and his family associated with such notable abolitionists as William Lloyd Garrison, John H. Andrew, and Wendell Phillips. The Shaws later moved to New York City for a short time but moved back to Boston in the 1850s. Robert attended Harvard for three years but withdrew to join his uncle's business in New York City. After the bombardment of Fort Sumter, he immediately volunteered in the Seventh New York National Guard Regiment in April 1861 and marched to defend Washington, D.C. (Burchard 1965:4–5; Sturman 1997:3).

The Seventh New York Regiment lasted for only thirty-seven days, and Shaw immediately joined the Second Massachusetts. During his service, he reflected on his strong abolitionist upbringing. He wrote to a friend while encamped on Maryland Heights, outside Harpers Ferry,

> Isn't it extraordinary that the Government won't make use of the instrument that would finish the war sooner than anything else—viz. the slaves? I have no doubt they could give more information about the enemy than anyone else, and that there would be noth-

> ing easier than to have a line of spies right into their camp. What a lick it would be to [the rebels], to call all the blacks in the country to come and enlist in our army! They would probably make a fine army after a little drill, and could certainly be kept under better discipline than our independent Yankees. (Quoted in Duncan 1992:123)

Shaw had echoed the sentiments of Frederick Douglass, who had said in his *Monthly* that a lenient war would be a costly war. He claimed that the war would end earlier "by carrying the war into Africa. Let the slaves and free colored people be called into service, and formed into a liberating army to march into the South and raise the banner of Emancipation among slaves" (quoted in Burchard 1965:45).

About a year later, Shaw wrote about his ambition to team up with Major Copeland to command an African American regiment:

> It would be much wiser to enlist men in the North, who have had the courage to run away, and have already suffered for their freedom, than to take them all from contrabands at Port Royal and other places. . . . Copeland wants me to take hold of the black regiment with him, if he can get permission to raise it, and offers me a major's commission in it. . . . Copeland thinks [it would be] the greatest thing that has ever been done for the negro race. (Quoted in Duncan 1992:202)

The War Department did not allow African Americans to enlist since they considered it "a white man's war," although African Americans had previously served in the military. African Americans had served in the American Revolution and the War of 1812. But they had been barred from the state militias since 1792, and they could not enroll in the regular army. The administration also refused to accept the organization of black regiments in Kansas, occupied Louisiana, and the South Carolina sea islands during the summer of 1862. The Union navy, however, accepted African Americans from the outset of the conflict in the capacity of fire-fighters, coal heavers, cooks, and stewards. In August 1862, a group of freed slaves served as a gun crew on the *U.S. Minnesota* (McPherson 1988:563–64).

The War Department initially interpreted Lincoln's Emancipation Proclamation in a way that saw black troops in limited supporting roles for the white troops. This attitude soon changed. Major General David Hunter, commanding the Department of the South, had been an enthusiastic supporter of the development of African American troops. "Thomas Wentworth Higginson's contraband regiment, the First Regiment of the South Carolina Volunteers, was [developed under] Hunter" (Burchard 1965:92; see also Higginson 1971). Recruitment was slow since many newly freed African Americans received conflicting information from both their former owners and white recruiters who opposed their incorporation into the army. Before the Emancipation Proclamation, they were not guaranteed freedom for military service. According to Higginson's (1971:272–73) autobiography, the freed slaves believed that once recruited by the Union, they would be sold to Cuba, dissolving whatever relations they had already established. The recruiters also told them that they would work without pay and that they would be sent to the front lines.

Despite the obstacles, by the summer of 1862 other regiments of free African American troops formed in Louisiana, and a regiment of freed blacks developed in Kansas. Before the end of the year, two more Louisiana regiments, along with the authorized South Carolina regiment, had formed (McPherson 1988:564).

The War Department authorized Colonel James Montgomery, along with Thomas Wentworth Higginson, to organize a second regiment of newly freed African Americans in South Carolina. In 1870, Higginson (1971:4) wrote, "I had been an abolitionist too long, and had known and loved John Brown too well, not to feel a thrill of joy at last on finding myself in the position where he only wished to be." Burchard (1965:92) explains, "Montgomery was now in the South with his cadre of Northern officers bagging contrabands for the Second Carolina Volunteer Infantry. He was taking the word 'volunteer' with a grain of salt." Montgomery created the Second Carolina Volunteers, a regiment of African Americans, under conditions not usual for Union recruitment (Burchard 1965:53, 98; Higginson 1971:1). He forced slaves from their fields without giving them a chance to say good-bye to their families. Montgomery never told them that their new status meant pay and furlough time to visit with their families.

Higginson led the First South Carolina on a successful raid along the South Carolina coast in January 1863. He wrote a letter to the War Department that eventually ended up in the newspapers. "Nobody knows anything about these men who has not seen them in battle," he stated. "No officer in this regiment now doubts that the key to the successful prosecution of the war lies in the unlimited employment of black troops" (from McPherson 1988:565). The *New York Tribune* commented that these reports would "shake our inveterate Saxon prejudice against the capacity and courage of negro troops" (from McPherson 1988:565).

Governor John A. Andrew of Massachusetts had a strong desire to form the first "model regiment" of African Americans in the eye of world opinion (quoted in Duncan 1992:26). In February 1863, Governor Andrew asked Shaw to lead the 54th Massachusetts Volunteer Infantry. In a January 30, 1863, letter to Shaw's father, the governor spoke of a "colored regiment" that could serve as a model for the organization of other African American troops. Using Captain Shaw of the Second Massachusetts Infantry was important since many Republicans would recognize "him as a scion from a tree whose fruit and leaves have always contributed to the strength and healing of our generation" (Berlin 1982:97). Shaw's father, Francis, wrote to Governor Andrew and claimed, "The only fear I have is in regard to his opinion of his own competency. In all other points I know he is right and true" (Francis Shaw, quoted in Burchard 1965:72; see also Duncan 1992:22). His father then traveled to Stafford Courthouse in Virginia and presented Robert with the governor's offer (Blight 1989b:158).

Shaw Takes Command

Much was on the line for Robert Gould Shaw. A contemporary author (quoted in Burchard 1965:72) remarked, "In this new negro-soldier venture, loneliness was certain, ridicule inevitable, failure possible; and Shaw was only twenty-five; and although he stood among the bullets at Cedar Mountain and Antietam, he had till then been walking socially on the sunny side of life."

Shaw initially refused the offer, and his mother saw his response as a rejection of her work as a lifelong abolitionist (Duncan 1992:24). Shaw explained to his fiancée, Annie, "If I had taken it, it would only have been from a sense of duty; for it would have been anything but an agreeable task" (quoted in Duncan 1992:283). Shaw's mother wrote to the governor about her son's decision. She informed him that if Robert had accepted,

> it would have been the proudest moment of my life and I could have died satisfied that I had not lived in vain. This being the truth, you will believe that I have shed bitter tears over his refusal. I do not understand it unless from a habit inherited from

> his Father, of self-distrust in his own capabilities. (Quoted in Burchard 1965:73; also in Duncan 1992:23)

However, Shaw had a change of heart the next day, probably after talking to his commander. He telegraphed his father and said, "Please destroy my letter and telegraph to the Governor that I accept. Stafford Court House, Feb. 5, 1863" (quoted in Burchard 1965:74). His mother was overjoyed and wrote Robert, "Now I feel ready to die, for I see you willing to give your support to the cause of truth that is lying crushed and bleeding" (quoted in Duncan 1992:23). Robert wrote to Annie and claimed, "I feel that what I have to do is to prove that a negro can be made a good soldier." Later in the letter he explained, "I shan't be frightened out of it by its unpopularity; and I hope you won't care if it is made fun of" (quoted in Duncan 1992:285–86).

The Forming of the 54th Massachusetts

On learning about the Emancipation Proclamation, Confederate General Pierre Beauregard, threatened by the raising of African American troops, called for the "execution of abolition prisoners [i.e., captured Union soldiers] after 1st of January. . . . Let the executions be with the garrote" (quoted in McPherson 1988:565–66). Jefferson Davis, in a message to the Confederate Congress, stated that captured Union officers leading black troops should be punished for "inciting servile insurrection, and shall, if captured, be put to death or be otherwise punished at the discretion of the Court" (Emilio 1969:7; see also McPherson 1988:566).

There are several incidents where Jefferson Davis and Secretary of War James A. Seddon approved the execution of captured black soldiers. In another case, a Confederate colonel reported what had happened when his men captured a squad of African American soldiers in Louisiana. When some were reported to have attempted to escape, the colonel wrote, "I then ordered every one shot, and with my Six Shooter I assisted in the execution of the order." A North Carolina soldier wrote his mother that after a skirmish "several [were] taken prisoner & afterwards either bayoneted or burnt. The men were perfectly exasperated at the idea of negroes opposed to them & rushed at them like so many devils" (quoted in McPherson 1988:566).

In May 1863, the Confederate Congress sanctioned the policy that captured officers leading African American troops should be tried and punished by military court (McPherson 1988:566). Despite the risks, Shaw was not discouraged in his efforts to establish his regiment.

After Shaw accepted the commission, he began the recruitment and training of the troops. About 40 percent of Boston's African American population eligible for military service had joined the 54th Massachusetts, but this mark fell short of filling the ranks. Therefore, recruitment continued throughout the United States and Canada (Burchard 1965:ix; Duncan 1992:38). Shaw knew the consequences of taking command of the regiment and wrote his mother, "I feel that there are more chances than ever of my not getting back" (quoted in Burchard 1965:87).

When Shaw left his Massachusetts regiment, he probably had some reservations regarding the competence of the fighting ability of African Americans. Russell Duncan (1992:35) compiled Shaw's letters and noted that while Robert corresponded to his mother and friends from the beginning of the war, he called African Americans "niggers" and "darkeys" (see, e.g., Shaw, quoted in Duncan 1992:293). He often avoided these terms when he wrote his abolitionist mother while training the 54th Massachusetts two years later. Shaw also made racist remarks based on stereotypes of physical attributes and poor language skills. However, after these men proved their abilities during training, he began to respect them. He wrote his mother on March 25, "The intelligence of the men is a great surprise to me. They learn all the details of guard duty and camp service, infinitely more readily than the Irish I had under my command" (quoted in Duncan 1992:313). "Shaw still wondered what they might do when they reached the battlefield, but he finally stopped calling them niggers" (quoted in Duncan 1992:35).

On May 6, Secretary of Treasury Salmon P. Chase reviewed the troops. The *Springfield Republican* reported, "They marched well, they wheeled well, they stood well, they handled their guns well, and there was about their whole array an air of completeness, and order, and morale, such as I have not seen surpassed in any white regiment" (quoted in Duncan 1992:36).

On May 18, 1863, ceremonies were held in Boston before the regiment sailed from the port. Frederick Douglass, William Lloyd Garrison, and Wendell Phillips spoke to a crowd of about 3,000 spectators. The governor presented the battle flag to Shaw. Shaw responded by saying, "May we have an opportunity to show you that you have not made a mistake in intrusting the honor of the State to a colored regiment,—the first State that has ever sent one to war" (quoted in Duncan 1992:333). On May 28, Shaw and the 54th Massachusetts Volunteer Infantry marched to Battery Wharf. Runaway slave Harriet Jacobs wrote about the account in *Incidents in the Life of a Slave Girl* in 1871. She explained, "How my heart swelled with the thought that my poor oppressed race was to strike a blow for Freedom! We're at last allowed to help in breaking the chains" (quoted in Duncan 1992:39). The troops passed the Shaw residence, and his sister wrote, "Rob . . . looked up and kissed his sword, his face was as the face of an angel and I felt perfectly sure he would never come back" (Quoted in Burchard 1965:94).

General Hunter, commander of the Department of the South, requested that the 54th Massachusetts be placed under his command. The troops set sail for the Sea Islands off Charleston, South Carolina. A few days later, Shaw wrote,

> Truly I ought to be thankful for all my happiness and success in life so far; and if the raising of coloured troops proves such a benefit to the country and the blacks, . . . I shall thank God a thousand times that I was led to take my share in it. (quoted in Duncan 1992:335)

The 54th Marches into Battle

The world watched the 54th Massachusetts, including its abolitionist supporters and its Democratic detractors. Fourteen days after sailing from Boston, the 54th Massachusetts participated in an event that became the regiment's worst moment. Shaw and his troops were on maneuvers with Colonel Montgomery of the Second South Carolina. Montgomery was in charge of the operations. Shaw described him as "an Indian in his mode of warfare . . . [and] I can't say I admire it. It isn't like a fair stand up such as our Potomac Army is accustomed to" (quoted in Duncan 1992:339). When they reached the deserted town of Darien, situated on the banks of the Altamaha River in Georgia, Montgomery allowed his men to break rank and loot at will. When Shaw protested, Montgomery advised him that they were acting under orders from General Hunter. Montgomery then ordered a company under Shaw's command to help burn the town. They burned churches, stores, and houses (Burchard 1965:105–9).

Writing his wife, Annie, Shaw (quoted in Duncan 1992:342–43) explained,

> Montgomery ordered all the furniture and movable property to be taken on board the boats. This occupied some time; and after

> the town was pretty thoroughly disemboweled, he said to me, "I shall burn the town." . . . I told him, "I did not want the responsibility of it," and he was only too happy to take it all on his shoulders; so the pretty little place was burnt to the ground, and not a shed remains standing. . . . One of my companies assisted in it, because he ordered them out, and I had to obey.
>
> The reasons he gave me for destroying Darien were, that the Southerners must be made to feel that this was a real war, and that they were to be swept away by the hand of God, like the Jews of old. . . . I myself don't like it.

Shaw spent the rest of his life trying to put behind him the incident at Darien. News of the event only marred his regiment's reputation and gave fuel to the Democrats, who believed that African Americans should not be fighting, for they would fall to these barbarian tactics.

The 54th Massachusetts met its first battle contest on James Island on July 16. The island, a strategic land mass, was key to holding Fort Wagner, guarding the main shipping channel to Charleston, South Carolina. Although outnumbered, the 54th Massachusetts rescued the 10th Connecticut Regiment from defeat by routing the rebels (Duncan 1992:49–50). Word spread of the heroics of the 54th in battle—African Americans could fight, and fight well.

Two days later, after a two-night march through rain and shifting sands with insufficient rations, Shaw accepted the order to lead an attack on Fort Wagner, although such an attempt had failed the week before. At dusk on July 18, the 54th Massachusetts led the assault. "More was riding on the 54th's first big action than the capture of a fort, important as that might be" (McPherson 1988:686). Colonel Shaw led only 600 troops across a narrow spit of sand against a strong earthwork. A large camp guard remained behind. Shaw was one of the first to fall, but his troops pressed on (see figure 4.2). More than half reached the inside of the fort, and they held Wagner's parapet for an hour before being driven off by the Confederates (McPherson 1988:686). Other regiments attacked that night, but they also failed. The assault on Fort Wagner that day left 1,515 Union casualties compared with only 181 on the Confederate side (Burchard 1965:149).

A Confederate lieutenant, Iredell Jones, reported, "The dead and wounded were piled up in a ditch together sometimes fifteen in a heap, and they were strewn all over the plain for a distance of three-fourths of a

Figure 4.2. Currier and Ives image of the attack on Fort Wagner (courtesy U.S. Department of the Interior, National Park Service, Saint-Gaudens National Historic Site, Cornish, New Hampshire).

mile" (quoted in Benson and Kirstein 1973:n.p.). The 54th Massachusetts received heavy casualties. Two-thirds of the officers and nearly half the enlisted men were either killed, wounded, or missing. This tragedy was only compounded by the wounded receiving poor medical attention and the Confederates' mistreatment and execution of the captives. Confederate commanders refused the assistance of the Union army to care for the wounded and the burial of the dead. They shipped the captured soldiers upriver to Charleston and paraded them through the streets amid jeers and catcalls (Burchard 1965:142).

One account of the 54th Massachusetts is Captain Luis F. Emilio's *A Brave Black Regiment: History of the Fifty-Fourth Regiment of Massachusetts Volunteer Infantry, 1863–1865* (1969). His is a firsthand account of the assault on Fort Wagner by the 54th Massachusetts and a stoic story of taking command after nearly all his superiors died in the battle.

John T. Luck, an assistant surgeon, wrote in the only northern account of the battle's aftermath that "all the officers killed in the assault were decently buried, excepting Colonel Shaw" (quoted in Burchard 1965:142).

Captain H. W. Hendericks, a Confederate officer, remarked that "his body was carried through our lines; and I noticed that he was stripped of all his clothing save under-vest and drawers. . . . His watch and chain were robbed from his body by a private in my company" (quoted in Emilio 1969:98). Hoping to disgrace him, they buried him in a mass grave with his troops. "Colonel Shaw was the only officer buried with the colored troops" (quoted in Emilio 1969:98).

When the Federals asked for Shaw's body for proper burial, a Confederate general reportedly said, "We have buried him with his niggers" (McPherson 1969:n.p.). Brigadier General Hagood, commander of the Confederate forces at Wagner, supposedly said, "I knew Colonel Shaw before the war, and then esteemed him. Had he been in command of white troops, I should have given him an honorable burial; as it is, I shall bury him in the common trench with negroes that fell with him" (from Emilio 1969:101; see also Burchard 1965:143). Hagood later denied he said those words.

News of the assault on Fort Wagner by the 54th Massachusetts became widely known in the North, and Shaw's deed transformed him into a martyr. Henry James wrote Shaw's parents, "I feel for you all, in truth, exactly what I should feel for myself—profound pity: and yet such a pride in the noble and beautiful boy, such a grateful sense of his finished manhood, as disdains that pity" (from Benson and Kirstein 1973:n.p.). The *New York Tribune* wrote that the battle "made Fort Wagner such a name to the colored race as Bunker Hill had been for ninety years to the white Yankees" (from McPherson 1988:686). The *Atlantic Monthly* wrote, "Through the cannon smoke of that black night the manhood of the colored race shines before many eyes that would not see" (from McPherson 1969:n.p.). General Grant also wrote,

> By arming the negro we have added a powerful ally. They will make good soldiers and taking them from the enemy weakens him in the same proportion they strengthen us. I am therefore most decidedly in favor of pushing this policy to the enlistment of a force sufficient to hold all the South falling into our hands and to aid in capturing more. (From McPherson 1969:n.p.)

The 54th Massachusetts had proven that African Americans could fight honorably, and enlistment of African American troops increased dramatically. By the end of the year, sixty black regiments were being organized (Duncan 1992:53).

In retrospect, W. E. B. Du Bois (1935:10) wrote, "How extraordinary . . . in the minds of most people . . . only murder makes men. The slave pleaded; he was humble; he protected the women of the South, and the world ignored him. The slave killed white men; and behold, he was a man."

Union troops took Fort Wagner on September 6, 1863, two months after Gettysburg. General James Gillmore proposed the recovery of Shaw's body to give it a special burial. The Shaw family refused, and his father noted that he could hope for "no holier place" for his body (from Duncan 1992:54). He wrote to Gillmore,

> We hold that a soldier's most appropriate burial-place is on the field where he has fallen. I shall therefore be much obliged, general if in this case this matter is brought to your cognizance, you will forbid the desecration of my son's grave and prevent the disturbance of his remains or those buried with him. (Quoted in Emilio 1969:102–3; see also Berlin 1982:787)

The family's insistence symbolized their disregard for preferential treatment and a sense of unity between the races.

After the attack on Fort Wagner, numerous problems and inconsistencies came to light. The usual preparations for an assault were not made, and the Union army did not make any provisions for cutting away obstructions, filling the ditch, or spiking the guns. Emilio (1969:78) notes,

> No special instructions were given stormers; no line of skirmishers or covering party was thrown out; no engineers or guides accompanied the column; no artillery-men to serve captured guns; no plan of the work was shown company officers. It was understood that the fort would be assaulted with bayonet, and that the Fifty-fourth would be closely supported.

Possible rivalry between the naval and land operations did not help the 54th's cause. The regiment did not receive support by any rearguard troops. Guns of the fleet stationed in the harbor also fell silent during the attack. In his own defense, the naval captain said he knew nothing of the attack. There is also speculation the commanders maliciously used the troops. Special correspondents of the *New York Tribune* testified before the American Freedmen's Inquiry Commission in 1864 that the commander deliberately placed the regiment before the other troops. They used the

54th Massachusetts both as a "decoy" and to "dispose of the idea that the negroes could fight" (Berlin 1982:535). When the attack plan had been formulated, General Truman Seymour commented to Gillmore, "Well I guess we will let Strong put those d——d negroes from Massachusetts in the advance, we may as well get rid of them, one time as another" (quoted in Duncan 1992:50–51). Major Smith, who gave the order to place the 54th at the beginning of the assault, had little confidence in black troops (Boime 1990:203; Williams 1969:192–204).

The 54th Massachusetts Volunteer Infantry was the first and most famous black regiment enlisted in the North. After its assault on Fort Wagner, the regiment compiled a distinguished war record. A detachment of the 54th was among the first troops to enter Charleston when the city fell in February 1865. As a result of the bravery of the men who charged Fort Wagner, more than 200,000 African Americans were mustered into the U.S. service. Yet even though the troops of the 54th are memorialized in bronze, they serve only as a backdrop for their white colonel.

Postbattle Memorialization

Immediately after the 54th Massachusetts failed in its attack on Fort Wagner, the Shaw memorialization began. Shaw represented the gallantry of the regiment not only because of his position as commander but also because he came from the Boston Brahman elite. His death became a family loss and a moral contribution by Boston to the preservation of the Union and the fight for emancipation (Lauerhass 1997:5).

As with the martyrdom of John Brown, many authors wrote about the great sacrifice Shaw made for the Union and the abolitionist cause. Charles Lowell described Shaw's death as "a perfect ending. I see now that the best Colonel of the best black regiment had to die, it was a sacrifice we owed,—and how could it have been paid more gloriously?" (quoted in E. Emerson 1907:285). Lowell later said that Shaw's death was for "a cause greater than any National one" (quoted in E. Emerson 1907:288). Lydia Maria Child wrote to Shaw's mother and echoed the sentiment of many other abolitionists. She said that Robert "died nobly in the defense of great principles, and he has gone to join the glorious army of martyrs" (quoted in Meltzer and Holland 1982:433).

Shaw became one of the Civil War's most celebrated legends, and newspapers published many of his letters soon after his death. Some of these selected letters explained his abolitionist views, and others defended his reluctant role in the burning of Darien (Duncan 1992:375). More than forty poems have been written about Shaw and his martyrdom. The most famous one is by James Russell Lowell (from Emilio 1969:n.p.):

> Right in the van,
> On the red rampart's slippery swell
> With heart that beat a charge, he fell
> Forward, as fits a man;
> But the high soul burns on to light men's feet
> Where death for noble ends makes dying sweet.

And Ralph Waldo Emerson (from Duncan 1992:55) wrote,

> So nigh is grandeur to our dust
> So near to God is man
> When Duty whispers low
> Thou must
> The youth replies
> I can

Plans for a Shaw Memorial began almost immediately after his death. Shaw's own regiment, although still unpaid at the time, raised $2,832 toward a memorial. T. W. Higginson's regiment added $1,000, and the African American population of Beaufort, South Carolina, added $300. The troops planned to erect a modest memorial near the battlefield. The Shaw family insisted that the monument be a plain shaft with a simple inscription. Shaw's father wrote, "It seems to me that the monument, though originated for my son, ought to bear, with his, the names of the brave officers and men, who fell and were buried with him. This would be simple justice" (quoted in Benson and Kirstein 1973:n.p.).

Because of shifting sands and general hostility among the local population to the idea of a monument to the 54th Massachusetts, a monument was never erected near Fort Wagner. Instead, the funds were used to create the first free African American school in Charleston, named after Shaw (from Benson and Kirstein 1973:n.p.).

After the Civil War, the monument-building craze began, commemorating the bravery of fallen soldiers and their leaders. One African American veteran, George W. Williams, who enlisted in the Union army in 1864, claimed that remembrance did not extend to the black participants

(Blight 2001:168). He noted (1969:328) in *A History of the Negro Troops in the War of the Rebellion,*

> Nowhere in all this free land is there a monument to brave Negro soldiers, 36,847 of whom gave up their lives in the struggle for national existence. Even the appearance of the Negro soldier in the hundreds of histories of the war has always been incidental. These brave men have had no champion, no one to chronicle their record, teeming with interest and instinct with patriotism.

Williams predicted that one day a painter would commemorate the assault on Fort Wagner, but Americans would remember only one name, Colonel Robert Gould Shaw (Williams 1969:202). He exclaimed,

> Looking back over the centuries, there would be little else to record of the poor, patient Negro save his suffering and degradation were it not for the luminous flashes of his martial glory, which cast a light upon the background of an otherwise somber picture. But a monument such as is here proposed would surely and safely elevate the Negro to a proud place in the history of the nation. (Williams 1969:331–32)

Williams proposed that a monument be placed in front of Howard University that would contrast with contemporary portrayals of African Americans, which often depicted African Americans as "dreamy-eyed and fatigued" (Boime 1990:212). He proposed a memorial that would represent African Americans as standing erect, proud, and tall. The monument would stand in a park named after Colonel Robert Gould Shaw. It would be

> surmounted by a private soldier in great-coat, equipment, fixed bayonet, gun at parade rest, looking south towards the capital. . . . At the four corners the arms of the field-service and the navy would be represented. *First figure,* a Negro artilleryman in full-dress uniform, with folded arms, standing by a field-piece. *Second figure,* a cavalryman in full-dress uniform, with spurs and gloves, and saber unhooked at his left side. *Third figure,* an infantry man in full-dress uniform, accouterments, and musket at in-place rest. *Fourth figure,* a Negro sailor in uniform standing by an anchor or mortar. (Williams 1969:328–29)

Williams commented that commemoration in the form of creating monuments would live in America's memory for a long time. He remarked,

> Centuries might pass, treasures corrode, cities disappear, tribes perish and even empires whose boast was duration might crumble, but a republic that remembers to defend its defenders in tracing their noble conduct in monumental marble and brass can never decay. Heaven and earth may pass away, but God's word endures forever. Truth is immortal. (Williams 1969:332)

Working with Senator George F. Hoar of Massachusetts, Williams helped draft a bill for federal funding of a black-soldier monument to be erected near Howard University in the Shaw neighborhood. In 1887, the bill was introduced in both houses of Congress. The bill passed the Senate in December 1887, but the House of Representatives failed to act (Blight 2001:196).

In 1916, Freeman Henry Morris Murry, an African American, published *Emancipation and the Freed in American Sculpture* and wrote a critique of African American representation in art. Insightfully, he wrote that the idea of "art for art's sake" was a way for the elite to maintain their cultural and social hegemony:

> Hence, when we look at a work of art, especially when "we" look at one in which Black Folk appear—or do not appear when they should,—we should ask: What does it mean? What does it suggest? What impression is it likely to make on those who view it? What will be the effect on present-day problems, of its obvious and also of its insidious teaching? In short, we should endeavor to "interpret" it; and should try to interpret it from our own peculiar standpoint. (Murry 1916:xix)

Murry noted the importance of public art, especially since it is highly visible. He saw the reinforcement of racist ideology in the absence of African Americans in sculpture. When whites created sculptures with black representation, they merely presented stereotypes (Boime 1990:154).

Saint-Gaudens and the Making of the Shaw Memorial

Plans for a Shaw monument in Boston began with a formal meeting held in the autumn of 1865. Joshua Smith, a carter, formerly a fugitive slave and once a servant of the Shaw family, was one of the original proponents. He pledged $500 of his own money and raised several thousand dollars in the African American community in Boston (Savage 1997b:196–97). Soon after, a committee of twenty-one was formed, chaired by Massachusetts Governor John Andrew. They intended to "not only mark the public gratitude to the fallen hero, who at a critical moment assumed a perilous responsibility, but also to commemorate the great event, where he was a leader, by which the title of colored men as citizen-soldiers was fixed beyond recall" (Atkins 1897:7). Progress slowed after the deaths of Governor Andrew and Senator Charles Sumner of Massachusetts, the chief political supporters of the memorial. The Shaw family did not press the project. By the 1870s, Joshua Smith's role had diminished significantly, and a commemorative project that had its genesis in the African American community had been usurped by Boston's Brahman elite (Savage 1997b:197). More than $16,000 was raised by the early 1880s, and on February 23, 1884, more than twenty years after the assault on Fort Wagner, the committee appointed a young, well-known artist, Augustus Saint-Gaudens, to the Shaw Memorial project and offered him $15,000 for the work (Benson and Kirstein 1973:n.p.; Lauerhass 1997:12).

Saint-Gaudens began his career as an apprentice to a cameo cutter and later attended the École des Beaux-Arts in Paris. Some believe that he won his place as one of the great American sculptors because of his attention to detail and knowledge of his subjects' personalities. He began his illustrious career in 1873 in New York, where he received great acclaim for his statue of American Civil War hero Admiral Farragut (1875–1877), situated in Madison Square Park. He was also lauded for his work *Standing Lincoln* (1884–1887), located in Lincoln Park in Chicago (Dryfhout 1982:158; Sturman 1997:6).

Saint-Gaudens initially planned to create a conventional equestrian monument, a soldier on horseback. However, Shaw's family objected, stating that the monument would be pretentious since their son's inexperience hardly merited such high praise. A single equestrian monument, they also felt, would ignore the role of the troops in the 54th Massachusetts (Saint-Gaudens 1913:332). The family also pointed out that Shaw did not lead the charge mounted but was on foot, with his men beside him (Benson and Kirstein 1973:n.p.; Boime 1990:212). Saint-Gaudens labored sporadically for thirteen years and did not regret the length of time it took to complete his commission since he claimed to be underpaid. He perceived the Shaw Memorial as a "labor of love" (Saint-Gaudens 1913:333).

Saint-Gaudens did not complete and unveil the memorial until 1897. It was the first soldier's monument to honor a group rather than a single individual (Dryfhout 1982:226). The Shaw Memorial placed the colonel in the center among his marching troops. Shaw is wearing his fatigue cap, and the soldiers are ready for battle with rifles over their shoulders. The procession is led by a drummer boy, and above them is an allegorical figure with laurel branches in one hand and poppies in the other (Dryfhout 1982:222).

In 1897, *Century Magazine* described the work: "No poet's dream of heroism, glory, or devotion . . . could be realized in material form as this is . . . this beautiful work of art" (quoted in Lauerhass 1997:53). An article in the magazine said,

> In this sculptured picture we see the awakening of a race, the dark, determined mass moved by a common impulse of daring endeavor; lifted above these, the high-bred form, the delicate, intense, intellectual visage, the fair Anglo-Saxon head of their heroic leader; and high above all, the everlasting ideal, the symbol of the spiritual purpose, which beckons, inspires, and gloriously rewards. (Quoted in Savage 1997b:204)

Lorado Taft (1969:302), in his pioneering history of American sculpture, wrote in 1903 that "there is nothing like it or even suggestive of it, in the annals of art." He then explained that it was an "adequate expression of America's newborn patriotism" (Taft 1969:304). In 1916, Freeman Murry lauded the sculpture as a "memorial to man, race, and a cause." He later noted that it seemed "strangely providential that the greatest of American military memorials should have been inspired primarily by the valor and devotion of Negro-American soldiery" (Murry 1916:172). He claimed that Saint-Gaudens's work will "tower above the color line" (Murry 1916:166). Murry's endorsement of the Shaw Memorial remains puzzling to some scholars of modern art, such as Albert Boime. Boime (1990:205–6) points out that Saint-Gaudens was a racist. He created the Shaw Memorial in the context of strong racial and ethnic tensions in the late nineteenth century, an era when many Americans felt threatened by the massive waves of immigrants entering the United States. Although freed and American born, African Americans received no better—and often worse—treatment than immigrants. The development of Jim Crow legislation in the late nineteenth century in the South and the North made it increasingly difficult for African Americans to achieve equality.

Saint-Gaudens wrote that while he searched for African American subjects to photograph for his sculpture, "the darkeys were more exciting in the entertainment they furnished . . . while those that I did succeed in trapping, trembled and perspired in utter terror as I stood them up with guns over their shoulders and caps on their head" (Saint-Gaudens 1913:333–34; see also Boime 1990:207). A friend suggested to Saint-Gaudens that they probably thought he was a physician and that he wanted to kill them and use their parts for anatomical study. Their terror, explained Saint-Gaudens, was "augmented by seeing plaster heads, painted a brown color lying about" (Saint-Gaudens 1913:334).

Saint-Gaudens filled his studio in New York with models chosen from the residents of the surrounding neighborhood (see figure 4.3). He noted that while many of the African Americans who came to his studio were born after the Civil War and did not even know how to hold a gun, they "described to me in detail the battle of Fort Wagner and their part in it" (Saint-Gaudens 1913:335). Reinforcing a contemporary stereotype, Saint-Gaudens noted that "they ranged in character from a gentle Bahama Islander to a drummer-boy who, while posing for the figure in the foreground, told me how he had just been released from prison. . . . On the whole, however, they are very likable, with their soft voices and imaginative, though simple, minds" (Saint-Gaudens 1913:334–35; see also Boime 1990:208).

In an 1893 letter to his brother, Saint-Gaudens wrote about two possible models for the monument. He described the subjects as though he could purchase them at will, or at least purchase their time from a restaurant (Boime 1990:208):

> There are two gorgeous darkeys, so gorgeous that I wish to put them in the Shaw Monument. . . . I shall select the one that best suits my purpose. . . . The one that I keep will have two weeks to a month's work with me at three dollars a day. . . . I may find that . . . they are no better than the hundreds of Seventh Avenue darkeys, and I may send 'em both back. That should be understood. (Saint-Gaudens 1913:337–38)

Saint-Gaudens's son, Homer, describes another incident of his father's substandard treatment of African Americans. In *The Reminiscences of August Saint-Gaudens,* Homer (1913:133) noted, "I believe he could detect a change of two degrees from his favorite amount of heat, when woe betides the darkey who tended stove."

Figure 4.3. Sketch model for African American soldier's head (courtesy U.S. Department of the Interior, National Park Service, Saint-Gaudens National Historic Site, Cornish, New Hampshire).

While contemporary critics claimed his sculpture was an act of "newborn American patriotism" (Taft 1969:304) and that it would "tower above the color line" (Murry 1916:166), Saint-Gaudens was probably less optimistic in his feelings about African Americans. Albert Boime (1990:209) feels that Saint-Gaudens's treatment of African Americans was "more akin to that of General Gillmore, who ordered the 54th to lead the charge on Fort Wagner."

Another critic of modern art, Charles Caffin (1913:11), wrote that Saint-Gaudens

> portrays the humble soldiers with varying characteristics of pathetic devotion. [The sculpture is] distinguished by virile contrasts and repetition of line and by vigorous handsomeness of light and shade. Mingled with our enjoyment of these qualities is the emotion aroused by intent and steadfast onward movement of the troops, whose doglike trustfulness is contrasted with the serene elevation of their white leader.

There is no doubt that the white officer is the central figure in the monument, elevated as he is on horseback and "sharing the upper zone with the allegorical Angel of Death who bears Victory and Sleep" (Boime 1990:209). It is not the egalitarian statue that his parents had hoped for.

Shaw, the troops, and the allegorical angel all move laterally, in differing levels of relief. Shaw is portrayed as noble and sits erect in his saddle. He is a three-dimensional figure, while the troops are further from view and take on less of a three-dimensional quality. The soldiers are cropped out from both sides of the memorial (Dryfhout 1982:X). The horse's head is erect and complements Shaw's torso. His rumpled-looking troops are somewhat listless. Their postures are less certain and less energetic than Shaw's. The troops' movement is in sync with the horse. The horse and Shaw's torso block the images of many in the regiment. Some of them are recognized only by their boots. The net result, according to Boime (1990:209), "is to visually promote the identification of troops and animal, who moved in obedience to Shaw's command, further reinforced by his diagonally thrusting riding crop."

Saint-Gaudens's inscription on the relief honors only Shaw. It reads, "Omnia relinquit servare rempublicam" (He forsook all to preserve the public weal). Saint-Gaudens added the following inscription underneath the relief:

> Robert Gould Shaw
> Colonel of the Fifty Fourth Regiment of Massachusetts Infantry
> Born in Boston 10 October MDCCCXXXVII
> Killed while Leading the Assault on Fort Wagner South Carolina
> 18 July MDCCCLXIII

Boime (1990:211) concludes that Saint-Gaudens succeeded "in establishing a visual 'color-line' that guarded white supremacy."

The unveiling of the monument took place on Decoration Day, May

31, 1897. A platform was erected on the statehouse steps facing the monument. Sixty-five veterans of the 54th Massachusetts marched up Beacon Hill, in the opposite direction they had marched leaving town, almost thirty-four years to the day earlier. The soldiers marched to the monument as thousands of onlookers greeted them. Veterans of the 54th Massachusetts laid a wreath of lilies of the valley before the monument (Lauerhass 1997:26–27). African American veterans of the 55th Massachusetts and the Fifth Cavalry also attended the event (Lauerhass 1997:26–27). One Shaw Memorial committee member wrote that the "bas-relief permits us to make it a memento for those who fell at Fort Wagner, . . . but always with Col. Shaw the leading figure in the Memorial" (quoted in Savage 1997b:200) (see figure 4.4).

Saint-Gaudens wrote about the scene later:

> Many of them were bent and crippled, many with white heads, some bouquets. . . . The impression of these old soldiers passing the very spot where they left for the war so many years before, thrills me even as I write these words. They faced and saluted the relief, with the music playing "John Brown's Body," a recall of what I heard and seen thirty years before from my cameo-cutter's window. They seemed as if returning from the war, the troops of bronze marching in the opposite direction, the direction in which they left for the front, and the young men there represented now showing these veterans the vigor and hope of youth. It was consecration. (Saint-Gaudens 1913:83)

William James, a prominent moralist and philosopher, made the principal address. With some firsthand knowledge of the event (since his brothers, Robertson and Wilkinson, received wounds in the Fort Wagner assault), he remarked,

> There on foot go the dark outcasts, so true to nature that one can almost hear them breathing as they march. . . . There they march, warm-blooded champions of a better day for man. There on horseback among them, in his very habit as he lived, sits the blue-eyed child of fortune. . . . Onward they move together, a single resolution kindled in their eyes. . . . The bronze that makes their memory eternal betrays the very soul and secret of those awful years. . . .
>
> And this, fellow citizens, is why, after the great generals have

Figure 4.4. Veterans of the Massachusetts 54th Regiment marching past the Shaw Memorial at its 1897 dedication (courtesy U.S. Department of the Interior, National Park Service, Saint-Gaudens National Historic Site, Cornish, New Hampshire).

> had their monuments, and long after the abstract soldiers'-monuments have been reared on every village green, we have chosen to take Robert Shaw and his regiment as the subject of this soldiers'-monument to be raised to a particular set of comparatively undistinguished men. The very lack of external complication in the history of these soldiers is what makes them represent with such typical purity the profounder meaning of the Union Cause. (Quoted in Benson and Kirstein 1973:n.p.)

Booker T. Washington, head of the Tuskegee Institute, who had received an honorary degree from Harvard the year before, spoke at the ceremony. He remarked that

> it would be hard for any white man to appreciate to what extent the negro race reveres and idolizes the name of Colonel Shaw. Not so much for what he did as for the principle for which he stood . . . Shaw succeeded in making the negro soldier because he had faith in him as a man. (Quoted in Lauerhass 1997:55)

In his speech, he noted the contributions of both black and white to the development of the 54th, but he particularly spoke about memorializing Shaw. The *Boston Evening Transcript* wrote,

> The multitude, shaken out of its usual symphony-concert calm, quivered with an excitement that was not suppressed. A dozen times it had sprung to its feet to cheer and wave and hurrah, as one person.
>
> To you, to the scarred and scattered remnants of the Fifty-Fourth, who with empty sleeve and wanting leg, have honoured the occasion with your presence, to you, your commander is not dead. Though Boston erected no monument and history recorded no story, in you and the loyal race which you represent, Robert Gould Shaw would have a monument which time could not wear away. (From Benson and Kirstein 1973:n.p.)

Late Twentieth-Century Memorialization

Until the Civil Rights movement, blacks had a very limited role in the collective memory of the United States. From the 1970s on, there was a gradual process of inclusion in terms of both written symbols and commemorative activities that recognized black contributions to the American landscape (Kook 1998:154–78). This process is evident in the commemoration ceremonies that surrounded the Shaw Memorial in the late twentieth century. Until 1981, only Shaw is recognized in the monument, and the rest of the regiment are anonymous characters that fill the background of the composition. Some African Americans raised the issue that Shaw had significant representation in the monument but that the soldiers who died with him are not known. A committee raised about $125,000 for restoration of the monument and for adding the names of those who fell with Shaw to the back of the statue (Dryfhout 1982:226; Lauerhass 1997). Some African American committee members argued unsuccessfully that the names of the black soldiers should remain omitted as "a reminder of the racial prejudice that had characterized the late nineteenth century" (Whitfield 1987:3). A rededication of the monument placed a stone on the back of the monument with the names of the 281 soldiers who died in the assault on Fort Wagner. The names do not include those who died afterward of wounds and diseases or those who were listed as missing after the battle (Whitfield 1987:3–4).

Additional text inscribed on the back of the monument states,

> The white officers taking life and honor in their hands cast in their lot with men of a despised race unproven in war and risked death as inciters of servile insurrection if taken prisoners besides encountering all the common perils of camp march and battle.
>
> The black rank and file volunteered when disaster clouded the Union Cause. Served without pay for eighteen months till given that of white troops. Faced threatened enslavement if captured. Were brave in action. Patient under heavy and dangerous labors. And cheerful amid hardships and privations.
>
> Together they gave to the Nation and the World undying proof that Americans of African descent possess the pride, courage and devotion of the patriot soldier. One hundred and eighty thousand such Americans enlisted under the Union Flag in MDCCCLXIII–MDCCCLXV.

The text reinforces the hierarchy presented in the sculpture. The text on the "white officers" supercedes that of the "black rank and file." Thus, the placement of the text mimics and reinforces the hierarchy imposed by the sculpture on the reverse side.

In May 1997, a public ceremony and symposium sponsored by the National Park Service celebrated the one-hundredth anniversary of the unveiling of the Shaw Memorial. The event was titled "Hope and Glory: Centennial Celebration of the Augustus Saint-Gaudens Monument to Robert Gould Shaw and the Fifty-Fourth Massachusetts Regiment" (Blatt et al. 2001). At the symposium, historians Barbara Fields (1997) and William McFeely (1997) remarked that the monument is especially significant because it was the first monument to show that black men participated in the war. This representation is significant for its own era and for today. Art historian Kirk Savage (1997a) at the same conference disagreed with Boime's earlier critical interpretation. Savage remarked that the monument is significant as the first monument evidence showing African American participation in the war. He also feels that it is an excellent blend between soldier and general, and Shaw is not leading the procession. The soldiers look well drilled. Each soldier looks very different, with individuals wearing their uniform in various fashions. The horse glides and towers, and the soldiers are weighed down by their equipment as they lean forward. Savage argues that they are not "listless," as described by Boime, but rather determined. The troops do not lose their humanity. "Saint-Gaudens was able to elevate the white hero without demoting the black troops" (Savage 1997b:203). Savage disallows multivocal interpretation of the monument and claims that Boime's argument (1990) "cannot be sustained without a serious misreading of the sculpture itself" (Savage 1997b:256, n. 97). He notes that African Americans never had this representation of individuality before, and if they were white, they might not be interpreted as listless. Savage (1997a) also notes that Charles Caffin's (1913) description of "dog-like trustfulness" is a misreading of the monument. While Saint-Gaudens made racist remarks in his memoirs, Savage (1997b:201) claims, he made the infantrymen individuals, and thus it is not a racist monument (see figure 4.5). Savage (1997a, 1997b) proposes that what Saint-Gaudens was thinking about had no bearing on his sculpture, "nor does the lack of sympathy he showed in his memoirs invalidate the visual evidence of the sculpture" (Savage 1997b:202). He notes that Saint-Gaudens "treated racial differences openly and with dignity, asserting a 'brotherhood' of man. And yet it registered, compellingly and beautifully, the transcendence of the white hero in that brotherhood" (Savage 1997b:204).

At the one-hundredth anniversary's public ceremony, several prominent African Americans spoke. President Benjamin Payton of Tuskegee University, Professor Henry Louis Gates Jr. of the Du Bois Institute of Harvard

Figure 4.5. The Shaw Memorial (courtesy Paul A. Shackel).

University, and General Colin Powell all commented on the splendid beauty of the monument and saw the portrayal of the troops in a positive and uplifting light (Public Ceremony 1997). Powell (1997:1–2) remarked,

> I doubt if plaster and bronze have ever spoken more eloquently to us than the celebrated work by Augustus Saint-Gaudens. What a powerful image we see—proud, young, fatalistic Colonel Robert Gould Shaw and his Negro soldiers, heads high, rifles on their shoulders, resolution in their every step as they move southward with fortitude. The scene is May 28th, 1863, in front of the Statehouse in Boston, on their way to glory.
>
> Look at them. Look at them one more time. Soldiers looking to the front, marching solidly and straight ahead on a perpetual campaign for righteousness, led by their brave colonel. So let us too follow these heroes. Let us carry on the work to make this God-given beloved country of ours an even more perfect Union. A land of liberty and justice for all.

> And so thank you Augustus Saint-Gaudens, thank you Col. Robert Gould Shaw, thank you Colored volunteers of the 54th infantry, thank you to the great Commonwealth of Massachusetts, thank you my fellow citizens.

The newspaper *USA Today* reported on the ceremonies and did not even mention Robert Gould Shaw when describing the memorial. Shaw had faded to a role as supporting actor, and the heroism of the 54th Massachusetts had moved to center stage. The reporter stated that the members of the 54th Massachusetts "were honored during the weekend in a celebration of the 100th anniversary of the dedication of a memorial to them here" (Larrabee 1997:3A).

The Shaw Memorial's meaning, I think, will always be debated. It can be read in many different ways, and its meanings will be challenged and changed, depending on who is reading the object and the social and political context within which they are reading it. Is the statue about Saint-Gaudens's racist tendencies, is it about honoring one of Boston's antislavery Brahman members (Robert Gould Shaw), or is it about the Massachusetts 54th?

No longer do publicly funded institutions, such as the National Park Service, refer to the memorial as the Robert Gould Shaw Memorial, but they now include the name of the 54th Massachusetts Volunteer Infantry when referring to it. This is part of the dominant culture's changing view of the Civil War and its increasing willingness to include African American history in the public memory of the country.

Conclusion

After the Civil War, the government and other powerful groups commissioned monuments to reinforce a set of values prescribed by the dominant culture to justify their existence and unify their power. These monuments became very important in the late nineteenth-century xenophobia-dominated American society. The heroes usually "stood out against a backdrop of nationalism, inventions, industrialization, and great wealth" (Dryfhout 1982:28). The monuments embellished public places where they could be easily viewed.

For Murry and Williams, both writing in the early twentieth century, the creation of the monument was important because African Americans were steadily losing personal freedoms during the Jim Crow era. A monument gave them visibility and power in the official memory of the war. Boime, on the other hand, felt that Saint-Gaudens's monument with African Americans only served to reinforce the difference between whites and blacks. The hegemony of the powerful is explicit and noticeable (Boime 1990:217).

Only one monument dedicated solely to an African American, Frederick Douglass, was erected during the nineteenth century (Ruffins 1991:517). While it was originally conceived of as a memorial to the fallen soldiers of the Civil War, the plan changed when Douglass died in Rochester in 1895. There was little support for the erection of a Douglass monument in Rochester. The black community raised only $500, although the government of Haiti, a country where Douglass served as U.S. minister, contributed $1,000. Finally, by 1899, $10,000 was raised, and Sidney W. Edwards unveiled a monument to the distinguished orator. The monument portrays Douglass addressing a Cincinnati crowd shortly after the ratification of the Fifteenth Amendment. The statue stands on a nine-foot-high pedestal. While most whites in the Rochester community did not see Douglass as their social equal, the imposing statue counters the visual tradition of bigotry and symbolically elevates Douglass far beyond any living being (Boime 1990:217; B. Thompson 1903:34–35).

During the late nineteenth century, statues with black representation were rare. Newly arrived immigrants, also the target of racism and xenophobia, knew that they needed to compete with blacks for menial jobs, and they did not support any idea that gave blacks representation on the American landscape. In fact, a proposed statue design for the U.S. capitol with Abraham Lincoln and a kneeling slave beside him was rejected by a committee "because of fear that the figure of a negro in a public monument would arouse the resentment of the Irish citizens" (Savage 1997b:81–82). During the nineteenth and into the early twentieth century, the Irish were marginalized by racism, and the dominant white society often saw them as black and very close to African Americans on the evolutionary scale. A marble relief panel created in the 1860s on a monument in the Allegheny Cemetery in Pittsburgh is the first interracial monument dealing with emancipation (Savage 1997b:70–72).

Thomas Ball's Freedmen's Memorial to Abraham Lincoln, also known as the Emancipation Monument, was placed in Lincoln Park in Washington, D.C., in 1876, and a replica was erected in Park Square in Boston in 1879. The statue depicts a freed black, half stripped and kneeling at the feet of Abraham Lincoln. The black person is clearly subordinate to Lincoln (Savage 1997b:70–90).

There is only one monument with a single standing soldier who has African American features, and it is located in Norfolk, Virginia. In the South, even though blacks may have outnumbered whites in communities, they often avoided taking the risk of erecting a Union monument in former Confederate territory. Norfolk was an anomaly because Union forces recaptured it during the war, and it had a large federal presence even after Reconstruction. The effort to create an African American soldier monument developed in the 1880s, led by a former slave and black veteran, James Fuller. He succeeded in creating a section in the local cemetery for black veterans, outside the main wall of the cemetery. By 1906, he had a small pedestal erected, but not until after his death in 1920 was a figure installed. At this time, a new inscription was added to include the commemoration of World War I veterans, but the Union soldier on top of the pedestal, at parade rest, has African American features (Savage 1997b:187).

There are two other nineteenth-century monuments that depict blacks in military service, one in Cleveland and the other in Brooklyn. In both cases, there are large groups of white military men, and the blacks are one member of the larger group. Unlike their white counterparts, the blacks are seminude without a recognizable uniform. They appear to be in states of transition—from slavery to freedom. "Thus their status remains uncertain: like many actual black sailors during the war, they are easily assimilated into the category of contraband, fugitives from slavery pressed by circumstances into unofficial or ambiguous roles" (Savage 1997b:192). A new Civil War memorial with black representation now sits in the Shaw neighborhood of Washington, D.C., which celebrates the valor of the African Americans who participated in the conflict.

Thus, it is easy to see that Saint-Gaudens's monument stands as one of only a few Victorian-era public memorials in which African Americans had some form of representation without an overt racist tone. It is no wonder, as Boime (1990:218) suggests, that Murry validated Saint-Gaudens's monument. A critical reading of Saint-Gaudens and the Shaw Memorial, however, provides a contrasting view. Saint-Gaudens, creator of the memorial, held derogatory views toward African Americans commonly held by whites in the late nineteenth century. At best, African Americans were seen as passive children who needed to be guided. At worst, African Americans were seen as shiftless subhumans who needed to be controlled and subjugated. Saint-Gaudens's attitudes appear to fall between these two negative extremes, and these feelings are expressed in the Shaw Memorial.

The Shaw Memorial has had various meanings to different groups of people over the past century. Whites and blacks from varying socioeconomic stations see the monument in different ways, and it is clear that it does not have a single meaning to all groups. Rather, ethnic groups and social classes mold and reshape the view of the monument as social and political circumstances change within the group as well as within the country.

5

Contradictions on the Landscape: Myth and Creation at Manassas National Battlefield Park

THE SITE OF THE First and Second Battles of Manassas (known in the North as the First and Second Battles of Bull Run) is known for its Confederate victories. While the federal government established national military parks in Chickamauga, Chattanooga, Shiloh, Gettysburg, and Vicksburg in the 1890s, Manassas had to wait almost half a century for federal recognition. The Grand Army of the Republic, a northern veterans group, unanimously resolved at their National Encampment at Minneapolis in 1906 that "the United States should acquire title to the land on which the Bull Run Monuments were erected and such roadways and adjacent areas as are necessary to enable comrades and citizens of our country to see the first battlefield of the great war without trespassing on private property" (quoted in Round 1917:n.p.). Their resolution fell on deaf ears. Congress continually thwarted southern preservationists' efforts and neglected to recognize the site. Southern heritage groups struggled for years to have Manassas placed in the national public memory. The image and meaning of this land were heightened in the national memory only after the federal government acquired it and made it a national park.

The public memory and commemoration of Manassas continue to change into the twenty-first century, and the understanding of African American history related to the national park continues to be in flux. Before the Civil War, the Bull Run community embraced European American planters, poor servants and overseers, freed African American families living on small farms, and enslaved plantation workers. Representation of all these groups on the landscape has been systematically erased in favor of a history that emphasizes troop movements and southern victories.

Manassas National Battlefield Park has always been about the history of the battles, and National Park Service (NPS) historians in the park have been unwilling to expand the interpretation of the park to include a more dynamic social history of the people who once inhabited these lands. Today, the boundaries of the national park include the remains of several plantations as well as free African American communities and farmsteads. The story of slavery and accounts of how African Americans survived on the landscape before the Civil War and how they endured prejudice and discrimination after the war—during the Jim Crow and the Reconstruction eras—are noticeably missing from the park's interpretation. As African American history has played an increasingly important role in social history, it is fitting to recognize the contributions of African Americans on our national landscapes. Understanding the outcome and consequences of the Battles of Manassas provides a rich history of commemoration and the creation of public memory in this national park in northern Virginia.

The First Battle of Manassas

By July 1861, three months had passed since the opening event of the Civil War, the bombardment of Fort Sumter. No major Union force of consequence had yet crossed into Virginia. Federal Major General Patterson maneuvered against Confederate Brigadier General Johnston. Confederate troops under the command of General Beauregard were within twenty miles of Washington, D.C., where the Union General McDowell was drilling his army for a move on Richmond.

McDowell moved his army of 35,000 men against Beauregard's 20,000, where they stood concentrated near Centreville, Virginia. McDowell's success hinged on Patterson preventing Johnston from supporting Beauregard at Centreville. On July 16, McDowell marched out of Washington, and the Confederate troops fell back to a point on the west bank of the Bull Run. Finding the Confederates well entrenched along the Bull Run, McDowell attacked their left flank. The Confederates were thrown back. Jackson brought his Virginia regiment to their support. The troops regrouped on high ground near the Henry House, where, if sufficiently behind the crest, they could be somewhat protected from Federal fire. Imboden's battery stood in front of Jackson's infantry regiment.

The Federals made a charge, but they were repelled, and the Confederates received further reinforcements. Federal batteries, in full range of infantry and artillery fire, were soon wiped out. Union troops withdrew, leaving the battery in the hands of the Confederates. Johnston's supporting troops had arrived and joined the Confederates, giving them the field. McDowell's brigade fell back in disorder and failed to reorganize until they reached the defenses of Washington.

The Second Battle of Manassas resulted in a similar end—a Union defeat. After the war, developing a national military park to commemorate these Confederate victories met with some resistance in both the North and the South. While Congress continually rejected the idea of creating a park that commemorated southern victories, many southerners did not want federal monies to control a southern park. Southern heritage groups worked tirelessly to celebrate the war events at Manassas and feared that if the land became federally owned, northerners would dictate the terms and interpretations of the site. Manassas has a rich history of commemorative activities that celebrate the events of the battle rather than the area's social history. This focus has led to the removal of many traces of African American material remains from the battlefield and thus the removal of African Americans from public memory of the event.

Early Commemoration at Manassas

Commemoration at Manassas occurred almost immediately. Only six weeks after the First Battle of Manassas, soldiers from Colonel Francis S. Bartow's brigade placed a marble column on Henry Hill to honor Bartow's memory. Union soldiers consecrated two additional monuments on June 11, 1865. At Henry Hill, Lieutenant James M. McCallum of the 16th Massachusetts Battery supervised troops from the Fifth Pennsylvania Heavy Artillery in constructing a twenty-foot obelisk adorned with five 200-pound shells. Henry Hill is a significant piece of real estate in Civil War history because it was the center of the First Battle of Manassas, and it became the focus of subsequent preservation movements. The same soldiers constructed a similar monument, although only sixteen feet high, at Groveton, where troops experienced heavy action during the Second Battle of Manassas. The troops decorated this monument with relic shot and shell found on the surrounding battlefield (Zenzen 1998:2).

The Henry Hill and Groveton monuments bear the inscription, "In memory of the patriots who fell." The patriots are the northern dead, and the monument expresses northern sentiment on a battlefield that witnessed two significant Union defeats. These two monuments are the only memorials ever erected by Union soldiers themselves, and it was their last service before their final discharge. This commemoration, like all others, was meant to show that their comrades' death was not in vain, although local southerners were offended by a northern presence on the battlefield (Zenzen 1995, 1998:2).

Since the turn of the twentieth century, groups have placed other markers and monuments on the Manassas battlefield (Round 1917:n.p.). In 1904, the Bull Run Chapter of the United Daughters of the Confederacy (UDC) erected a monument in the Groveton cemetery (Zenzen 1995, 1998:3). In 1906, New York State added three granite monuments to honor the 5th New York Volunteers, the 10th New York Volunteers, and the 14th Brooklyn (84th New York), each of which had experienced substantial losses during the Second Battle of Manassas. The New York monuments were placed close to Confederate monuments that honored the southern dead. Both Union and Confederate former commanders shared the ceremonial podium for their unveiling of the New York monuments, a gesture that supposedly symbolized reunification (Zenzen 1998:3–4).

Commemorating Southern Victories and Reconciliation

The Manassas Peace Jubilee

The local chapter of the UDC, wanting to keep the memory of the Confederate victories alive in the national consciousness, held well-attended annual commemorations for each battle throughout the early twentieth century (Zenzen 1995). Commemoration activities were often veiled in the tone of reconciliation. It is no mistake that the UDC did not invite African Americans to these events, and their absence reinforced their exclusion from the changing public memory of the war.

The Manassas Peace Jubilee commenced on July 16, 1911, for a week of commemorative activities to celebrate the First Battle of Manassas. All veterans received a medallion badge that contained the U.S. colors, the Confederate battle flag, and the flag of Virginia (O'Donnell 1986:16–17). On July 21, 1911, 350 Confederate and 125 Union veterans met on Henry Hill, where they embraced each other. A newspaper account in the *Manassas Journal* (1911:1) described,

> The climax of the grand Peace Jubilee week reached, Friday noon, when a multitude of veterans, on both sides in the great

> Civil War, met upon the historic plains of Bull Run and clasped hands with adversaries of half a century ago and greeted each other with assurances of good will and fellowship that would eliminate all future bitterness and animosity" (see figure 5.1).

The article continued, "To see a body of battle-scarred veterans advancing upon each other upon the field where, fifty years ago, they sough each others lives in the first great struggle of a four-years' bloody conflict, with none other than friendly demonstration, was a proceeding never before witnessed."

The crowd cheered as the veterans greeted each other. Governor Mann, a Confederate veteran, declared that the veterans joining hands in reunion "would go down in history as an incident unparalled [*sic*] in the annals of time" (*Manassas Journal* 1911:1). The *Manassas Journal* (1911:1) reported that General John Gilman, commander in chief of the Grand Army of the Republic, assured the governor that "all unfriendly spirit toward those who wore the Grey would be forever changed into those of fellowship so far as his efforts and influence would count." When General George W. Gordon, chief of the United Confederate Veterans (UCV), stood to speak, there was a loud burst of applause, and he could not be heard for a few moments. Both speakers shook hands.

Part of the opening address included a poem by Colonel Burkley:

> But did its destined purpose fill,
> Of carrying out our Master's will
> Who did decree, troubles should cease
> And his chosen land have peace;
> And to achieve this glorious end
> We should four years in conflict spend;
> Which done the world would plainly see
> Both sides had won a victory. (*Manassas Journal* 1911:1)

Other congressmen made speeches, and President William Howard Taft delivered a keynote address to about 10,000 visitors (Zenzen 1995) (see figure 5.2). President Taft crafted reconciliatory speeches prior to and during the Civil War Centennial. While his attitudes were not new for the era, it reinforced the tones and views of the dominant ideology (Blight 2001:357).

The ceremonies ended after Taft's speech. The public could purchase

Figure 5.1. The Peace Jubilee of the Blue and the Grey: Fiftieth anniversary of the First Battle of Manassas at the Henry farm, July 1911 (courtesy Manassas National Battlefield Park).

Figure 5.2. The Peace Jubilee Celebration with President Howard Taft, July 1911 (courtesy Manassas National Battlefield Park).

a limited number of official souvenirs that had the "White Ribbon of the Veterans Badge, with the Olive Branch and Dove; the Blue and Grey shaking hands; 'Let Us Have Peace,'—Grant. 'Duty, the Sublimest Word of Human Language.'—Lee" (Round 1911:n.p.).

George Carr Round (1911:3–4), a main organizer of the Peace Jubilee, summarized the event in a four-page pamphlet by quoting a newspaper article:

> The real reunion had been accomplished already, and that we now live in a united country and enjoy that peace which springs from the hearts and intelligence of the people. [The veterans] met there again on the battlefield in peace and concord and by their reunion and the fraternal spirit which characterized that reunion, demonstrated to the world that finally and definitely not only the war, but the hatred, resentments, misunderstandings and injustices which had provoked that mighty struggle, were buried, forgotten and forever settled.

The success of the Peace Jubilee encouraged Round to pursue his dream of getting federal recognition for the battlefields associated with the First and Second Battles of Manassas.

The Making of Manassas Battlefield Confederate Park

For many years, Round failed to convince Congress to commemorate the battlefield at Manassas. In 1900, a bill introduced by Representative Peter J. Otey of Lynchburg, Virginia, proposed the establishment of a "National Battle Park." Congress failed to act on this measure. In 1902, Round testified, along with Brigadier General George Breckenridge Davis, before a congressional subcommittee in support of the federal government's acquisition of the Virginia battlefield. The bill never left the subcommittee (Zenzen 1995, 1998:7–8).

Development of the battlefield park finally seemed imminent when Congress passed and the president signed into law the Manassas Bill on March 3, 1913, which enabled the War Department to appoint a board to survey the site, interview landowners, and establish a reasonable purchase price for lands. The War Department recommended that the federal government repair the two 1865 monuments and purchase the lands on which they stood, and they decided that the acquisition of additional lands from local farmers for memorialization was not necessary. Congress failed to act on the board's recommendations (Zenzen 1995, 1998:10–11).

"We were whipped at Bull Run, I don't like to vote money for monuments there," one northern congressman remarked to Round. "Not so thought the soldiers themselves," responded Round in a pamphlet. "Of all possible sites between the Susquehanna and Rio Grande, the veterans of Appomattox selected Henry Hill for their first monument to their fallen brothers" (Round 1917:n.p.).

Round's background and intentions concerned longtime Manassas residents since he had served in the Union army and settled in the Manassas area after the war. His attitudes and perceptions of the war differed significantly from those in local Confederate organizations who were later responsible for memorializing the battlefield. In a letter that Round wrote to Senator Cross about Fletcher Webster (of Massachusetts), he made his northern sentiments clear. "What did Fletcher Webster and his comrades of 1861–65 accomplish? 1st Liberty for all. 2d An Indestructible Union for all Time and 3d Universal Education for all races" (Round 1918:n.p.). Round's opinions alienated him from many southerners, and their animosity toward him impacted his plea for community support to commemorate the battlefield. A local resident cautioned that Round's cause was supported by Manassas businessmen, "descendants of Carpet-baggers or scallywags, who were willing to sell their birthright for a few paltry dollars that they might gather from the sale of souvenirs" (Anonymous 1927). While he gained some local and legislative support for federal recognition of the battlefield, Round died in 1918 without even seeing his dreams come to fruition.

In 1921, the Sons of Confederate Veterans (SCV), led by Major E. W. R. Ewing, committed themselves to establishing a Confederate Park at the Henry farm. They developed the Manassas Battlefield Corporation, which represented the first successful attempt by an organization to preserve a segment of the battlefield. While the park's mission sought cooperation and fairness between the North and the South, it also promoted the South's "distinct, wonderful, equally thrilling, all-important story." The corporate directors wanted to change the direction of contemporary histories that portrayed their ancestors as "enemies of [their] country" (Zenzen 1995:42–43). The corporation saw the Confederate Park as a way to tell their story and convey what they perceived as the "full truth" since "truth shall make our children free" (Ewing 1921:4–8,12,15–16).

An editorial in the *Confederate Veteran* (1921b:237) remarked that

> the object of this movement is to establish a perpetual park as the South's memorial to all Confederate soldiers and as an expression of Southern love and veneration of the glorious and devoted women of the South during the dread era. The battle of Manassas resulted in a Southern victory. Other fields on which the South was victorious have been nationalized, with the result that the South is practically ignored in memorials. It is said, for instance, that in after years the world will wonder whether or not the Southern army made an appearance at Chickamauga, whereas now it is known by students, if not schoolchildren, that the battle was won by the South.

A prospectus written by Ewing for the development of a Confederate Park at Manassas noted that the development of a park could commemorate the southern cause. The cause, according to Ewing and other Confederate sympathizers, was not about slavery but about states' rights. The South, "from first to last, was the more devoted to the principles of government by written constitution, and to proclaim the great truth that secession did as much for American constitutional government as did the Revolution which made the constitution possible" (Ewing 1921:4).

Ewing noted that because of the Union defeat at Manassas, it is the "birthplace of the first real and general respect the North ever entertained for the South and without which there could be no greater national solidarity which today exists" (Ewing 1921:4). But Ewing contended that the park needed to be established in order to counter any misrepresentation of the southern story. He noted,

> Yet so persistent is the propaganda which seeks to distort the historical truth, the North and South people are more and more coming to regard our Confederate ancestors as enemies of our country. . . . Shall the children of the South be taught that our Confederate ancestors fought to 'extend and perpetuate slavery.' . . . Such an argument is so wanting in evidential support that it is astounding. (Ewing 1921:11–12)

Manassas Battlefield Confederate Park, under the leadership of Ewing, "acquired 130 acres of those renowned and sacred fields to build to *all* Confederates, not forgetting the *Blue* who fell there" (Ewing 1927:3). The land cost $25,000, of which $12,000 was raised by the corporation; the state gave $10,000, provided that the organization could raise the remaining $3,000 (Ewing 1927:9). The center of the park included Henry Hill, the main focus of the First Battle of Manassas. The Henry House served as the park's visitor center. Adjacent to this tract, and in view of the Henry House, lived the Robinsons, an African American family who had lived on this land from the 1840s and became one of the wealthiest African American households in the county. Based on existing literature, the Manassas Battlefield Confederate Park never mentioned the family or even recognized that their farmstead was part of the Civil War battlefield landscape.

At the inauguration ceremonies on July 21, 1921, speakers projected confidence that the project to memorialize the battleground would be successful. One speaker, Dr. Owens, explained, "There are those who refer to Gettysburg as the Waterloo of the Confederacy. The South, however, will be able to point to her Austerlitz, her Manassas" (*Manassas Journal* 1921:1).

Pleading for money and hoping that each Confederate state would pledge $500 in order to buy the land and meet their debts for the Confederate Park, Ewing (n.d.:1) wrote, "If we are to do anything like justice to our Confederate fathers and mothers in presenting correctly the causes and right of their brilliant fight, it demands a financed educational central power and source about which all Confederate organizations may cling for real help." Ewing also remarked, "In simple justice to our Confederate ancestors, in the love of truth which we want taught [in] the future, we must not leave to the Federal Government all such memorials! We must build at least one on the famous fields of Manassas" (Ewing, n.d.:1).

A pamphlet, written to gain support and money for the Confederate Park, asked rhetorically, Why a Manassas Battlefield Confederate Park? It responded, to celebrate "courage, brain, and individual initiative, not yet surpassed" (Manassas Battlefield Confederate Park 1923:3). The pamphlet noted that the "descendants of Confederate soldiers owe their ancestors at least one fitting battlefield memorial, fair to the Blue, yet empathetically Confederate in perpetual emphasis; and teaching, without bitterness or prejudice, of that which the Confederacy fought" (Manassas Battlefield Confederate Park 1923:3). This tribute should stand as "a symbol of Confederate purpose and valor" (Manassas Battlefield Confederate Park 1923:4). The "Park shall forever stand as the supreme battlefield memorial to all Confederate soldiers" (Manassas Battlefield Confederate Park 1923:8).

Field guides gave tours, and plaques were in place on the field while the organization operated a small museum in the Henry House. Every year, on the anniversary of the First Battle of Manassas, the park held a "well attended Confederate field-day." Ewing wrote that the events surrounding Manassas were "slowly but surely moving into national proportions" (Ewing 1927:9). These ceremonies were fitting at Manassas Battlefield, claimed Ewing (1927:3–4), because

1. Those fields are in Dixie
2. Today there lie in unknown graves boys from every Southern State
3. There, first under Beauregard and Johnston, and then a year later, on the same fields, under Matchless Lee, lads from every Southern State, by courage, brain *and individual initiative,* not yet surpassed, won two signal and most brilliant Confederate victories,—"typical of the imperishable glory of Southern arms," said ex-Gov. Trinkle, of Virginia, when commending this Confederate Park.
4. *Descendants of Confederate soldiers owe their ancestors at least one fitting battlefield memorial,* fair to the Blue, yet emphatically Confederate in perpetual emphasis; and *teaching,* without bitterness or prejudice, *of that which the Confederacy fought.*

5. [The park should] stand a symbol of Confederate purpose and valor; nowhere better found a great educational, historical and charitable work, to be maintained in the interest of broader Americanism through a fuller story of the South's contribution to government and history.

Ewing invited soldier organizations to erect monuments at the new park (Ewing 1927:8), but they were slow to answer his invitation. In fact, Union organizations erected large markers for their fallen at Manassas, while the Confederate groups were conspicuously absent. Small printed boards marked the spots where "General Bee fell, where Jackson was positioned where he received his name 'Stonewall.'" "Yet," Ewing remarked, "beautiful monuments speak of Northern heroism and sacrifice. . . . Shall the story thus remain unfinished? . . . Nothing there recalls to the visitor that fine Southern courage which thus triumphed over numbers and resources, nor of the brilliant strategy by which Lee brought on that battle" (Manassas Battlefield Confederate Park 1923:18). The Federals have their stories "in marble and bronze . . . , at Gettysburg and Sharpsburg (Antietam) one sometimes wonders what the Confederates really did" (Manassas Battlefield Confederate Park 1923:18).

Judge Howry, active in the local organization of the SCV, had a similar opinion as Ewing. He wrote (in Ewing 1927:11) that "a recent visit to Gettysburg brought home to me more than ever that it would be a reflection on our entire people to longer delay to monument Manassas to the valor of the Southern soldier."

The Manassas Battlefield Corporation struggled to finish collecting the necessary funds to obtain the Henry farm, and they made their final payment in June 1927. Maintenance left the corporation financially strapped, and these difficulties hampered the park's operations. The Great Depression made it even more challenging to stay out of debt. In an undated document from the Depression era, the Bull Run Chapter of the UDC passed a resolution that noted the prohibitive cost of fifty cents for the entrance fee. They asked the Virginia Commission of Conservation and Development to acquire the Confederate Park, by gift or otherwise. They requested that the lands should be "made available to the general public as a monument to Stonewall Jackson and his soldiers" (Dogan, n.d.:1).

In 1933, the National Park Service (NPS) obtained control over the War Department's historic parks and monuments. Correspondence soon began between the Manassas Battlefield Corporation and the NPS. By

1935, the federal government had established more than 1,400 acres for the Bull Run Recreational Demonstration Area. They acquired, through eminent domain, many small farmsteads owned by both whites and blacks. The land acquisition was part of the New Deal policy to develop recreational areas close to cities to better the lives of urban residents. Northern Virginia's representative, Howard V. Smith, saw this as an opportunity to preserve significant historic sites, provide recreational facilities for area residents, and make submarginal land productive in the form of a military park (as well as winning favor with his constituents, especially since he opposed many New Deal reforms). History, recreation, and work relief combined to develop this land. The recreational area did not include the Henry Hill tract, and some members of the Manassas Battlefield Corporation resisted incorporation into the Recreational Demonstration Area. They held reservations about the federal government taking a park that southern money had created. The following year, in 1936, they agreed to donate the property, although the transfer was not completed until 1940. That year, the secretary of interior used the authority of the 1935 Historic Sites Act to create Manassas National Battlefield Park, which included the Bull Run Recreational Area and the former Manassas Battlefield Confederate Park (Zenzen 1995, 1998:13–24). In order to celebrate this event, managers thought it would be fitting to stage a reenactment to commemorate the seventy-fifth anniversary of the First Battle of Manassas.

The 1936 Reenactment

The seventy-fifth-anniversary event included a briefing on the battle to the public and a description of the accidental and tragic killing of two figures at the Henry House. The Henry's house stood in the center of the battle, and Mrs. Judith Henry, eighty-five years old and bedridden, remained in the house during the fighting. Confederate snipers positioned themselves in her house, and Federals fired at the house in retaliation. The crossfire killed Mrs. Henry and severely damaged the house. Many of the pre-celebration news releases related to the battle claimed that "not only was she a martyr to the cause, but the Negress, servant to the family, fell in action by her side" (*The Chronicle* 1936; see also *Fauquier Democrat* 1936). The story of the fallen servant by her mistress's side is not mentioned in any other previous or subsequent commemorative events at Manassas. An African American servant did not die during the First Battle of Manassas, and Mrs. Henry was the only civilian death in the battle. The emphasis of the death of a faithful servant during the Jim Crow era is consistent with the UDC's attempt to construct a faithful-slave myth. They claimed that slaves were satisfied with their place in a plantation society and that they remained faithful to their white masters throughout the Civil War, even though they had a chance to revolt and/or escape. During the 1920s and 1930s the UDC received considerable publicity for their cosponsorship of a faithful-slave monument in Harpers Ferry (discussed in chapter 3).

Southern sentiment for the Lost Cause flowed in local and regional Virginia newspapers. The *Manassas Journal* wrote, five days before the 1936 reenactment, about the

> spot sacred to the memory of the Southern cause. It was a proud day, indeed, that bright, hot Sunday afternoon of long ago. Had not the invading horde of what they contemptuously referred to as "Lincoln's hireling band" been turned back in confusion and in disgrace? Was not this vindication of their prowess sufficient to strike terror into the hearts of those who sought to smother the soft handed Southerners in their supposed ease of idleness?

The reenactment is to honor and "uphold the dignity and justice of the cause for which these men and women contended even to the loss of everything they held dear in life" (*Manassas Journal* 1936).

About 1,500 Army and Marine troops were engaged to stage the reenactment. The Civilian Conservation Corps constructed viewing stands for 5,000 spectators (O'Donnell 1986:24–25). The Manassas–Prince William Chamber of Commerce, the Manassas Battlefield Confederate Park Association, and the NPS sponsored the event, with monetary support from the Virginia Assembly (H. Tucker 1936:2).

The day began with a luncheon sponsored by the UDC and then, at 1:30, featured music by the Fifth United States Marine Band. The Right Reverend H. St. George Tucker followed with an opening invocation, welcoming people to the commemorative ceremonies. Before 31,000 people, he described the general context of the battle, including the position of "our beloved Stonewall Jackson" (H. Tucker 1936:1). The place where Stonewall Jackson won his fame was unmarked, except for a board nailed to a tree. Tucker remarked that Manassas "is one of the few great battlefields of this war that remains unmarked, neglected and uncared for. We feel it is a disgrace to Virginia and the entire nation" (H. Tucker 1936:2). State Senator John Rust of Fairfax presided and introduced several prominent guests. One of them was Wilbur C. Hall, chairman of the Virginia State Commission on Conservation and Development. He declared that the creation of a historic battlefield did not serve the glorification of war. It was "for the purpose of memorialization. . . . It is intended to commemorate permanently and fittingly the heroism of Americans who made the supreme sacrifice for causes they believed right" (*Richmond News Leader* 1936). Governor George C. Peery of Virginia echoed these feelings (Folliard 1936:14).

At 2:00, Douglas Southall Freeman, winner of the 1935 Pulitzer Prize for his biography of Robert E. Lee, provided a narrative account of the Battle of Manassas. His speech was interrupted by the reenactment because the preceding guest had spoken too long, and the sham battle began at 2:30 sharp.

Stonewall Jackson, a major in the 12th United States Infantry at Fort Washington and relation to his namesake, played the role of the famous general. The Federals dressed in blue denim and were represented by the First Battalion of the Fifth Regiment of the United States Marines, including the 10th Artillery of that regiment. Those portraying the Confederates—the Reserve Officers' Training Corps, the Third United States Cavalry, and Battery B 16th Field Artillery—dressed in grey denim. Various historical associations from around the country loaned some of the original flags from the First Battle of Manassas for the reenactment.

The regional and local newspapers reported news of the event. "A wild rebel yell arose from the grandstand as Jackson's men, bayonets out, rushed down on the Federals in the last successful charge, and J. E. B. Stuart's cavalry tore out of the woods to hasten their flight to Washington" (Folliard 1936:1). At 4:00, the sham battle was followed with drills by the Third United States Cavalry and the Battery B 16th Field Artillery (see figure 5.3). As part of the finale, fifty-five Marine Corps aircraft performed aerial combat stunts (O'Donnell 1986:24–25; *Washington Post* 1936).

The *Washington Evening Star* (1936) headline announced: "35,000 Watch Confederates Conquer Yankees at Manassas." The *Manassas Journal* (1936b:1, 10) reported that "the battle was unique in every sense of the word because it represented the initial clash of ideals and an exhibition of ignorance of conditions that existed in both fighting bodies." The article later stated that

> Dr. Owen deplored the action of the committee which eliminated Southern heroes entirely in naming the honor roll for the memorial amphitheater in Arlington, recalling the action of

Figure 5.3. The seventy-fifth-anniversary celebration and reenactment of the First Battle of Manassas, 1936 (courtesy Manassas National Battlefield Park).

> President McKinley, who ordered that the graves of North and South in the national cemetery be decorated alike. "Had the North understood the South, there would have been no war," he said.

The paper later described Senator Williams's reaction to the events. He referred to himself as "a Tennessean by birth, a Mississippian by residence, and a Virginian by love." He noted, " 'There is no Lost Cause.' The men of the South fought for constitutional rights, he said, and got what their fathers stood for" (*Manassas Journal* 1936b:10).

Letters to the editor of the *Washington Post* questioned the meaning of the reenactment. One person wrote that the reenactment glorified war. J. O. Knott wrote,

> Why not reenact the hanging of John Brown, the burning of Joan of Arc, the beheading of Lady Jane Grey. The fact is, we have become a people that for some reason want entertainment

> which thrills, no matter how the thrills come or what are the results on moral principles. (Knott 1936)

Another letter also questioned the "glorification of war":

> It was an open rebellion against the United States Government, and we as a people, regardless of section, cannot afford to put a stamp of approval on treason. . . . Loyalty to country, not to a section, should be emphasized now as perhaps never before. . . . Rebellion is a vicious word and is never justified . . . [except] to end intolerable rule, as was the case with our forefathers in the American Revolution. (Patriot 1936)

The 1961 Centennial

In the 1950s, the Department of the Interior authorized the NPS to undertake Mission 66, an extensive program for the development of various parks, including Civil War parks "so that fitting observances may be held at each as its centennial occurs" (from Kammen 1991:609).

Centennial celebrations occurred at Manassas National Battlefield Park from July 21 to 23, 1961. Sponsors of the event included the Virginia Civil War Centennial Commission, the Defense Department, and the NPS. Planning for the event began on September 25, 1958, when Karl Betts, executive director, and Virgil Carrington "Pat" Jones of the Civil War Centennial Commission; Dr. J. Walter Coleman, historian, and Francis F. Wilshire, superintendent of Manassas National Battlefield Park; and G. P. Oakley and R. Jackson Radcliffe of the Greater Manassas Chamber of Commerce met to discuss the details of the event (First Manassas 1960:12). An estimated cost for the reenactment in 1960 was placed at $200,000 (First Manassas 1960:5–9; Wilshire 1960).

The NPS promised, through a cooperative agreement with the First Manassas Corporation, to provide the facilities and technical assistance (Cooperative Agreement 1961). Wilshire called on higher motives for the reenactment. He remarked,

> It is believed that the event can be staged with such colorful and dramatic realism as to provide an arresting stimulus to a better evaluation and appreciation of the principles of freedom and democracy on which this Nation was founded—principles which today hold the hope of the Free World. (Wilshire 1960)

Many community groups quickly supported the event. The president of the Civil War Round Table of the District of Columbia, Rex B. Magee, wrote that his organization fully supported the reenactment since "The Round Table's purpose is to study without bias the War Between the States and to help preserve the glorious traditions of the conflict a hundred years ago." Claiming pride in the Confederate battle flag, chosen after the First Battle of Manassas, he stated that "this Confederate flag, along with the U.S. Stars and Stripes, can now fly with immunity from Cape Cod to Korea as a great nation's symbol of unity" (Magee 1960). In August 1960, President Dwight Eisenhower wrote the First Manassas Corporation that the event "will serve to remind all Americans that the bonds which now unite us are as precious as the blood of young men" (Eisenhower 1960).

A pamphlet advertising the event described the importance of the battle in American history. It stated that the "reenactment will commemorate in action, sight, and sound the courage and devotion demonstrated here in 1861 and the need for similar dedication in the years to come" (Grande Reenactment 1961).

The Centennial Commemoration program claimed that "today's commemorative spectacle has the objective of reminding you of our common heritage—and indeed of reminding the world—that our people have always been willing to fight and to die if need be for their beliefs—and their principles" (Centennial Commemoration 1961). Whether fighting for the Union or the Confederacy, "they were all deeply in love with their country. And the country they loved was America" (Centennial Commemoration 1961).

More than 3,500 people came to participate as reenactors. They included 1,200 members of the North–South Skirmishing Association, and the remainder were National Guard members (Onesty 1961:14). On Friday, the reenactors rehearsed before about 20,000 people. Saturday opened with a United States Army Band concert and a colorful Pageant of American Unity. It was the story of the U.S. flag as it grew from thirteen stars to fifty (Ashton 1961:2). The military band played war melodies of both sides (Wolfe 1961).

Despite the 100-degree temperatures, the crowd of close to 60,000 attended each day, many in authentic garb (Updike 1961). Spectators paid $4.00 for grandstand seating or $2.50 for rental of a folding chair, or they could stand for no charge (Abroe 1998:23). The events began at 10:00 AM with a display of clothing and gear. At 10:30, the men drilled. After lunch, dignitaries delivered speeches. Virginia Governor J. Lindsay

Almond Jr. opened the ceremonies by stating, "We re-enact this battle and commemorate the Civil War because it taught this young nation what it needed to learn . . . it taught us that united we stand, divided we fall . . . that we were ordained and destined to be one people" (Cox 1961:1). The governor also proclaimed that "we cherish with sacred devotion and unalloyed dedication to commemorate the valor, sacrifice, fiber, endurance, honor and conviction of principle woven indelibly and eternally into the fabric of a Union indissoluble composed of states indestructible" (*Journal Messenger* 1961:1).

After the speeches, the reenactment began, narrated over a loudspeaker by Virgil Carrington Jones, a Civil War history author. He described the struggle with a "rich southern drawl" (*Grit* 1961:6) (see figure 5.4). The sham battle was divided into two segments, representing the morning and afternoon events of the 1861 conflict. In the first part, the Union troops routed the Confederates. It ended with the death of Confederate General Bernard Bee as he called his disorganized men to "rally behind the Virginians!" The next act was an artillery exchange. The Confederates routed

Figure 5.4. The one-hundredth-anniversary celebration and reenactment of the First Battle of Manassas, 1961 (courtesy Manassas National Battlefield Park).

the northerners, who left their artillery and wounded behind (O'Donnell 1986:38–39). A partisan crowd viewed the event, and as the southern reenactors finally drove the Federal troops off of Henry Hill, the crowd let out a "sustained rebel yell" (Updike 1961; Wolfe 1961). The reenactment of the battle ended with both "Federals" and "Confederates" joining together on the battlefield to sing "God Bless America." A "superficial harmony belied a problem-filled affair. . . . A . . . fundamental issue was that many on both sides appeared intent on refighting the Civil War" (Abroe 1998:23).

On Saturday night, the National Guard sponsored a parade that proceeded down the streets of Manassas. National Guard units included a southern contingent from Fredericksburg, Richmond, Staunton, Leesburg, and Warrenton. Northern groups included those from New York, Michigan, Maine, and Wisconsin. Carried in a case were the "tattered colors of the 14th Brooklyn, New York Regiment which saw action during the July 1861 battle" (O'Donnell 1986:39). One newspaper reported that "the crowds stood solemnly at attention for the playing of both the 'Star-Spangled Banner' and 'Carry Me Back to Ole Virginny' " (J. White 1961).

When the weekend reenactment concluded, the NPS described the event as unplanned, "poorly organized," and having a "lack of coordination at the top. . . . As a result much of the planning work and actual accomplishment had to be assumed by NPS personnel" (Volz 1961:5). Financial commitment by the First Manassas Corporation fell short, and the NPS had to pay out more than $10,000 in expenses for sanitation facilities and trash disposal. This did not include other funds needed for visitor protection (Volz 1961:8–9). "Little was right about the planning and preparations for the Reenactment" (Volz 1961:11).

One newspaper report commented on the value of such reenactments since they evoked patriotism. "This was a commemoration of the American heritage, a reminder of a spirit that must be ever renewed. The men of the Civil War, on both sides, had deeply rooted beliefs and were willing to fight for them. Their spirit is needed today" (Updike 1961).

While the reenactment received praise from the press, others criticized the event as "a celebration rather than an event commemorating a tragic event in our history. The 'Coney Island' atmosphere that concession stands created behind the spectator section was objectionable" (see Volz 1961:12). Another citizen noted "that even though great pains were taken to present a historically accurate event, and it was, comparatively few people came away really understanding what took place" (see Volz 1961:12).

An editorial in a Washington, D.C., newspaper the *Sunday Star* (1961:D4), wrote,

> The week-end child's play at the Battle of Bull Run is a harmless diversion, we suppose. . . . This silly business would perhaps have served a more useful purpose, however, if re-enactment of the battle itself could have been replaced by realistic scenes of the field after the battle had been fought, when death and suffering and the indescribable tragedy of war had taken command—as they always have and always will.

At the end of the centennial celebrations at Manassas, there were plans to create a Civil War hall of fame. A campaign to raise $5 million got under way, with the assumption that any net profits from the First Manassas Corporation would be donated to the undertaking (Updike 1961). "No dead museum of the old-fashioned type, it would include such features as revolving chairs from which visitors could watch battles unfold on devices mounted on the walls. It would stress, not old enmities, but present amity" (Associated Press 1961). It would be about the commitment to a cause (Associated Press 1961). The proposed name—Civil War Hall of Fame—was probably derived from the many generals who fought at Manassas. These included the commanders, Irvin McDowell (Union) and Pierre Gustave Toutant de Beauregard (Confederacy). Other notable Confederates included James E. Longstreet, Joseph E. Johnston, Thomas "Stonewall" Jackson, Edmund Kirby-Smith, Fitzhugh Lee, C. P. Ewell, J. E. B. Stuart, Jubal A. Early, and Wade Hampton. Another Union leader involved in the battle was William Tecumseh Sherman. Another newspaper reporter wrote that the profits from the centennial celebration would be donated for a Civil War memorial at Manassas National Battlefield Park (*Journal Messenger* 1961:1). There were no profits from the reenactment, and hope for a hall of fame diminished as the memory of the centennial events faded.

Commemoration and African Americans on the Battlefield Landscape

The Robinsons, a free African American household, occupied a portion of what became Manassas National Battlefield Park from the 1840s through 1936. Their longtime presence on the landscape gave the NPS a chance to expand on their traditional, essentially synchronous interpretation of the area's national significance to one that is more inclusive and diachronic. The original Robinson House was built in the late 1840s. An 1850 agricultural census indicates that the Robinson family had a 150.5-acre farm. They owned $175 in livestock, including four horses, three milk cows, and six swine. They also had a hundred pounds of wool, seven bushels of Irish potatoes, 200 pounds of butter, and five tons of hay (Turner 1993).

The Robinsons escaped injury during both battles at Manassas, although their house served as a significant landscape feature during the events. General Franz Sigel, commanding the First Corps of Pope's Army of Virginia, established his headquarters on the Robinson farm during the First Battle of Manassas (U.S. War Department 1880, 1885:32). Union forces also used the building as a field hospital (U.S. War Department 1880, 1885:302; see also *Irish-American* 1863; Lyon 1882). Family tradition notes that the Robinsons returned to their house to find blood stained floors (Wilshire 1948).

The Robinsons constructed several additions to their home from the 1870s through the twentieth century. They lived in a comparatively small dwelling for several decades, even though they had become the third-wealthiest African American family in the county. According to the agricultural censuses from 1850 through 1880, the Robinson family had two to six times more wealth than the Henry family, their closest neighbor (Agricultural Census 1850, 1860, 1870). Robinson's house stood in clear view of the Henry House. The Henrys were not only part of the dominant, white society but also descendants of Robert "Councilor" Carter. Even with the Robinson's superior wealth, their dwelling remained comparable in size to the Henry House (Martin et al. 1997:160).

The battles of Manassas significantly damaged the Henry House, and shortly after the war the Henrys rebuilt a substantially larger dwelling on the same site. The Robinsons waited several years, until the 1870s, to build additions to their home, doing so only after the Henrys had enlarged their house. The Robinsons may not have wanted to appear socially equal to or wealthier than the Henrys, as the Robinson's house and additions still stood smaller than the Henry House. Apparently, the Robinsons used existing forms of material culture, such as their house, to reassure the white community of their subordinated position, thus reducing potential conflict (Martin et al. 1997:171). This strategy became an important survival tactic during the Reconstruction and Jim Crow eras. The Robinsons knew that they could always be under the surveillance of their neighbors since the Henrys lived only about a quarter of a mile away and inhabited grounds that were slightly higher in elevation. Family oral traditions claim that the Robinsons were discreet in their use of new farm equipment and other materials, and they made sure that they kept them out of view, placing the items in barns or storage areas when they were not in use (Martin et al. 1997:171; Robinson 1996).

A fire in 1993 destroyed much of the wood frame structure, and some community members felt that arsonists intentionally set fire to the house in order to erase African Americans and any signs of the Robinson family from the battlefield landscape. Most of the destroyed house dated from the postbellum era, and the Williamsport Preservation Training Center, a branch of the NPS, eventually documented and dismantled much of what was left (Sandri 1994). Only the chimney and foundations survived the arson and dismantling (Martin et al. 1997:158) (see figure 5.5).

Archaeology, performed around these remaining ruins, provided additional information for park management regarding the depth of African American history within the park boundaries (see Martin et al. 1997).

Figure 5.5. Remains of the Robinson House, dismantled by the National Park Service after the frame structure was destroyed by fire (courtesy Paul A. Shackel).

Archaeological evidence shows that family members played active roles in shaping and creating their lives and their surrounding environment. It also provides park managers with the information necessary to be more inclusive in interpreting the various histories of subordinated groups. It allows them to share with the public a history of a people who have often been overlooked in traditional NPS interpretation.

Preserving the Robinson House ruins has met with varying degrees of success. There has been some resistance from the Manassas National Battlefield Park staff members to preserving and interpreting the remaining foundations since they believe that the postbellum additions to the Robinson House do not follow the mandate of the park's congressional enabling legislation: to interpret the First and Second Battles of Manassas. The resistance to recognizing the presence and importance of the Robinson family on the Manassas battlefield landscape has a long history. Susan Morton, in her 1939 guidebook to the battlefield, noted that the Robinson House had "no interesting history connected with this house before the war, it then became quickly famous, and it was not far from here, on a part of the Henry farm, that General Jackson won his immortal sobriquet of STONEWALL" (S. Morton 1939:n.p.).

The NPS interpretations for both the Henry House and the Robinson House are also telling of how the park views the importance of these two houses. The park maintains the interpretations of these properties that were developed during the Jim Crow era. At the Robinson House site, you can read from an interpretive plaque that the house (now foundations) does not fit in with the battlefield landscape that the visitor is experiencing. Park interpretation states that at best you are seeing the remains of an 1880s structure (although, in reality, additions to the original structure, which exist only in the archaeological record, were made in 1871, 1888, and 1926).

In comparison, the Henry House was destroyed during the Civil War and rebuilt soon thereafter. On-site park interpretation is not explicit about the building's postbellum construction date. The visitor is not informed that the existing structure did not exist during the battles of Manassas. The NPS uses the Henry House, a noncontributing structure to the historic landscape (since it was built after the war), as an important symbol and marker for the First Battle of Manassas. It is interesting that the NPS downplays the role of the Robinson family and house, with the justification that the house was built after the Civil War, while the Henry House, rebuilt after the Civil War, is given a prominent place on the Manassas landscape.

After the Robinson House burned and the wood framing was dismantled, only the postbellum stone foundations and chimney remained. The foundations and chimney helped convey the story of an African American family's struggle to survive in a racist society. It seems appropriate that this family's contributions to the area's local and regional history be recognized. The foundations and chimney are a testament to their postbellum effort to rebuild in a battle-worn landscape and persist through Reconstruction and the Jim Crow era while maintaining their cultural identity.

It might be fitting that the foundations of the Robinson House be used to not only commemorate the Robinson family's struggle to survive under racist conditions but also to represent and commemorate the many unknown African American families who struggled under similar circumstances. Their story is about how they aspired to be accorded the full rights of American citizenship without rejecting or being stripped of their African identity.

A discussion between park management and the NPS's chief historian in 1996 resulted in an agreement that only the top brick portion of the chimney, constructed in 1926, be dismantled (Pitcaithley 1996). The rest of the chimney ruins were to stand as a monument to the Robinsons and the African American presence on the landscape.

In September 1998, the NPS's director, Robert Stanton, an African American, wrote a memo to all NPS employees about the importance of our national parks. He insisted that our national parks should be inclusive of the rich cultural diversity that can be found within them. He noted,

> As we look toward the future, the ultimate preservation of our parks will rest on the degree to which Americans value our natural legacy and our multicultural heritage. Parks teach us that while recognizing and respecting our differences, we as a nation should come together as one. National parks are representative of the cultural, natural, recreational, historical, and professional diversity that has shaped our nation, taught our history, and united us as a people. (Stanton 1998:1)

In the following year, Representative Jesse Jackson Jr. (D-Ill.) added new language to the Department of the Interior's appropriation bill, which passed in November 1999. The new law asks park managers "to recognize and include in all of their public displays . . . the unique role that the institution of slavery played in causing the Civil War and its role, if any, at the individual battle site" (Mauser 2000:1).

Unfortunately, these directives came too late. The management of Manassas National Battlefield Park claimed in 1998 that the remaining chimney at the Robinson House was unstable. Without consultation from outside experts, the park's cultural resource manager and chief historian told the great-grandson of the original Robinson family that the chimney was unstable and a threat to visitors (Robinson 1998). The park did not propose any alternatives, such as stabilization, even though the NPS has at its disposal emergency stabilization money for significant cultural resources. An NPS historic architect said that it would have cost between $15,000 and $20,000 to stabilize the chimney, arguably a small price for such an important social and cultural symbol on the Manassas landscape (Vitanza 1999). Since the remaining chimney was constructed in the 1870s, the park felt that it did not conform to their synchronous mission of interpreting the First and Second Battles of Manassas. Therefore, the NPS dismantled the chimney in August 1998 (see figure 5.6). Afterward, the stones from the Robinson House chimney lay in a pile in the park's maintenance yard, being used for access ramps and the capping of the

Figure 5.6. Remains of the Robinson House foundations after the removal of the chimney, 1998 (courtesy Paul A. Shackel).

Stone Bridge. One NPS historian (not affiliated with Manassas National Battlefield Park), appalled and in disbelief at the park's actions at the Robinson House, remarked that "safety is the last refuge for scoundrels" (Anonymous 1998). Surprisingly, there has been no outcry from the historic preservation or African American communities. Without any challenge, the park may continue its policy of only interpreting a synchronous dimension of the area's history.

Removing the Robinson House ruins can be interpreted by many as a racist action since African American representation is being erased from the landscape. Without these symbolic representations to remind us of their presence, it becomes increasingly difficult to remember the story of African Americans in some of the most significant events of American history, such as the Civil War, Reconstruction, and Jim Crow. Removing the Robinson's heritage from the battlefield is shocking, especially after the NPS director's call for recognizing our multicultural heritage.

Remembering Landscapes of Conflict 6

Controlling Meaning

Frequently there is no one agreed-on interpretation for the historical landscapes and monuments of America. They have different meanings for different people, and it is the struggle for control over meaning that makes the American historical landscape so dynamic and interesting. While creating a particular memory of an event helps make it part of society's corporate history, the act of marking off and preserving land, or creating monuments, sanctifies the memory. Kenneth Foote remarks that there must be some type of public ceremony that describes why an object is important and why the site should be remembered. These places, or monuments, then serve to remind future generations "of a virtue or sacrifice or to warn them of events to be avoided" (Foote 1997:8).

Sanctified sites and memorials have a distinctive appearance in the landscape:

> First, they are often clearly bounded from the surrounding environment and marked with great specificity as to what happened where. Second, sanctified sites are usually carefully maintained for long periods of time—decades, generations, and centuries. Third, sanctification typically involves a change of ownership, often a transfer from private to public stewardship. Fourth, sanctified sites frequently attract continued ritual commemoration, such as annual memorial services or pilgrimage. Fifth, sanctified sites often attract additional and sometimes even unrelated monuments and memorials through a process of accretion. That is, once sanctified, these sites seem to act as foci for other commemorative efforts. (Foote 1997:9)

Minority groups often struggle to assert their view through commemoration, although sometimes their views are overpowered by those of the dominant group. One example is the commemorative events that followed the 1886 Haymarket Riot, a clash between labor and capital. While both sides produced martyrs and claimed that their ends justified their means, the two groups still fight today over the meaning of commemoration of the event. Capitalists claimed that the policemen who died were the "protectors of Chicago," even though they helped ignite the riot that killed some of their own colleagues. Eight of the strikers were tried, and four of the labor organizers were falsely accused and executed in one of "the great miscarriages of justice in U.S. history" (Foote 1997:11). The labor organizers became martyrs for the labor movement, while industrialists saw the police as martyrs. Businessmen quickly moved to commemorate the policemen in order to prevent labor from memorializing its martyrs. Its monument, "The Protectors of Chicago," was raised on the site of the 1886 riot, and the city denied labor organizations the right to erect a monument within the city limits. Decades of vandalism eventually forced the city to remove the statue to a protected indoor location at the police academy in the 1970s. Today, all that remains is the pedestal. Labor raised a monument at the grave site of its martyrs at the Waldheim Cemetery in Forest Park, Illinois (across the Chicago city line), after one of the largest funerals in Chicago's history (Foote 1997:11–14).

Control over meaning constantly infiltrates our daily lives, and it is dynamic and always changing. Another good example of this is the conflict between Anglos and American Indians over the meaning of the battle at the Little Bighorn. The official memory of the event has changed dramatically since the late nineteenth century. Soon after Custer's final battle, military officials criticized his tactics as reckless and careless. But journalists from 1876 through the mid-twentieth century countered this criticism and portrayed his outcome as a heroic death. Much like Masada, the Alamo, and the Confederacy's defeat, the Last Stand was transformed into a moral defeat: Custer died for timeless ideals while facing overwhelming odds in bringing civilization to the frontier. A more critical view of the battle of the Little Bighorn arose in the 1960s amid American Indian protests for equal representation. Today the Custer myth is no longer supported by the National Park Service (Linenthal 1993:267–81). The name "Custer National Monument" was changed to "Little Bighorn National Monument" by an act of Congress in 1991, and the American Indians' perspectives on the historical events have played an important role in the park's interpretation.

In a similar vein, the struggle to control the meaning of the Civil War began at Appomattox, and blacks have struggled ever since to subvert the white hegemonic interpretation of the event. Immediately after the war, sections of the United States became deeply divided over the reasons and causes of the war. In the late 1890s, the official memory of the war began to stress patriotic and courageous motives in order to preserve a tangible past and to provide a coherent white cultural identity (Rainey 1983). This change is very noticeable at national battlefields, such as Gettysburg. John Patterson (1989:138 ff.) outlines the different stages in the history of creating and preserving a national battlefield at Gettysburg in the context of the changing meaning of the Civil War. The earliest stage of preservation favored northern sentiment, and African Americans veterans were sometimes part of Gettysburg encampments. After 1895, Confederate views were increasingly represented at the expense of African Americans. By the turn of the twentieth century, black veterans were no longer invited to reunions, and rather than remaining a monument to the northern cause, the Gettysburg battlefield eventually became a symbol of reunion, progress, and peace among whites.

In contemporary preservation, Civil War battlefields and monuments play a variety of roles that are continuously being negotiated. They are places where blacks and whites and northerners and southerners are struggling over meaning and sanctification as the collective memory of race is being challenged. Competing groups clash over who should provide the "legitimate and true" interpretation of the event. Whether the challenge to the collective memory succeeds depends on the political strength and perseverance of subordinated groups. Sometimes, challenging the entrenched views of powerful institutions can be an overwhelming task.

Promoting the Lost Cause

Much of the tension over control of the national public memory of the Civil War stems from trying to subvert the ideology of the Lost Cause. Following the war, the South suffered tremendously, and its economic recovery was slow. Many southern values were transformed by Reconstruction, and traditions such as segregation became illegal. After economic recovery and the establishment of Jim Crow legislation in the 1890s, southerners looked to the future with a hope that relied on revitalizing southern heritage and tradition (Coleman 1891:333).

Anthropologists have studied revitalization movements among American Indians, but this phenomenon was evident among Confederate southerners after the Civil War, and its movement continues, to some extent, today. After the war, southerners did not launch a political movement for the re-creation of the ways of the Old South. Rather, an ideology infiltrated southern communities that were dissatisfied with their defeat as they recalled the antebellum days of the South. Anthony F. C. Wallace (1956:264–81) defines "revitalization" as a "conscious, deliberate, organized effort on the part of some members of society to create a more satisfying culture" by restoring "a golden age"—an attempt "to revive a previous condition of social virtue." Ralph Linton (1943:233) observes that these movements occur "almost without exception, associated with frustrating situations and are primarily attempts to compensate for the frustrations of the society's members. The elements revived become symbols of a period when the society was free, or, in retrospect, happy or great." This southern revitalization movement reminded the aristocracy of the antebellum South and justified slavery and their defense of states' rights.

With the development and strengthening of the Lost Cause, from the late nineteenth century through most of the twentieth, the memory of African American participation in the war became rather limited in American literature. Southern whites gained tremendous political and social power after Reconstruction and developed a southern patriotic past that could overcome historical humiliation. They created a glorious past of honor and dedication to a cause that excluded African Americans from the story. African Americans' participation in the Civil War vanished from the American consciousness (Aaron 1973:332–33).

Reunions became a place to ritualize and create sentimental versions of the past; the sense of tragedy was eliminated, and reconciliation became the predominant talk at these events (McConnell 1992:178–79). At the fiftieth-anniversary celebration of the battle of Gettysburg, U.S. Vice President Thomas Marshall noted that "there is now no difference between North and South except cold bread and hot biscuits" (*Confederate Veteran* 1913:380). Speaker of the House Champ Clark noted that "it was not Southern valor, or Northern valor. It was, thank God, American valor" (quoted from Reardon 1997:190). And a clergyman wrote, "Never before in the world's history have two armies that stood against each other like two castles with cannon shotted to the muzzle, met in friendship, good will, and with a common enthusiasm for the same flag" (quoted in Reardon 1997:190).

Southern tradition was redisplayed in public arenas in ceremonies, and white southerners created new monuments to their heroes and war dead. Pageantry became another means to display public pride and rekindle a particular memory of the past. "Public historical imagery is an essential element of our culture, contributing to how we define our sense of identity and direction" (Glassberg 1990:1). In the 1920s, historical pageantry blossomed in the Northeast and Midwest but flourished as never before in the Deep South and the West (Glassberg 1990:231):

> Public historical imagery is both a reflection of the larger culture, and its prevailing ways of looking at the world, and a major element in the shaping of that culture. Since every way of seeing the world—past and present—excludes hundreds of alternatives from view, the power to define what particular version of history becomes the public history is an awesome power indeed. (Glassberg 1990:2)

The fiftieth-anniversary celebrations of the Civil War ended in 1915 with a tone of reconciliation that incorporated northern and southern views (Kammen 1991:416). The general mood of the celebration included the feeling that

> secession had been wrong and preserving the Union right; blacks were not equal to white men, but terminating the moral blot of slavery was a good thing; Reconstruction was misguided because attempts to provide equal rights for former slaves resulted in injustices against white southerners. [These] themes appeared in a surprising number of histories, fictional works and films of the period. (Logan 1996:E4)

Southerners took a renewed interest in writing their own histories and presenting the views of the Confederacy in order to instill local pride. For example, in Montgomery, Alabama, in 1926, southerners reenacted the inauguration of Jefferson Davis. A later production saw southern troops, represented as the "Spirit of the South," led into battle by "Chivalry," which was later invoked to lead southern troops into battle during World War I. The United Confederate Veterans in Charlotte, North Carolina, reenacted the Confederate victory at Manassas. In Atlanta in 1920, a pageant showed the defeat of Reconstruction as Ku Klux Klan members entered the stage and chased carpetbaggers and blacks out of town. Music from the score to *The Birth of a Nation* played in the background. Some of the pageants had messages of reconciliation between northern and southern troops, although sectional hostility was often portrayed, showing northerners looting and drinking. These pageants portrayed blacks as comic buffoons, happy under the system of slavery. Several pageants did not even offer a rationale for slavery. In one display, a slave begged to accompany his master to the front lines of the war; in another instance, a slave protested that he did not want to be freed (Glassberg 1990:252–53).

African Americans responded to these degrading portrayals. One such work is W. E. B. Du Bois's *Stars of Ethiopia,* which premiered in 1926 at the Sesquicentennial International Exposition in Philadelphia. It included a 500-voice chorus from the Hampton and Fisk University Quintets. The pageant depicted five epochs and six episodes of African and African American history. They include the "gift of iron" from prehistoric African society, the "gift of the Nile" from ancient Egyptian society, the "gift of the faith of Mohammed," the "gift of humiliation," and the "gift of struggle toward freedom." The final episode is the "gift of freedom" with William Lloyd Garrison, John Brown, Abraham Lincoln, David Walker, Frederick Douglass, and Sojourner Truth, along with marching black Union soldiers (Blight 2001:375). Marian Anderson also gave a solo performance. Another pageant included *The Answer: A Symbolic Pageant Showing the Contributions to America's Growth and Greatness Made by Negroes.* It was presented as a history of black oppression on the 110th anniversary of Wendell Philips's birthday (Glassberg 1990:254–55, 351).

With the aim of rewriting the histories of the Reconstruction era, the United Daughters of the Confederacy along with the Sons of Confederate Veterans worked diligently to construct the "faithful-slave" myth, which becomes apparent in two of the case studies presented in this book. Planning for a faithful-slave memorial started at the national annual meeting of the United Daughters of the Confederacy in 1905, and such a memorial was finally erected at Harpers Ferry in 1931. The Heyward Shepherd Memorial celebrates the institution of slavery and the aristocracy of the Old South. The message of the memorial divided both white and black communities, and neither group spoke with a unified voice. White and black civil rights advocates condemned the white president of Storer College, Henry McDonald, for participating in the unveiling ceremonies. Some blacks criticized the Reverend George F. Bragg for playing a role at the monument's dedication, and a descendant of Heyward Shepherd who was honored at the unveiling ceremonies denounced blacks who protested the event. At Manassas, the faithful-slave myth emerged during the seventy-fifth-anniversary celebration of the First Battle of Manassas in 1936, an era when Jim Crow legislation had taken hold of the country and racist groups such as the Ku Klux Klan thrived.

Even today, southern heritage groups continue to fight for the memory of the faithful slave, while African American groups struggle to erase this idea from the American landscape. For instance, a new exhibit at the Tennessee Civil War Museum in Chattanooga claims that more than 35,000 African Americans fought in the Confederate army—an estimate that James McPherson, a Civil War historian and Pulitzer Prize winner, calls absurd (*Washington Post* 1999:A16).

Forgetting and Subverting the Official History

Memories can be public as well as private, and they serve to legitimize the past and the present. Public history exhibits, monuments, statues, artifacts, national historic parks, commemorations, and celebrations can foster myths that create a common history, allowing for divergent groups to find a common bond. Therefore, a shared history and the creation of community create a complex set of interactions. Elements of the past both remembered and forgotten in common are essential for group cohesion and the fostering of a particular ideology (Glassberg 1996:13).

While collective memory can be about forgetting a past, this is often at the expense of a subordinated group. Those who are excluded may try to subvert the meaning of the past, or they may strive for more representation in order to create a new memory of a more pluralistic past. At other times, subordinated groups may not call attention to their absence in the collective memory. Reflection on the meanings associated with our collective national memory shows that they have usually focused on elites and white traditional heroes. The perception has been that American history is linear and straightforward. However, this uncomplicated version occurs only when we leave "others" out of the picture.

Creating white hegemony depends on erasing signs of material culture that may reflect an image of African, Asian, Latin American, and American Indian pasts. If Americans tour some of the Civil War battlefields today, they will see a sanitized and trivialized version of history that often omits African American views. The history of the war covers little more than troop movements and embellishment of heroic acts. It becomes easy to ignore stories of racism and slavery when the material culture that represents African American ideals is erased from the landscape. Forgetting can be a form of symbolic violence and a tactic of white hegemony—a tactic used at Manassas National Battlefield Park. Symbolic representation and material culture related to the story of the Robinson family were removed from the landscape in order to simplify the story of the battles. The complex human story at Manassas has been trivialized as interpreters discuss only troop movements and the valor of heroic figures. The issues of slavery, oppression, racism, Reconstruction, and Jim Crow are prevented from becoming part of the national story by having all evidence removed. Yet in the Manassas community, African Americans have not been vocal about this removal.

Displaced Africans in America have used different strategies to keep alive and perpetuate African beliefs, values, and ideas in often hostile environments. For instance, George Lipsitz (1998:130) shows how enslaved Africans often kept their culture alive by meeting secretly in remote corners of the plantation to chant songs. They buried their dead facing east, toward their homeland. They integrated African words and phrases into their speech. They "made music based on the West African pentatonic scale rather than on the European diatonic scale" (Lipsitz 1998:130). African Americans "kept part of Africa alive in America. African retentions helped them understand their captivity as a crime; it encouraged them to resist the European American ideology that defamed them as less than human, that attributed their subordination to their own nature rather than to historical actions of their oppressors" (Lipsitz 1998:130).

Lipsitz (1998:130–31) explains that since Africans were denied their language and explicit forms of their cultural heritage, they turned to implicit uses of their culture as a form of covert resistance. One example, noted by Leland Ferguson involves an enslaved African American who tried to build an African-style hut on his master's land, but the plantation owner made him tear it down. Ex-slave Ben Sullivan explained,

> Old man Okra said he wanted a place like he had in Africa, so he built himself a hut. I remember it well. It was about 12 by 14 feet, it had a dirt floor, and he built the sides like a woven basket with clay plaster on it. It had a flat roof that he made from brush and palmetto, and had one door and no windows. But Master made him pull it down. He said he didn't want an African hut on his place. (Cited from Ferguson 1992:75)

After emancipation, African Americans continued to build their lives to reflect their African heritage:

> They built shotgun houses that resembled dwellings in West Africa and protected their dwellings through a variety of traditional practices from their home continent—placing mirrors on outside walls, setting ceramic jars on both sides of front doors, ringing yards with white washed stones, and decorating inside walls with a dynamic script called "spirit writing." (R. Thompson 1989:121)

Charles Joyner (1984:xxi) points out that even when enslaved and freed African Americans used European material culture, they used it in a distinctly African fashion, and the materials had a distinctively African meaning. Africanisms have helped shape American culture. Two of the case studies in this book show how African Americans applied their own meaning to white material culture. From the beginning of the Jim Crow era, the meaning of John Brown and the John Brown Fort changed dramatically within the dominant white culture. From the late 1880s, the official memory no longer considered Brown to be a martyr and saint, and his deeds were strongly condemned, especially with the emergence of southern revisionist history. African Americans embraced their hero for being willing to fight for their cause, and in 1910 the fort was removed to Storer College, an institution that developed for the education of newly freed slaves. Through the Jim Crow era, the fort was a distinctive African American symbol.

The Robert Gould Shaw Memorial is also about African Americans co-opting the meaning of a symbol on the American landscape. After its unveiling in 1897, many claimed that the work was one of America's greatest pieces of art. The meaning of the memorial was clear. It praised the deeds of Robert Gould Shaw, the white colonel who rides on horseback with his black troops marching at his side. Some art historians claimed that the memorial was racist because Shaw is raised on horseback when, in fact, he charged Fort Wagner with his troops on foot. From the civil rights era on, blacks increasingly claimed ownership of the memorial. Names of the dead soldiers were placed on the rear of the memorial in the 1980s, and in the 1990s the National Park Service and other official organizations began calling the memorial the Robert Gould Shaw and the 54th Massachusetts Volunteer Infantry Memorial. In fact, at the one-hundred-year rededication ceremonies in 1997, Robert Gould Shaw was not mentioned, and many dignitaries praised the deeds of the black foot soldiers.

Since many white Americans are willing to simplify the story of the

Civil War and forget or even dismiss some of the issues related to African Americans, it becomes even more important that blacks co-opt material culture and make it represent issues that are important to them. The John Brown Fort during the Jim Crow era and the Robert Gould Shaw Memorial during the post–civil rights era, are important material representations where the black voice came to be heard on the national scene.

Revitalization and the Neo-Confederate Movement

Confederate History and Heritage Month and the Heritage Preservation Association

Today people celebrate the Civil War and use symbols related to the event, but their intentions are not necessarily national unity. Rather, the meanings of these celebrations are local, ethnic, and regional. The Civil War remains prominent in politics, and it is part of the popular memory of American history. It is still common to search the newspapers and see organizations, such as the Ku Klux Klan, use Confederate symbols for their racist message. In 1997, the *Washington Post* (1997b:B5) covered a rally of fifty Klan members who were from the Stonewall Jackson Society. They wore their white hoods and displayed a Confederate flag. In 1994, Oliver North's campaign for Virginia senator supported those who wished to retain the Confederate flag as an emblem of southern pride. His opinions ignited an emotional war between those who see it as a symbol of racism and those who honor it as an emblem of southern heritage. As recently as 1995 in Richmond, Virginia, the placement of the Arthur Ashe monument brought attention to the racial divide in that state and in the United States. Proponents of the monument wanted to place it on Monument Row, where Confederate generals are honored. Ironically, Ashe was unwelcome in that part of town when he grew up in 1950s segregated Richmond. Many whites sympathetic to the ideals of the Confederacy did not think that the monument should be placed in the row, and ultimately it was placed at the end of Monument Row with its back toward the generals.

Governor George Allen of Virginia proclaimed April as Confederate History and Heritage Month to honor the southern "cause of liberty . . . and preserving the self-determination of the bond of States." He signed proclamations in 1995, 1996 and 1997, drafted by the Sons of Confederate Veterans, calling the Civil War a "four-year struggle for [southern] independence and sovereign rights." The documents never mention slavery (Hsu 1998:C1, C7; *Washington Post* 1997b:B3). One reader of the *Washington Post* responded to Allen by writing that the governor was "trying to bring back the '50s—the 1850s" (Coyner 1997:A12). However, a survey performed by the Mason–Dixon Political/Media Research found that 72 percent of those polled in Virginia approved of Allen's actions (*Washington Post* 1997a:B3).

On April 9, 1998, the 133rd anniversary of the surrender at Appomattox, Governor James S. Gilmore III of Virginia also declared April as Confederate History and Heritage Month, but during his declaration he also condemned slavery. Gilmore praised southern generals and soldiers but also honored "the ordinary men and women, free and not free," who made the Confederacy part of American history. The governor declared that the war was a

> four-year tragic, heroic and determined struggle for deeply held beliefs. He also noted that slavery was a practice that deprived African Americans of their God-given inalienable rights [and] which degraded the human spirit. . . . We honor our past and draw from it the courage . . . to reconcile ourselves and go forward . . . together as Virginians and Americans. (Hsu 1998: C1, C7)

His proclamation angered both defenders of white Confederate heritage and civil rights leaders. R. Wayne Byrd Sr., president of Virginia's Heritage Preservation Association, called Gilmore's proclamation "an insult" and stated that the governor gave in to "racist hate groups such as the NAACP [National Association for the Advancement of Colored People]." Byrd continued by stating, "I don't see why these people [in the NAACP] have a right to tell me how to honor Southern heritage" (Hsu 1998:C7).

The NAACP stated that they appreciated Gilmore's condemnation of slavery, but they worried that the governor sanctioned the celebration of the Confederacy. Tommy J. Baer, president of B'nai B'rith International and a Richmond lawyer, said that Gilmore's proclamation is "like Germany having a World War II—I won't even call it Nazi—history month, but [saying], 'We're going to include the suffering of the Jews.' It doesn't pass the common sense test" (Hsu 1998:C7).

In March 2001, Governor Gilmore discarded Virginia's Confederate History Month proclamation and replaced it with a proclamation "In

Remembrance of the Sacrifices and Honor of All Virginians Who Served in the Civil War." The proclamation recognized those who served in the Confederacy and also states, "It is fitting to recognize the historical contributions of great Virginians who served the Union with honor, such as Sergeant William H. Carney of the 54th Massachusetts Volunteers, a son of Norfolk who fled slavery." It also states, "The practice of slavery was an affront to man's natural dignity, deprived African-Americans of their God-given inalienable rights, degraded the human spirit and is abhorred and condemned by Virginians" (quoted in Melton 2001:A19).

Confederate heritage groups quickly denounced Gilmore's revised proclamation, noting that the governor succumbed to the NAACP's threat of a statewide tourism boycott. Bragdon Bowling, holding the second-highest office in the state's chapter of the Sons of Confederate Veterans, claimed that Gilmore had done the bidding of the NAACP "by honoring people who invaded this state and murdered, raped and pillaged. It's a cop-out, a sellout (quoted in Melton 2001:A1).

Started in 1993, the Historic Preservation Association was one of the first nationwide neo-Confederate organizations to develop in the post–civil rights era. In 2000, they had members in forty-nine states and six countries with chapters in ten states with the goal of preserving the symbols, culture, and heritage of the American South. The goal of the Historic Preservation Association is to fight "political correctness and cultural bigotry against the South" (Historic Preservation Association 2000b). They claim victory in Virginia since they were able to fight against the NAACP to keep Confederate History and Heritage Month. They claim that the NAACP's fight against honoring Confederates is "racial, anti-southern bigotry and hatred" (Historic Preservation Association 2000b).

In Alabama, Governor Fob James proclaimed the month of April Confederate History and Heritage Month. The Historic Preservation Association has been successful in obtaining this proclamation from the Alabama governor since 1998. The proclamation calls for "Alabamians to become more aware of the Confederate Heritage in Alabama and encourages our schools and citizens to join efforts to become more knowledgeable of the true role of the Confederate States of America in the history of our country" (Historic Preservation Association 2000a).

The League of the South

In 1994, a group of scholars, journalists, and political activists sympathetic to the neo-Confederate cause created the League of the South, headquartered in Tuscaloosa, Alabama. The league was founded by Michael Hill, a professor at Stillman College in Tuscaloosa, and several other pro-Confederate scholars (Roberts 1998:67–68).

The League of the South believes that secession is neither premature, impractical, nor illegal. The group believes that "the right of secession is nothing more than the right of sovereign states to recall the powers they delegated to the federal government when they ratified the constitution. This right cannot be renounced because the right to liberty and self-determination is an inalienable right given by God" (League of the South 2000). The League of the South notes that if the southern states secede, they would be an economically sound country. If the thirteen states of the old Confederacy were a nation, its gross national product would place it among the top five or six nations of the world. In its position statement, it claims that secession would mean that the new Confederacy "could leave the United Nations and oppose the Bush–Clinton New World Order. We could stop foreign aid. We could once again reward merit. We could get government out of our children's education. In a word. We could again seize control of our destiny" (League of the South 2000).

The group, formerly known as the Southern League, changed its name because a baseball minor league had the same name and threatened to sue. The name comes from two of their philosophical inspirations. First is the League of United Southerners, an antebellum pro-slavery group formed in 1858 that advocated secession. Its founders included Alabaman William Lowndes Yancey, a declared secessionist as early as 1851, and Virginian Edmund Ruffin, who fired the first shot at Fort Sumter. After the Confederate surrender at Appomattox, he wrote of "unmitigated hatred . . . to the malignant and vile Yankee race" and then wrapped himself in a Confederate flag and committed suicide with a pistol (Roberts 1998:68). The second group is the modern Northern League of Italy, a right-wing separatist group that is advocating an independent "Republic of Padania," a region from Turin to Venice. The Northern League has done well in recent elections, and their results have fueled the ambitions of the League of the South to one day field candidates in U.S. elections (Roberts 1998:68). In a recent bid for Congress in 1997, State Senator Charles Davidson of Alabama, although not a member of the league, reaffirmed its philosophy. Davidson argued that slavery was justified in the South since it was mentioned in the Bible, and thus the abolitionists cannot "call something evil that God obviously allowed." Davidson continued:

> to say that slaves were mistreated in the Old South is to say that the most Christian group of people in the entire world, the Bible Belt, mistreated their servants and violated the commandments of Jesus their Lord. Anyone who says this is an accuser of the Brethren of Christ. Not a very good position to take. (Quoted in Roberts 1998:102)

The League of the South wants Confederate battle flags flying over statehouses and a federal holiday for Robert E. Lee, and their president desires to establish "the natural social order of the south" (Roberts 1998:68). In its founding proclamation, the League of the South explains their desire for states' rights and home rule. The organization's charter asserts that it has a dream of

> a free and prosperous Southern Republic. Our own nation founded on private property, free association, fair trade, sound money, low taxes, equal justice before the law, secure borders, and armed and vigilant neutrality. Self-governing states and local communities invoking the favour and guidance of Almighty God. A bold, self-confident civilisation based on its European roots.
>
> From the beginning the League of the South has fearlessly stated its basic purpose: *We seek to advance the cultural, social, economic, and political well-being and independence of the Southern people by all honourable means.*

The document proclaims that the organization honors the courage and forthrightness that made the South the envy of the world. The League of the South stands by ten principles:

1. Advance the interests and independence of the Southern people.
2. Define the historic Christian faith of the South and return the regulation of religion and morals to the jurisdiction of states and local communities.
3. Educate Southerners (and other Americans of good will) about our history and our civilisation.
4. Protect the symbols and heritage of the traditional south.
5. Maintain our link with the great civilisations of Europe, especially that of the Anglo-Celts, from which the South has drawn its inspiration.

6. Encourage the development of healthy local communities and institutions by seceding from the mindless materialism and vulgarity of contemporary American society.
7. Restore the traditional rights reserved to the states under the Constitution.
8. Form friendships and alliances with sympathetic movements, and independence for authentic nations and regions, both inside and outside of the United States.
9. Stimulate the economic vitality and self-sufficiency of the Southern people.
10. Pledge our lives, fortunes, and sacred honour to the cause we have undertaken.

In this document, the League of the South warns of the "American Empire," which is run by "corrupt politicians [and] tyrannical judges." The empire, the league claims, has imposed an oppressive bureaucracy "in the form of welfare and affirmative action programs that squander our wealth and incite racial strife." The American Empire

> has enacted legislation and issued judicial edicts to legitimate moral perversity and persecute religion; it has assumed control over the education of our children, who are taught little except to hate their ancestors and to despise their own people; and ultimately, it has—while pursuing empire abroad—refused to defend its people against an epidemic of crime, the invasion of our borders by illegal aliens, and the international agencies that are bit by bit chipping away at the sovereignty of the United States. These enormities are sufficient to nullify whatever moral authority the central government once had.

Claiming that the federal government has stripped the people of the South of their rights, the document ironically states that "the sons of free men have become slaves." In closing, the document reads, "We revere our Southern ancestors because they were *right* and because their ideas have consequences for our future."

The League of the South is an organization that fights to keep its southern heritage, even if it means displaying Confederate battle flags, an act that offends most African Americans (Reingold and Wike 1998).

Michael Hill, president of the League of the South, and Thomas Fleming (Hill and Fleming 1995:C3) wrote that

> legislatures in Southern states are under pressure to rename streets and destroy monuments that honor Confederate soldiers. Corporations headquartered in Southern states have refused to fly state flags that contain a Confederate emblem; public schools have forbidden the display of the Confederate battle flag as if it were an example of gang colors.

Both Hill and Fleming describe the outcry over the use of southern symbols, such as Confederate battle flags, as a form of "cultural genocide." They called South Carolina Governor David Beasley a coward for deciding that the battle flag should no longer fly over the Capitol. In 1993, the flag was taken down in Alabama at the request of black lawmakers and a largely white chamber of commerce who feared convention boycotts (Roberts 1998:69).

Roberts argues that the League of the South sells hysteria, not history, when it comes to their most treasured symbol, the battle flag:

> It doesn't matter to them that the Confederate battle flag didn't fly over the Alabama Capitol in Montgomery until George Wallace hoisted it in 1963 to spite Bobby Kennedy and fellow integrationists. They act like the thing has been flapping in the breeze above the dome ever since Jeff Davis stood on those white marble steps and proclaimed secession. It doesn't matter to them that there were (large) parts of the South that did not secede, that were not Anglo-Celtic, that were not even English speaking. (Roberts 1998:102)

It is worth noting how Hill and others aligned with his cause are using the language of cultural victimization, terms that one often expects from groups other than southern white males. A pure southern culture, which the League of the South aspires to, is nothing more than a misconception. Many southern cultural traits, such as speech, foodways, and music, are a product of centuries of cultural interaction. "The League of the South clearly longs for a time when men were men, women were ladies, and black folks knew their place" (Roberts 1998:102).

The Southern Party

While groups such as the League of the South and the Heritage Preservation Association provide the academic and intellectual core for arguing about issues such as states' rights and southern heritage, the Southern Party is the political mechanism for secession. The Southern Party, founded in 1999, is a fledgling conservative political party that hopes to create an independent southern nation. It held its first convention in Charleston, South Carolina, from June 30 to July 1, 2000 (Southern Party 2000b). In 2000, it had about 2,000 members, and it plans to model itself on the secessionist movement in Quebec by the Parti Québécois and the Scottish Nationalist Party, both of which advocate full independence for their regions. They believe that a Southern Party would speak for the interests of the South. "Dixie has had no truly unified political voice since the demise of the formerly Solid South. With the Democrats now transformed into a party of Leftism and the Republicans representing primarily the interests of global/corporate capitalism, it is clear that something new is needed" (Southern Party 2000c). The party wants to restore "the unique cultural, social and religious foundations of the Southern People" (Southern Party 2000b).

They plan to support local and state candidates who will vote to secede from the United States. Its goal, according to the constitution of the Southern Party, is "complete independence for the Southern people from these United States." The southern party will "strive to preserve and protect our culture, our principles, our right, and our persons, all of which are threatened by a central government that refuses to abide by the limitations placed on it by its own Constitution." The constitution of the Southern Party also claims that its ultimate goal is for the "complete, permanent separation of the Southern States from these United States of America and the restoration of the southern republic, the Confederate States of America, to its rightful place among the nations of the earth" (Southern Party 2000a).

Remembering History and Racism

People tend to reconstruct the past according to the needs of contemporary culture (Kammen 1991:3). Reconstruction of the past may occur immediately after an event, and it continues to happen as long as reconstruction serves some viable need to the present. Celebration and sanctification of sites sometimes develop without recognizing alternative views and minority participants. In the United States, this situation often occurs when subordinated groups, such as Indians and African Americans, were participants in an event. Kenneth Foote (1997:322) recognizes that celebrating Native American heroism and their fight to preserve their culture often contradicts the frontier mythology that celebrates western expansionism. He also remarks that to celebrate African American resistance to slavery and racism helps to recognize the failure of democracy and egalitarianism, virtues celebrated by our national story. Therefore, the celebration and recognition of minority histories make us question our national memory and make many members who subscribe to the dominant white official history feel uneasy about the past and the present.

For more than a century, scholars have written extensively about how Americans choose to remember the events and causes of the American Civil War. The changing memories of the conflict have influenced and shaped racial relations from Reconstruction through the Jim Crow and the civil rights eras and continue to impact the way we interpret the Civil War today. In this book, I have examined the context and meaning of several Civil War landscape features to show the changing dynamics of public memory of these places for whites and blacks. The meaning of these landscapes and features are filled with contradictions and are part of a continuing struggle that is rooted in racism. Historian Eliot J. Gorn graphically illustrates these contradictions when he points out that historians argue that it was an "'irrepressible conflict' and an avoidable one; an ideological war to end slavery and a war that had nothing to do with slavery; a war waged by a rising bourgeoisie against a proto-aristocracy and a war of capitalism fighting each other" (Gorn 2000:B4).

Sacred objects, such as battlefields, monuments, and structures, are part of the ritual of dedication to the memory of an event or a person. They are publicly consecrated and widely venerated. Whether internally coherent or contradictory to the dominant view, memories validate the holders' version of the past. Understanding how and why some groups tend to remember a particular past while others forget or ignore a past is an important issue for critically evaluating and understanding the development and meaning of racism and the American landscape. As a group, people decide which experiences to collectively remember and which ones to forget as well as how to interpret these experiences. People develop a collective memory by molding, shaping, and agreeing on what to remember, and this often reflects current social and political circumstances.

The cases examined in this book show how groups create and control the collective national memory of revered sacred sites and objects. Different group agendas may clash, causing the established collective memories to be in continuous flux. While some subordinated groups can subvert the dominant memory (Shaw Memorial), other groups compromise and become part of a multivocal history (John Brown Fort). Others struggle but fail to have their story remembered (Heyward Shepherd Memorial), while others take limited action to have their history recognized (Manassas National Battlefield Park). The tensions between and within groups who struggle for the control over the collective public memory are ongoing since the political stakes are high. Those who control the past can command the present and the future.

Epilogue: Approaches to Changing the Meaning of Commemoration

Applied Approaches to Challenging the Official History

Local, regional, and national museums and history organizations continually face the dilemma of addressing the changing meaning and focus of their exhibits, interpretations, and/or commemorative activities. Following, I offer examples of strategies that different organizations have implemented to establish alternative or multivocal histories at sacred places. At times, broadening the focus of the meaning of the site is not complicated, but often the entrenched views of various interest groups impede the representation of alternative perspectives. Sometimes, new or alternative views remain on the periphery of the central theme. In other instances, there are compromises and integration of alternative histories. Or groups may even refuse to compete or will create alternative views on their own terms and in their own territory.

In the preface, I remarked that when Congress or the president created a national park or when a historic site was developed, the site's meaning would be associated with the contemporary social, political, and economic national values. For instance, in the first half of the twentieth century, the United States commemorated great men in order to reinforce the national ideology of power and unity based on white Anglo ideals. The glory of industry and capitalism was also reinforced through commemorative activities. After the Civil Rights movement, Americans experienced a growing pressure to be more inclusive. New laws enabled minority groups, once left out of the national story, to take their place beside entrenched histories. This transition has not been smooth, and in many cases the discussion about inclusiveness and multivocality at historic sites continues today. As we move into the twenty-first century, it is apparent that debates over meaning at sacred sites will continue, and one question that is likely to arise repeatedly is, Should local, state, and national parks continue to support a memory of the era in which historic sites were created—in the name of American heritage—or should these sites be seen as dynamic, fluid, and changing places that serve the needs of contemporary society?

When we reflect on the traditional meanings associated with collective national memory, we see that the memory has focused on elites and traditional heroes, and the perception is that American history is linear and straightforward. This is an interpretive strategy that has a long tradition, and in many cases it is easier to interpret only one story. Unfortunately, this uncomplicated story can happen only when groups, such as African Americans, American Indians, Asian Americans, women, the poor, and labor, are downplayed or ignored (Leff 1995:833; see also Nash et al. 1998:100). Those who believe in recognizing only the dominant view may think that

> it is difficult . . . to see how the subjects of the new [social] history can be accommodated in any single framework, let alone a national and political one. . . . How can all these groups, each cherishing its uniqueness and its claim to sovereign attention, be mainstreamed into a single, coherent, integrated history? (Quoted in Nash et al. 1998:100–1)

Historical events are usually complex, entangling different people and groups with varying views and interests. History is often political, and historical constructions are embedded in the needs of the modern community (Breene 1989; Hobsbawm 1983a; Norkunas 1993). To ignore the complexity of history is to disregard the various responsible agents associated with any sacred site. However, there are several strategies for groups to use in commemorating an inclusive past. I have noted a few of these in the previous chapters related to the African American presence on the landscape, and now I want to expand on these ideas by providing a broader context for understanding the meaning of commemoration. The illustrations that follow demonstrate ways that underrepresented groups have taken steps to become part of the public memory of a particular event or a specific site. While there are undoubtedly additional schemes, I hope that those presented here will provide some ideas for groups trying to create a more representative approach to remembering and commemorating the past.

Refuse to Be Subsumed by the Dominant Ideology: Labor versus Capital at Lawrence, Massachusetts

The story of Lawrence, Massachusetts, furnishes a good lesson in how a minority group (in this case labor) refuses to be subsumed by a more powerful group (industrial capitalism). The official memory of the city of Lawrence does not encompass too many of the industrial themes expressed by the National Park Service at Lowell. In the midst of Lawrence's decaying industrial core, there is a museum with two floors of exhibit space devoted almost entirely to labor issues, including the story of the Bread and Roses Strike of 1912. The Bread and Roses Strike was the impetus for closing most of the Northeast's mills until slightly better wages and conditions could be obtained by labor. The exhibit does not place industry on a pedestal; rather, it provides a memory of labor strife. Lawrence, like many other northeastern industrial cities, suffered as textile mills fled the region during the 1920s to the South because of cheaper, unorganized labor. These former textile industrial centers lost significant capital. It was not until the 1970s that some northern industrial cities retooled and revitalized. Despite its claim to a well-known strike against capital, Lawrence remains one of the poorest cities in Massachusetts, as it still suffers from the loss of its major economic base.

The official memory can be challenged as competing groups celebrate contrasting values. Whether the challenge to the official memory succeeds depends on the political strength and the perseverance of the subordinated group. While the official history of the United States has a long tradition of emphasizing and glorifying industry and capitalism, Lawrence is an example of a place that remembers the struggle of labor.

Use an Interdisciplinary Approach to Build a Case for Inclusiveness: Labor versus Capital at Harpers Ferry, West Virginia

Finding a balance between labor and capital has also been difficult at Harpers Ferry National Historical Park, although an interdisciplinary approach to studying the past has allowed for a more comprehensive story to be told. The park celebrates many themes, including industry, transportation, John Brown, the Civil War, the U.S. Armory, and Storer College.

As visitors enter the park, they can go to specific exhibits that highlight particular fragments of Harpers Ferry history; but the topics are not necessarily interrelated.

For instance, one exhibit at Harpers Ferry presents the development of industrial technology, with the implementation of machinery and "time-saving devices" that revolutionized the manufacturing of weapons. The use of waterpower is presented as an important development in the progress of industry, and products are displayed and interpreted as material advancements resulting from the new industry developments. People are not mentioned, and the impact of the implementation of the division of labor on social and work life is ignored. The stories that strengthen the ideals of industry and capitalism are based on selective data; the written record and the histories of the working class are neglected.

Part of a new exhibit, "Harpers Ferry: A Place in Time," provides an account of the living conditions among boarders who lived and worked in Harpers Ferry. The exhibit uses materials found in a recent archaeological excavation of a boardinghouse, and the artifacts help supply scenarios of everyday life that could not be extracted from the historical record. For instance, more than 1,000 medicine bottles discovered in a privy indicates a reliance on self-medication to cope with poor working conditions during an era when capitalists were not required to be concerned about the health of their workers. Evidence of high concentration of parasites is another example of how poor living conditions influenced workers' health. The predominance of calves heads and the finding of few fruit and vegetable remains in the excavated privy matter give evidence of the generally poor diet.

The new exhibit on boardinghouse life provides a glimpse into the everyday life of working-class people during the Victorian era. The story is separate from the thematic presentations of "great men" and technological innovation found elsewhere in the park. Inroads are made into traditional interpretations when new information and additional disciplines are used to create a more inclusive history of a place.

Accept Minority Views as Equal: Tradition versus Scientific Methods at Sand Creek, Kiowa County, Southeastern Colorado

The story of the Sand Creek massacre provides an excellent example of how minority views are accepted as equal when commemorating an event.

The story of the Sand Creek massacre began on the eve of the American Civil War. Tensions between Europeans and Americans Indians in the Colorado Territory mounted when gold was found in 1858 and Europeans wanted to prospect on unclaimed land. In November 1864, approximately 500 Cheyenne and Arapaho lived along Sand Creek, outside Fort Lyon, under the protection of the U.S. Army. Without warning to Native Americans or soldiers stationed at the fort, Colonial John M. Chivington and approximately 700 soldiers of the Colorado First and Third Volunteers arrived at the fort unannounced and began an attack on the Cheyenne and Arapaho village (Scott 2003:55–65).

During the ensuing killing spree, U.S. soldiers gunned down women, children, and the elderly, and those who escaped and dug trenches to protect themselves were shelled by howitzers. One lieutenant wrote that "a great many started toward our lines with hands raised, as if begging for us to spare them," but the U.S. soldiers murdered them anyway (Cramer, quoted in Schultz 1990:135). In a letter, Captain Silas Soule wrote his account of the attack: "It was hard to see little children on their knees have their brains beat out by men professing to be civilized" (quoted in Fong 2000:5A). Between 150 and 200 Cheyenne and Arapaho were murdered in the incident, and the militia mutilated the dead, taking scalps and body parts as trophies to be displayed in Denver. Several of the Cheyenne corpses were beheaded. Their bones were defleshed and crated for shipment to the East or the new Army Medical Museum in Washington, D.C. (Schultz 1990:145; Scott 2003; Thomas 2000:53).

More than a hundred years later, on October 6, 1998, President Bill Clinton signed the Sand Creek Massacre National Historic Site Study Act as Public Law 105–243 (Scott 2003). The exact location of the massacre was not known, so the National Park Service's chief archaeologist, Douglas Scott, began an archaeological survey on five plots of land. The areas determined for the survey were based on historical and oral accounts, including those from American Indians and descendants of the soldiers. Archaeologists found what they believe to be the location of the massacre, discovering such artifacts as howitzer shrapnel, musket balls, spoons, knives, a coffee pot, iron arrowheads, hide scrapers, tinkler bells (from clothing), and other camp debris. It was the only significant deposit found in the three-and-a-half-mile length of the creek surveyed, and these items were not found at any other place in the study area. Finding the howitzer shrapnel is key since Sand Creek is the only recorded location in that region where the U.S. Army used howitzers. The site, however, is about seven-tenths of a mile north of the massacre site as known in Southern Cheyenne and Southern Arapaho traditions (Frazier 1999; Greto 1999; Scott 2003).

Archaeologists surveyed the area traditionally believed to be the massacre site but found no significant artifacts related to the massacre or campsite remains. While the tribes accept that the larger study area contains the massacre site, they do not agree with the archaeologically identified village site, north of the traditionally known massacre site, because it does not fit their oral tradition. A powerful Cheyenne Arrow Keeper blessed the traditional site, and the Cheyenne feel that it would be disrespectful to acknowledge that he blessed the wrong site (Scott 2003). Since the Cheyenne will not disagree with their oral history, the archaeologists and the Cheyenne have agreed to disagree on the location of the massacre, and they agreed that the entire study area should be commemorated. On November 7, 2000, President Clinton signed the bill that created Sand Creek Massacre National Historic Site, encompassing both the traditional and the archaeological sites within its boundaries. At a powwow celebration, Senator Ben Nighthorse Campbell, who sits on the Northern Cheyenne Council of Chiefs, discussed the Sand Creek massacre in the context of other tragedies, such as My Lai in Vietnam, the Nazi Holocaust, and the war in Bosnia (Hughes 2000).

The Sand Creek Massacre National Historical Site is about the clash of two cultures and the control over memory of the past. Often one group's story is told while the other's is excluded or subordinated, but the interpretation at Sand Creek is unique since both groups decided to agree to disagree and the Sand Creek National Historic Site boundary includes both the traditional site and the archaeologically identified massacre site. It is a compromise that allows both versions to be legitimated.

Make a Moral Lesson Out of a National Disgrace: Manzanar and Japanese Internment (Manzanar, Eastern Sierra, near the Town of Lone Pine, California)

Since the 1960s, the stories of minority groups have increasingly taken their place in our national story. Many of these minority histories are about struggle, racism, and tragedy. One way to commemorate these stories and make them part of the national memory is to create a moral lesson from these misfortunes. Many Americans continue to struggle with the commemoration of minority histories, while minority groups see their commemoration as vital since it allows them to claim a part of the public memory.

In the case of Manzanar National Historic Site, Japanese Americans continue to fight to make the official memory recognize the atrocities committed against them by the U.S. government. For decades prior to the formal entrance of the United States into World War II, anti-Asian sentiment had intensified in the United States. From the post–Civil War era on, Congress passed many legislative acts that limited the immigration of Asians into the United States, including the Immigration Act of 1924, which barred immigration from Japan into America (Conrat and Conrat 1972; Daniels 1971; Dubel 2001).

During World War II, the federal government forced Japanese Americans living on the West Coast into concentration camps. They were presumed to be a threat simply because of their ethnicity. At the height of its use, one camp at Manzanar had thirty-six blocks of wooden barracks for living quarters. With a population that peaked at about 10,000 people, it was the largest population center between Reno and Los Angeles. After the war, the complex was abandoned, and it has all but disappeared into the desert since the U.S. Army Corps of Engineers bulldozed the camp in 1946. Only two of the eight sentry posts and the wood-frame auditorium still stand (Booth 1997:D1). One journalist wrote, "The camp was dismantled and the remains sank back into the sagebrush. We had won the war, after all, and history is written by the winners. In this case, we decided to let Manzanar fade from memory, as if it didn't really happen" (Jones 1996:B2).

On March 3, 1992, President George H. W. Bush signed the enabling legislation that established Manzanar National Historic Park (Unrau 1996). At the same time that Japanese Americans insist on making the events at Manzanar part of the national collective memory, other groups are fighting to suppress the memory and commemoration of this site. Some groups argue that since the Japanese were our enemy during the war, the federal government was justified in the surveillance and internment of Japanese Americans. In 1996, the National Park Service released a plan to interpret the site, and since then it has received many anonymous threats (Forstenzer 1996:A20). Another controversy centers on the California Historical Landmark plaque that refers to Manzanar as a "concentration camp" (Forstenzer 1996:A20). It has been both defaced and defiled by camp opponents, and one man, claiming to be a World War II veteran, remarked that he had driven more than 200 miles for the sole purpose of urinating on it (Forstenzer 1996:A20; see also Dubel 2001).

There are others who believe that commemorating Manzanar is a way to remind future generations that in times of crisis the Constitution can be dangerously fragile (Rogers 1997). Bill Michael, director of the Eastern California Museum, which sponsors an exhibit on Manzanar, explains, "History is not just the things we like. Very seldom do the darker parts of history, and there were several at Manzanar, get commemorated. We can't learn from history if we don't acknowledge it" (quoted in Ross 1991:57; see also Dubel 2001). A former superintendent at Manzanar, Ross Hopkins, remarked that many citizens think there is a hidden agenda behind the interpretation of the site. "It's obvious that many of them feel that if we tell the story of Manzanaar as it relates to the war relocation camp with negative connotations that represents 'American-bashing'" (quoted in Forstenzer 1996:A20).

Recently, Minadoka, another internment camp in Idaho, became the 385th national park. These parks are taking an issue that is considered a national disgrace and interpreting the missteps of past government policies. The story of Manzanar is painful to interpret in a public forum, and some people continue to deny that the internment of Japanese citizens even happened. The creation of Manzanar National Historic Site has allowed the story of past injustices to become part of the national memory and has provided an opportunity to learn from past mistakes.

Persistence in Lobbying: Making the Women's Suffrage Movement Part of the Official Memory at the U.S. Capitol in Washington, D.C.

Women have fought long and hard to have the women's suffrage monument part of the national public memory. Suffrage groups tried to get a statue that represented three influential women of the movement—Elizabeth Cady Stanton, Susan B. Anthony, and Lucretia Mott—displayed in the U.S. Capitol building, along with the other statues of great people—all men. The statue, known as the Group Portrait Monument and the Suffrage Monument, commemorates the passing on August 26, 1920, of the Nineteenth Amendment, which enfranchised women. The statue was donated to the U.S. government in 1921 and displayed briefly in the Capitol rotunda, but the Capitol architect immediately removed it to a basement closet and later to the crypt. In 1928, 1932, and 1950, women's groups unsuccessfully lobbied Congress to have the statue returned to a prominent place (Workman 2001).

In 1995, the seventy-fifth anniversary of the ratification of the Nineteenth Amendment, many women's groups renewed their efforts to relocate the monument to a more prominent place, although this movement met strong opposition. For instance, Representative Sue Myrick (R-N.C.) explained, "I only deep-sixed moving it with public money. I don't think it's very attractive either" (Brooke 1996:A18). George Will, columnist for the *Washington Post,* also commented on the looks of the women portrayed in the statue, saying, "The answer to Freud's famous question—'What does a woman want?'—is an unattractive statue in the Capitol Rotunda" (Will 1997:C7). In response to these critics, Congresswoman Carolyn Maloney (D-N.Y.) replied,

> Dismissing the statue's importance by calling it "unattractive" belittles the accomplishments of the women who are depicted. Mr. Lincoln is not in the Rotunda because of his beauty. He is there because of his contributions to the nation. Leading the battle to enfranchise half the population of the United States is no minor feat. It is one of the most significant accomplishments in our nation's history. (Quoted in Workman 2001:54)

On July 17, 1995, the Senate unanimously voted to raise the statue back into the Capitol rotunda, although Representative Myrick temporarily stalled the resolution because she objected to using federal funds ($75,000) to relocate it (Love 1995:3). The Women's Suffrage Statue Campaign mobilized seventy-eight women's organizations to raise the money, and on May 12, 1997, the statue was lifted into the rotunda. It was rededicated in a ceremony on June 26, 1997 (Workman 2001).

Today, the Suffrage Monument sits in the Capitol rotunda with a temporary-looking plaque that fails to recognize the accomplishment of Stanton, Anthony, and Mott. The original legislation allowed for the relocation of the monument for only one year and also stated that funds to raise and lower the statue had to be contributed by private groups. So far, no groups have begun to raise money to lower the statue.

Of the 2,200 National Historic Landmarks across the country, only 5 percent are dedicated to women (Brooke 1996:A18). Inside the Capitol, there are approximately 200 statues, of which eleven include women. "The

Rotunda is filled with male statues and women are virtually invisible—the implicit message is that women don't count" (Workman 2001:62). The chronicle of the Suffrage Monument is about many years of lobbying to get the suffrage movement commemorated and make it a part of the official history and public memory. Lobbying persistence in the wake of the anniversary of the Nineteenth Amendment gave white women and the suffrage cause a presence in the rotunda and a place in the official history. Legislation allows the statue to be displayed in the rotunda for only one year, and some activists may see this action as an impermanent solution, but Congress would quite likely face many irate voices, both male and female, if they allowed it to be moved to an inaccessible place again.

Compromise with Minority Groups: The Franklin Delano Roosevelt Memorial, West Potomac Park, Washington, D.C.

While the United States continues to create monuments to great men, it becomes increasingly difficult to justify that historical meaning is owned by one group. The Americans with Disabilities Act of 1990 gave to disabled people what the Civil Rights Act made possible for minority groups: a vehicle to claim a piece of the public memory.

The FDR Memorial was dedicated in West Potomac Park in Washington, D.C., fifty-two years after his death. The debate over the FDR Memorial arose soon after the monument, which shows FDR sitting in a wheelchair with a cape over his shoulders and draping to the floor, opened to the public showing. Only small roller wheels at the rear of the chair are visible; otherwise, there is little evidence that Roosevelt used a wheelchair.

Since the unveiling, people have debated whether Roosevelt should be shown as the commander in chief who led the United States through the Great Depression and World War II, disguising his disability, or whether he be portrayed as a great man who accomplished many feats while in a wheelchair. Some groups argue that to show him in a wheelchair would be inaccurate because many Americans never saw him as disabled (Glastris 1997:1). Since the passing of the Americans with Disabilities Act, groups such as the National Organization on Disability have become more vocal and have argued that a memorial to Roosevelt should serve contemporary values and show him in a wheelchair (N. Tucker 2001:C1, C8).

Many of Roosevelt's grandchildren remarked that they approve of a statue of Roosevelt in a wheelchair. However, David Roosevelt, who takes the role as family spokesperson for Roosevelt's descendants, remarked, "I believe in the integrity of history, and I believe that this memorial should depict him as he was then. I don't believe his disability should become a focal point of what the historical reference is here" (Bierbauer 1997:3). The National Park Service placed a cane-bottom wheelchair, one that Roosevelt would have used, in the visitor's center with a brief explanation of the president's disability from polio.

Because of the vocal opposition by the National Organization on Disability to the portrayal of Roosevelt cloaked in a chair, on July 24, 1997, the 105th Congress reached a joint resolution to add a new statue to the memorial with Roosevelt seated in a wheelchair. The new statue, the resolution states, provides "recognition of the fact that President Roosevelt's leadership in the struggle by the United States for peace, well-being, and human dignity was provided while the President used a wheelchair (Public Law 1997).

The new statue was unveiled in January 2001, and Alan Reich, president of the National Organization on Disability, exclaimed, "The unveiling is a major national monument, the removal of a shroud of shame that cloaks disability" (quoted in N. Tucker 2001:C1). It is clear that persistent lobbying, being vocal, and getting the attention of Congress allowed this minority group to have their story told at a nationally significant place. Having a representation of Roosevelt in a wheelchair at this national monument allows the public to become more aware of the struggles, hurdles, and accomplishments of disabled Americans. It is clear that the memorial serves not only as a reminder of the past but also current social needs.

Understand the Power of Dissenting Groups: Patriotism and the Enola Gay Exhibit at the Smithsonian Institution, Washington, D.C.

While groups may strive to change the official meanings of the past, they do not always succeed, as the notions of patriotism and commemoration can supersede any ideas for a pluralistic past. The Enola Gay exhibit at the Smithsonian Institution is an excellent example of how the government suppressed an alternative view on the grounds that it was not patriotic. The original plans for the exhibit ran counter to the collective memory of powerful lobby groups, and it showed the strain of our country's political culture (*Journal of American History* 1995). The original designers of the exhibit underestimated the power of dissenting lobbying groups to control the intellectual contents of a national exhibit.

In January 1994, the Smithsonian made public a draft of their Enola Gay exhibit. The exhibit plans showed the effects of the atomic bomb, displaying pictures of the victims at "ground zero," and questioned the use of the bomb (Cornell 1994). Lobbying groups such as the Veterans of Foreign Wars, the American Legion, and the Air Force Association felt that the Smithsonian bowed to "political correctness" and felt the exhibit was pro-Japanese. They believed that the use of the atomic bomb was necessary to save millions of American lives and that the proposed Smithsonian exhibit would tarnish all World War II American servicemen (Harwit 1996:245). It is interesting to note that the Air Force Association is not a veteran's group like the American Legion or the Veterans of Foreign Wars but rather a lobbyist group backed by manufacturers of aviation technology utilized by U.S. military units. They are a voice for defense contractors (M. Wallace 1998:328).

These lobbying groups successfully captured the attention of politicians, and the Senate Committee on Rules and Administration conducted a Capitol Hill hearing to investigate the Smithsonian's management of the Enola Gay exhibit. Representative Tom Lewis of Florida threatened to cut federal funding for the Smithsonian (Lifton and Mitchell 1995:285). Congressman Sam Johnson stated that the Smithsonian was "disregarding history in order to promote their own agenda." He also noted that the United States should teach our children what was "good about America . . . and reflect the values on which this great country is based" (S. Johnson 1995). Political pressure from Congress, the president, vice president, the Senate majority leader, the speaker of the House, the chief justice of the Supreme Court, and the Smithsonian Board of Regents reduced the exhibit to a story about the crew of the Enola Gay and the necessity of the dropping the bomb in order to save numerous lives (Lifton and Mitchell 1995:296; Nobile 1995:xiii). In the final exhibit, the Smithsonian omitted the story of destruction and death associated with the event. The exhibit consisted of the plane's front fuselage and a videotape of crew members reminiscing about the flight. The text was short and uninformative, and it did not place the plane within a larger and more comprehensive historical context. The exhibit mentioned the atomic bomb only when mentioning the technology associated with the weapon.

As inferred by Congressman Johnson's statement, American history produces obedient, patriotic citizens. "The argument," notes Michael Frisch (1989:1253), "has traveled a long way from its humanistic origins, arriving at a point where education and indoctrination—cultural and political—seem almost indistinguishable." The Organization of American Historians issued a statement that criticized the museum for changing the exhibit because of congressional pressure (Nobile 1995:xxxvii–xxxviii). Other scholars called the change a product of "New McCarthyism (Dower 1998:378). Edward Linenthal, an adviser to the exhibit, warned that these changes were "a very dangerous precedent for the way we do public history" and that "powerful lobby groups who apparently fancy themselves historians and curators as well as public servants can . . . change the nature of how we present history" (quoted in Lifton and Mitchell 1995:291).

The Enola Gay exhibit heightens our awareness of how histories are remembered, forgotten, and created. The exhibit makes explicit the role of public history and the function that interest groups play in creating collective memories in a very contentious arena. Telling the story of the past has many views, and compromise is often not a middle ground between groups. In the case of the Enola Gay controversy, it became a matter of political power, and the curators underestimated the power of Congress to control public history. Academic freedom may have its limits if opposing lobbying groups can muster the backing of politicians.

Ignore Minority Viewpoints: The Don Juan de Onate Statue in Alcalde, New Mexico

In Alcalde, New Mexico, sits a larger-than-life bronze statue of Don Juan de Onate, erected in 1991, outside the Onate Visitors Center (Loewen 1999:119). Statues such as this one that honor the Spanish conquistadors are common throughout the American Southwest. In 1998, the New Mexico government promoted the Cuarto Centenario, the 400th anniversary of the settling of New Mexico by the Spanish. The state sponsored special events throughout the year to heighten awareness of Hispanic influence within the state (Apodaca 1998:1).

Onate is considered the first conquistador of New Mexico. He received permission from the Spanish crown to conquer and settle the land north of New Spain, and in 1598 he set out from New Spain on his mission with wagons of supplies, livestock, and 200 colonists (Jimenez 1998:118; Simmons 1991:58–96). When the expedition reached San Juan Pueblo, he chose it to be the capital of his new colony. He left his nephew Juan de Zaldivar in charge of the town and went off to conquer the rest of the pueblos and search for minerals (Simmons 1991:125). At the Acoma Pueblo, Onate assembled the elders and had them swear loyalty to the Spanish. He moved on, but the Acoma, growing tired of submission, revolted and killed Onate's nephew and ten of his men. Onate declared "war by blood and fire" and sent seventy-two soldiers to conquer the Acoma (Loewen 1999:120). They attacked the pueblo of about 500 Acoma. Hundreds died, and the remainder surrendered. Onate placed the Acoma on trial, making himself judge. Onate found the Acoma guilty and sentenced all men over age twenty-five (twenty-four individuals) to have one foot amputated and condemned them to twenty years of slavery. The amputations were done on the spot, and the Spanish forced the Acoma to San Juan, where they were distributed as slaves. Two Moquis Indians captured in the raid had their right hands amputated but were set free to take home news of their punishment for revolting against the Spanish. All men twelve to twenty-five years of age and all women over twelve were condemned to twenty years of slavery. Onate gave children under twelve to priests for a Christian upbringing, and sixty girls were later sent to Mexico City and never saw their relatives again (Simmons 1991:145).

By 1601, many of the colonists had abandoned Onate's leadership, and in 1606, King Philip III ordered Onate to return to Mexico City, where he was detained until his crimes could be investigated. A court found Onate guilty of many crimes against the Acoma and Spanish settlers (Simmons 1991:178–93).

Onate's achievements are celebrated by many Hispanics, and Marc Simmon, Onate's biographer, believes that "Onate is nothing less than New Mexico's George Washington" (quoted in Griego 1998:14A). Onate is credited as the founder of the livestock and mining industries, and he created the territory's first major roads. He also introduced peach, apple, and plum trees to the region (Baldauf 1998:3; Brooke 1998:10A).

Nevertheless, many American Indians remember Onate as a criminal, and the 400th anniversary of the Spanish settlement of New Mexico brought mixed emotions. The right foot of the Onate statue in Alcalde was removed in protest. This action served as a reminder of the horrors Onate perpetrated four centuries earlier (Griego 1998:14). After the amputation of the foot from the statue, a message was sent to the museum, stating, "We took the liberty of removing Onate's right foot on behalf of our brothers and sister[s] of Acoma Pueblo. We see no glory in celebrating

Onate's fourth centennial and we do not want our faces rubbed in it" (quoted in Brooke 1998:10). Lee Francis, interim director of the Native American Studies Department at the University of New Mexico at Albuquerque, said that the celebration of Onate is like "asking the Jewish people to celebrate Hitler" (quoted in Baldauf 1998:3).

Some Hispanics believe it is time to move on. "I don't approve of it, but it happened 400 years ago," explained Orlando Romero of the Frey Angelico Chavez Historical Library (quoted in Baldauf 1998:3). Others see the attack on the Onate statue as an attack on all Hispanics. When a public meeting was held in Albuquerque about the fate of a proposed Onate statue in that city, resident Michael Sanchez remarked, "Not to build this memorial is to deny Hispanics their place in history. . . . How dare you, an Anglo, cut back funding for a statue for Hispanics" (quoted in Potts 2000:A1). Another citizen exclaimed, "These Indians want their sovereignty but they want to tell us what to do. . . . Unless you live here and pay taxes . . . don't come here and tell us what to do, because I do not intend to come to Acoma and tell them how to run their business" (quoted in Potts 2000:A1).

The debate over how to present the story of Onate to the public is not only about the past but also about how a group chooses to remember a past. It is about how neighbors view and treat each other and how they view themselves (Gonzales and Rodriguez 1999:G-02). Nothing has changed at the Onate Visitors Center. The foot was recast and replaced despite a suggestion that it remain off to remind visitors of the American Indian version of the story. Only on close inspection can an individual see the unevenly weathered seam. The statue retains its simple text—"Juan de Onate established New Mexico's first colony here in 1598." A pamphlet available at the Visitors Center does not mention the atrocities performed against the Pueblo Indians (Loewen 1999:121). People who go to the Visitors Center come away with the story of the "great conquistador," and the American Indian voice is not heard.

Legitimation of American Heritage

The development of a sense of heritage took several centuries to unfold in America. Citizens of the early American republic resisted the development of an American collective memory and frowned on the commemoration of a sacred past. Adherence to republican values in the early nineteenth century produced tensions between democracy and tradition. John Quincy

Adams noted, "Democracy has no monuments. It strikes no medals. It bears the head of no man on a coin" (quoted in Everett 1879:38). In the antebellum era, Americans saw the United States as a country with a future rather than a glorious past worth commemorating, and they believed in the value of succeeding without patronage or family influence. Ralph Waldo Emerson wrote that Americans were "emancipated from history, happily bereft of ancestry, untouched and undefiled by the usual inheritances of family and race" (quoted in Lowenthal 1997:55).

This notion of freedom from the past did not last for long, as large-scale commemorative activities began slowly after the middle of the nineteenth century. Women became the primary custodians of American heritage and proclaimed their patriotism for America's past. The Mount Vernon's Ladies Association (1856) and the Ladies' Hermitage Association (1889) were important early preservation groups involved in the American historic preservation movement. Those without specific ancestral roots could join other heritage groups, such as the Patriotic League of the Revolution (formed in 1894). They wanted to "create and promote interest in all matters pertaining to American history, to collect and preserve relics of the period of the American Revolution, and to foster patriotism" (from Kammen 1991:267). In the 1890s, Congress authorized the creation of Civil War and Revolutionary War battlefields as national military parks. By 1906, protection became available for prehistoric ruins with the establishment of the Antiquities Act. These events are an indication of America's increasing need to create a useable heritage, a need that was both nostalgic and political.

Heritage creates a usable past, and it generates a precedent that serves present needs. More recently, the political uses of heritage have been made very explicit within Western culture. We exist in a society that has a seemingly unquenchable craving for nostalgia and heritage. Kammen (1997:214–19) calls the creation of Americans' awareness for historic preservation since the 1950s the "heritage phenomenon." And since the 1960s, the celebration of heritage has become a more widespread phenomenon in the United States, although modifying the official meaning of any site sometimes comes with struggle and resistance. Whenever citizens and scholars try to present new and different interpretations that challenge the consensus history, they are often criticized by those who demand the status quo. The media often portray revisionist histories as unpatriotic, antigovernment, and anti-American. They are seen as left-wing radicals who are overly concerned with "political correctness," ignoring the real point of revisionist history: understanding a multivocal past. Mark Leff (1995:843) remarks,

> This epithet, "revisionist," . . . may be the key to understanding the current crisis of history. "Revisionist" meant the displacement of the more happy-faced, elite oriented view of American progress and destiny to which most Americans, particularly those raised on "consensus history" textbooks, had became accustomed. At the same time, the use of "revisionist" as a term of abuse suggests a rejection of the very notion of historical reinterpretation, under the assumption that the displaced version of history had been objective and factual, while revisions were subjective and faddish.

Subordinated groups may subscribe to the dominant interpretation, ignore the dominant view, or fight for representation in the public memory. Transforming the public memory of any sacred place does not come without persistence, hard work, and compromise. While there are often strong movements to eliminate subordinated memories from our national collective memory, some minority groups battle to have their histories remembered. The debate over the control of public history occurs at some of the most visible places on the landscape, and they are the places for negotiating meanings of the past (see, e.g., Linenthal 1993; Linenthal and Engelhardt 1996; Lowenthal 1996). The meaning of sacred sites on the American landscape is continually being negotiated and reconstructed.

REFERENCES

Aaron, Daniel
1973 *The Unwritten War: American Writers and the Civil War.* University of Wisconsin Press, Madison.

Abroe, Mary Munsell
1998 Observing the Civil War Centennial: Rhetoric, Reality, and the Bounds of Selective Memory. Understanding the Past. *CRM* 21(11):22–25.

Afro-American [newspaper, Baltimore, Maryland]
1931a Telegram to Henry T. McDonald. McDonald Collection, Box 4, Folder 3, October 6.
1931b Yankee Woman Steals Rebel Girls's Show: Confederate Daughters Gape as She Lauds John Brown. October 17, 1931. Henry T. McDonald Papers, Harpers Ferry National Historical Park, Harpers Ferry, West Virginia.
1932a No title. May 28, HAFE microfilm, reel 123, flash 9.
1932b No title. June 11, HAFE microfilm, reel 123, flash 9.

Agricultural Census (on file, Prince William Regional Library, Manassas, Virginia)
1850
1860
1870

Allan, Theodore W.
1994 *The Invention of the White Race,* vol. 1. Verso Press, London.

American Anti-Slavery Society
1969 *The Anti-Slavery History of the John Brown Year.* Reprint of 1861 edition. American Anti-Slavery Society, Beckman St., New York.

Anderson, Benedict
1991 *Imagined Communities: Reflections on the Origins and Spread of Nationalism.* Verso Press, London.

Anderson, Osborne
1972 *A Voice from Harpers Ferry. The Black Heritage Library Collection.* Reprint of 1861 edition. Books for Libraries Press, Freeport, New York.

Andrews, Matthew Page
N.d. *Heyward Shepherd: Victim of Violence.* Heyward Shepherd Memorial Foundation, Harpers Ferry, West Virginia.

Anonymous
1927 Letter, Anonymous to Mr. Moore, February 28. On file, Manassas National Battlefield Park, Manassas, Virginia.
1981 Letter, Heyward Shepherd Folder, Harpers Ferry National Historical Park, Harpers Ferry, West Virginia.
1998 Personal communication with Paul Shackel, September 20.

Anthony, Kate J.
1891 *Storer College, Harpers Ferry, W.Va: Brief Historical Sketch.* Morning Star Publishing House, Boston.

Apodaca, R.
1998 Searching for Roots. *Los Angeles Times,* November 21, C1.

Ashton, Betty Parker
1961 History Is Repeated in Manassas Fields. *Richmond Times-Dispatch,* July 22, 1–2.

Associated Press
1961 Civil War Hall of Fame Museum Near Realization. *Alexandria Gazette,* July 24. Newspaper clipping. On file, Manassas National Battlefield Park Archives, Manassas, Virginia.

Atkins, Edward (ed.)
1897 *The Monument to Robert Gould Shaw: Its Inception, Completion and Unveiling 1865–1897.* Houghton Mifflin, Boston.

Atlanta Constitution
1911 No title. May 18.

Ayers, Edward L.
1992 *The Promise of the New South: Life after Reconstruction.* Oxford University Press, New York.

Bailes, Marc
1995 NAACP Seeks Response from Park Service, Calls Monument Offensive. *The Journal,* October 1, A1–A2.

Bailey, Rebecca
1995 Harpers Ferry Sign Angers Some. *The Civil War News,* August, 22–23.

Baldauf, S.
1998 New Mexico's Year of Fiestas Dampened by a Diverse Past. *Christian Science Monitor,* May 27, 3.

Barber, Max
1906 The Niagara Movement at Harpers Ferry. *The Voice of the Negro*, October, 402–11.

Barry, Joseph
1979 *The Strange Story of Harpers Ferry with Legends of the Surrounding Country.* Reprint of 1903 edition. Shepherdstown Register, Inc., Shepherdstown, West Virginia.

Benson, Richard, and Lincoln Kirstein
1973 *Lay This Laurel: An Album on the Saint-Gaudens Memorial on Boston Commons Honoring Black and White Men Together Who Served the Union Cause with Robert Gould Shaw and Died with Him July 18, 1863.* Eakins Press, New York.

Berlin, Ira
1982 *Freedom. A Documentary History of Emancipation 1861–1867. Series II: The Black Experience.* Cambridge University Press, Cambridge, Massachusetts.

Bethel, Elizabeth R.
1997 *The Roots of African-American Identity: Memory and History in Free Antebellum Communities.* St. Martin's Press, New York.

Bierbauer, Charles
1997 FDR: A New Deal and Perhaps, Some New Wheels. *AllPolitics, CNN Time,* May 2, at allpolitics.com/1997/05/02/bierbauer (accessed June 5, 1999).

Blake, C. N.
1999 The Useable Past, the Comfortable Past, and the Civic Past: Memory in Contemporary America. *Cultural Anthropology* 14(3):423–35.

Blake, Walter H.
1913 *Hand Grips: The Story of the Great Gettysburg Reunion, July 1913.* G. E. Smith, Vineland, New Jersey.

Blakey, Michael L.
1987 Skull Doctors: Intrinsic Social and Political Bias in the History of American Physical Anthropology; with Special Reference to the Work of Alec Hrdlicka. *Critique of Anthropology* 7(2):7–35.

Blatt, Martin H., Thomas J. Brown, and Donald Tacovone
2001 *Hope and Glory: Essays on the Legacy of the 54th Massachusetts Regiment.* University of Massachusetts Press, Amherst.

Bledsoe, Albert Taylor
1866 *Is Davis a Traitor: Or Was Secession a Constitutional Right Previous to the War of 1861?* Innes & Co., Baltimore.

Blight, David W.
1989a "For Something beyond the Battlefield": Frederick Douglass and

the Struggle for the Memory of the Civil War. *Journal of American History* 75(4):1156–78.

1989b *Frederick Douglass' Civil War: Keeping Faith in Jubilee.* Louisiana State University Press, Baton Rouge.

1997a Changing Memories of the War, 1863–1897. Paper presented at Hope and Glory: Centennial Celebration of the Augustus Saint-Gaudens Monument to Robert Gould Shaw and the Fifty-Fourth Massachusetts Regiment. Boston, May 29.

1997b Quarrel Forgotten or a Revolution Remembered? Reunion and Race in the Memory of the Civil War, 1875–1913. In *Union and Emancipation: Essays on Politics and Race in the Civil War Era,* edited by David W. Blight and Brooks D. Simpson, 151–79. Kent State University Press, Kent, Ohio.

2001 *Race and Reunion: The Civil War in American Memory.* The Belknap Press of Harvard University Press, Cambridge, Massachusetts.

Boas, Franz

1911 *The Mind of Primitive Man.* Macmillan, New York.

1912 *Changes in Bodily Form of Descendants of Immigrants.* Columbia University Press, New York.

Bodnar, John

1992 *Remaking America: Public Memory, Commemoration, and Patriotism in the Twentieth Century.* Princeton University Press, Princeton, New Jersey.

Boime, Albert

1990 *The Art of Exclusion: Representing Blacks in the Nineteenth Century.* Smithsonian Institution Press, Washington, D.C.

Bonnett, Alastair

1998 Who Was White? The Disappearance of Non-European White Identities and the Formation of European Racial Whiteness. *Ethnic and Racial Studies* 21(6):1029–55.

Booth, W.

1997 A Lonely Patch of History: Japanese Americans Were Forced to Live Here. They Don't Want to Be Forgotten. *Washington Post,* April 15, D1.

Branch, Taylor

1988 *Parting the Waters: America in the King Years.* Simon & Schuster, New York.

Breene, Timothy H.

1989 *Imagining the Past: East Hampton Histories.* Addison-Wesley, Reading, Massachusetts.

Breene, Timothy H., and Stephen Innes

1980 *"Myne Owne Ground": Race and Freedom on Virginia's Eastern Shore, 1640–1676.* Oxford University Press, New York.

Brooke, James

1996 3 Suffragists (in Marble) to Move Up in the Capitol. *New York Times,* September 27, A18.

1998 Conquistador Statue Stirs Hispanic Pride and Indian Rage. *New York Times,* February 9, A10.

Burchard, Peter

1965 *One Gallant Rush: Robert Gould Shaw and His Brave Black Regiment.* St. Martin's Press, New York.

Caffin, Charles H.

1913 *American Masters of Sculpture: Being Brief Appreciations of Some American Sculptors and of Some Phase of Sculpture in America.* Doubleday, Page & Co., New York.

Campbell, Donald

1996 Notes. Meeting with Don Campbell, April 5.

Centennial Commemoration

1961 Centennial Commemoration: July 22–23, 1961; The First Battle of Manassas (Bull Run). Program. Manassas National Battlefield Park, Manassas, Virginia.

Chicago Tribune

1892 No title. August 28, 25.

1895a No title. April 1, 8.

1895b No title. August 5, 9.

1896 No title. May 31, 6.

Chronicle, The (Arlington, Virginia)

1936 Plans Complete for Battle Anniversary at Manassas: Event Recalls Death of Mrs. Judith Henry and Servant Girl, Occupants of Henry House, Center of Battle's Holocaust. July 10. Newspaper clipping. On file, Manassas National Battlefield Park Archives, Manassas, Virginia.

Cohodas, Nadine

1997 *The Band Played Dixie: Race and Liberal Conscience at Ole Miss.* Free Press, New York.

Coleman, Charles Washington

1891 Along the Lower James. *The Century* 41:333.

Confederate Veteran

1904 Monument to Faithful Slaves. 12(November):525.

1905 Monument to Faithful Slaves. 13(March):123–24.

1913 Gettysburg, Gettysburg. 21(September):377–86.

1920 The Houston Convention. 28(November):436.

1921a Sons of Confederate Veterans. 29(March):117.

1921b Confederate News and Notes. 29(June):237.

1930 The New President General, U.D.C. 36(January):4.

1931 Heyward Shepherd. 37(November):411–14.

1932 Heyward Shepherd Monument. 40(June):236.

Confederated Southern Memorial Association

1904 *History of the Confederated Memorial Associations of the South.* D. Graham Press, New Orleans.

Connelly, Thomas L.

1977 *The Marbleman: Robert E. Lee and His Image in American Society.* Louisiana State University Press, Baton Rouge.

Connelly, Thomas L., and Barbara L. Bellows

1982 *God and General Longstreet: The Lost Cause and the Southern Mind.* Louisiana State University Press, Baton Rouge.

Conrat, Maisie, and Richard Conrat

1972 *Executive Order 9066: The Internment of 110,000 Japanese Americans.* Anderson, Ritchie and Simon, Los Angeles.

Cooperative Agreement

1961 Cooperative Agreement between the Director, National Park Service and First Manassas Corporation, Incorporated, Relating to the Staging of a Re-Enactment of the First Battle of Manassas at Manassas National Battlefield Park. On file, Manassas National Battlefield Park, Manassas, Virginia, May.

Cornell, J. T.

1994 War Stories at Air and Space: At Smithsonian, History Grapples with Cultural Angst. *Air Force Magazine,* April 24, at www.afa.org (accessed January 4, 1999).

Coslovich, Marco

1994 *I Percorsi della Sopravvivenza: Storia e Memoria della Deportazione della "Adriatisches Kustenland."* Mursia, Milan, Italy.

Cox, Fletcher, Jr.

1961 50,000 See Bull Run "Fought." *Richmond News Leader,* July 22, 1–2.

Coyner, T. Peyton

1997 The Lost Cause. *Washington Post,* April, 29, A12.

Dabney, Robert

1867 *A Defense of Virginia (and through Her, of the South) in Recent and Pending Contests against the Sectional Party.* E. J. Hale & Son, New York.

Daniels, R.

1971 *Concentration Camps USA: Japanese-Americans and World War II.* Holt, Rinehart and Winston, New York.

Davis, Jefferson

1881 *The Rise and Fall of the Confederate Government.* 2 vols. D. Appleton and Company, New York.

Davis, Stephen

1982 Empty Eyes, Marble Hand: The Confederate Monument and the South. *Journal of Popular Culture* 16(3):2–21.

Daynes, Gary

1997 *Making Villains, Making Heroes: Joseph R. McCarthy, Martin Luther King, Jr. and the Politics of American Memory.* Garland Publishing, New York.

Deagan, Kathleen, and Darcie MacMahon

1995 *Fort Mose: Colonial America's Black Fortress of Freedom.* University Press of Florida/Florida Museum of Natural History, Gainesville.

Deutsch, Jack

1995 War of Words Erupts over Monument. *Charleston Daily Mail,* November 28, 1A, 9A.

Dogan, Frances B.

N.d. A Resolution. Bull Run Chapter of the United Daughters of the Confederacy. On file, Manassas National Battlefield Park, Manassas, Virginia (Acc. 261, 21425).

Douglass, Frederick

1881 *John Brown. An Address by Frederick Douglass at the Fourteenth Anniversary of Storer College, Harpers Ferry, West Virginia, May 30, 1881.* Morning Star Job Printing House, Dover, Hew Hampshire.

Dower, John W.

1998 How a Genuine Democracy Should Celebrate Its Past. In *Hiroshima's Shadow,* edited by Kai Bird and Lawrence Lifschultz, 377–80. The Pamphleteer's Press, Stony Creek, Connecticut.

Dryfhout, John H.

1982 *The Works of Augustus Saint-Gaudens.* University Press of New England, Hanover, New Hampshire.

Dubel, Janice

2001 Remembering a Japanese-American Concentration Camp at Manzanar National Historic Site. In *Myth, Memory and the Making of the American Landscape,* edited by Paul A. Shackel, 85–102. University Press of Florida, Gainesville.

Du Bois, W. E. B.

1932 No title. *Crisis* 41 (January):467.

1935 *Black Reconstruction in America: An Essay toward a History of the Part Which Black Folk Played in the Attempt to Reconstruct Democracy in America, 1860–1890.* Atheneum, New York.

1962 *John Brown.* [Orig. published 1909] International Publishers, New York.

1992 *Black Reconstruction in America 1860–1880: An Essay toward a History of the Part Which Black Folk Played in the Attempt to Reconstruct Democracy in America, 1860–1890.* [Orig. published 1935.] Atheneum, New York.

1998 Jefferson Davis as a Representative of Civilization. [Orig. published 1890.] In *Black on White: Black Writers on What It Means to Be White,* edited by David R. Roediger, 204–7. Schocken Books, New York.

Duncan, Russell (ed.)
1992 *Blue-Eyed Child of Fortune: The Civil War Letter of Colonel Robert Gould Shaw.* University of Georgia Press, Athens.

Dyer, Richard
1997 *White.* Routledge, New York.

Early, Jubal A.
1867 *A Memoir of the Last Year of the War for Independence of Confederate States of America.* Blelock and Co., New Orleans.

Eckhardt, C. F.
1995 We Don't Want 'Correct' Alamo. *San Antonio Express.* On file, Heyward Shepherd Folder, Harpers Ferry National Historical Park, Harpers Ferry, West Virginia.

Eisenhower, Dwight D.
1960 Letter, Dwight D. Eisenhower to Major General James C. Fry, First Manassas Corporation. On file, Manassas National Battlefield Park, Manassas, Virginia.

Emerson, Bettie A. C.
1911 *Historic Southern Monuments, Representing Memorials of the Heroic Dead of the Southern Confederacy.* Neale Publishing, New York.

Emerson, Edward W.
1907 *Life and Letters of Charles Russell Lowell, Captain Sixth United States Cavalry, Colonel 2nd Massachusetts Cavalry, Brigadier General United States Volunteers.* Houghton Mifflin, Boston.

Emilio, Luis F.
1969 [1894] *A Brave Black Regiment: History of the Fifty-Fourth Regiment of Massachusetts Volunteer Infantry, 1863–1865.* Arno Press and the New York Times, New York.

Epstein, C.
1999 The Production of "Official Memory" in East Germany: Old Communists and the Dilemmas of Memoir-Writing. *Central European History* 32(2):181–201.

Everett, Edward
1879 *Orations and Speeches on Various Occasions.* Little, Brown, Boston.

Ewing, E. W. R.
N.d. Letter, Dear Friend from E. W. R. Ewing. On file, Manassas National Battlefield Park, Manassas, Virginia.

1921 The Manassas Battlefield Confederate Park, Prince William County, Virginia. The South's Proposed Memorial to Valor and in the Interest of American History. 1415 Eye St. N.W. Washington, D.C. On file, Manassas National Battlefield Park, Manassas, Virginia.

1927 The Manassas Battlefield Confederate Park, On the Battlefield of Manassas (Bull Run): A Fitting Tribute, an Unsurpassed Confederate Symbol, an Endowed Educational Center, a National Asset. E. W. R. Ewing. Booklet. On file, Manassas National Battlefield Park, Manassas, Virginia (Acc. 52, 1911).

Fairbairn, Charlotte J.

1961 John Brown's Fort: Armory Engine and Guard House 1848–1961. Harpers Ferry, West Virginia. Manuscript, Harpers Ferry National Historical Park, Harpers Ferry, West Virginia.

Farmers Advocate

1902 No title. February 15, 3.

1920 No title. November 13, 2.

1923 No title. September 1, 2.

Fauquier Democrat

1936 No title. July 8.

Faust, Drew Gilpin

1988 *The Creation of Confederate Nationalism: Ideology and Identity in the Civil War South.* Louisiana State University Press, Baton Rouge.

1990 Altars of Sacrifice: Confederate Women and the Narratives of War. *Journal of American History* 76(4):1200–28.

Ferguson, Leland

1992 *Uncommon Ground: Archaeology and Early African America, 1650–1800.* Smithsonian Institution Press, Washington, D.C.

Fields, Barbara J.

1982 Ideology and Race in American History. In *Region, Race, and Reconstruction,* edited by J. Morgan Kousser and James M. McPherson, 143–77. Oxford University Press, New York.

1997 The Impact of African-American Soldiers on the Civil War. Paper presented at Hope and Glory: Centennial Celebration of the Augustus Saint-Gaudens Monument to Robert Gould Shaw and the Fifty-Fourth Massachusetts Regiment, Boston, May 29.

First Manassas

1960 First Manassas (a Prospectus), a Commemorative Reenactment of a Great Moment in History, a Ceremony Officially Opening the Civil War Centennial Years 1961–1965. On file, Manassas National Battlefield Park, Manassas, Virginia.

Flinn, John J.
1893 *Standard Guide to Chicago, Illustrated World's Fair Edition.* Standard Guide Company, Chicago.

Florescano, E.
1994 *Memory, Myth, and Time in Mexico: From the Aztecs to Independence.* Translated by Albert G. Bork. University of Texas Press, Austin.

Folliard, Edward T.
1936 40,000 Cheer Charging Troops in Restaging of Manassas Battle: Rebel Yells Rend Air as Muskets Rattle, Cannons Boom and History Is Turned Back to Defeat of Federals in 1861. *Washington Post,* July 22, 1, 14. Newspaper clipping. On file, Manassas National Battlefield Park Archives, Manassas, Virginia.

Foner, Eric
1988 *Reconstruction: America's Unfinished Revolution, 1863–1877.* Harper & Row, New York.

Foner, Philip S. (ed.)
1970 *W. E. B. Du Bois Speaks: Speeches and Addresses, 1890–1919.* Pathfinder, New York.

Fong, Tillie
2000 House OK's Sand Creek Designation: President Is Expected to Sign Bill Declaring Historic Site at Location of 1864 Indian Massacre. *Denver Rocky Mountain News,* October 24, 5A.

Foote, Kenneth E.
1997 *Shadowed Ground: America's Landscapes of Violence and Tragedy.* University of Texas Press, Austin.

Forstenzer, M.
1996 Bitter Feelings Still Run Deep at Camp. *Los Angeles Times,* April 4, A3.

Foster, Gaines M.
1987 *Ghosts of the Confederacy: Defeat, the Lost Cause, and the Emergence of the New South, 1865 to 1913.* Oxford University Press, New York.

Fraser, Gertrude J.
1998 *African American Midwifery in the South: Dialogues of Birth, Race, and Memory.* Harvard University Press, Cambridge, Massachusetts.

Frazier, Deborah
1999 Search Close on Exact Location of 1864 Indian Village Massacre. *Denver Rocky Mountain News,* May 26, A17.
2000 House Bill to Address Sand Creek Monument. *Denver Rocky Mountain News,* October 2, A4.

Freeman, Douglas Southall
1934–1935 *R. E. Lee, a Biography.* Charles Scribner's Sons, New York.

Frisch, Michael

1989 American History and the Structure of Collective Memory: A Modest Exercise in Empirical Iconography. *Journal of American History* 75(4):1131–55.

1990 *A Shared Authority: Essays on the Craft and Meaning of Oral and Public History.* State University of New York Press, Albany.

Gee, Clarence S.

1958 John Brown's Fort. *West Virginia History* 19(2):93–100.

Glassberg, David

1990 *American Historical Pageantry: The Uses of Tradition in the Early Twentieth Century.* University of North Carolina Press, Chapel Hill.

1996 Public History and the Study of Memory. *The Public Historian* 18(2):7–23.

Glastris, Paul

1997 Spoiling a Proper Memorial. *U.S. News,* May 5, at www.usnews.com.80/usnews/issues/970505/5week.htm (accessed June 5, 1999).

Gondos, Victor

1963 Karl S. Betts and the War Centennial Commission. *Military Affairs* 27:51–65.

Gonzales, P., and R. Rodriguez

1999 Bridges Needed to Unite Cultures. *Denver Post,* April 4, G-02.

Goodall, Heather.

1999 Telling Country: Memory, Modernity and Narratives in Rural Australia. *History Workshop Journal* 47:160–90.

Gorn, Elliot J.

2000 Professing History: Distinguishing between Memory and the Past. *Chronicle of Higher Education* 46(34):B4–B5.

Grande Reenactment

1961 Grande Reenactment: The Battle of First Manassas (Bull Run), July 22–23, 1961. First Manassas Corp. Pamphlet. On file, Manassas National Battlefield Park, Manassas, Virginia.

Grant, Ulysses S.

1885–1886 *Personal Memoirs of U.S. Grant.* Century, New York.

Graphic [newspaper, Chicago]

1892 John Brown's Old Fort. January 9. On file, Museum and Galleries, Chicago Historical Society, Chicago.

Greto, Victor

1999 "Reconnaissance-Level" Archaeology Digs up Artifacts Believed to Pinpoint Site of 1864 Massacre. *Houston Chronicle,* July 7, A6.

Griego, T.
1998 A Foot Note to History: Amputation of New Mexico Statue Underlines 400-Year-Old Grudge. *Denver Rocky Mountain News,* June 21, A14.

Grit
1961 Manassas Refought; This Time, Most of Casualties Are among Spectators. July 23, 6.

Handler, Richard, and Eric Gable
1997 *The New History in an Old Museum: Creating the Past at Colonial Williamsburg.* Duke University Press, Durham, North Carolina.

Handlin, Oscar, and Mary Handlin
1950 Origins of the Southern Labor System. *William and Mary Quarterly* 7(2):199–222.

Handy, Moses P. (ed.)
1893 *The Official Directory of the World's Columbian Exposition, May 1st to October 30th, 1893. A Reference Book of Exhibitors and Exhibits; of the Officers and Members of the World's Columbian Commission, the World's Columbian Exposition and the Board of Lady Managers; a Complete History of the Exposition. Together with Accurate Descriptions of All State, Territorial, Foreign, Departmental and Other Buildings and Exhibits, and General Information concerning the Fair.* W. B. Conkey, Chicago.

Hanley, Ray
1992 The Gray Reunion. *Civil War Times Illustrated,* January/February, 43.

Harris, Neil
1970 Introduction. In *The Land of Contrasts: 1880–1901,* edited by Neil Harris, 1–28. George Braziller, New York.

Harwit, Martin
1996 *An Exhibit Denied: Lobbying the History of the Enola Gay.* Copernicus, New York.

Hass, Kristin A.
1998 *Carried to the Wall: American Memory and the Vietnam-Veterans-Memorial.* University of California Press, Berkeley.

Hearn, Chester G.
1996 *Six Years of Hell: Harpers Ferry during the Civil War.* Louisiana State University Press, Baton Rouge.

Higginson, Thomas Wentworth
1971 *Army Life in a Black Regiment.* [Orig. published 1870.] Corner House Publishers, Williamstown, Massachusetts.

Hill, Michael, and Thomas Fleming
1995 The New Dixie Manifesto. *Washington Post,* October 29, C3.

Hinton, Richard
1894 *John Brown and His Men.* Funk and Wagnalls, London.

Historic Preservation Association
2000a Alabama Governor Fob James Declares April "Confederate History & Heritage Month." Historic Preservation Association, at www.hpa.org/alabamaheritage.html (accessed June 9, 2000).
2000b Guarding Our Future by Preserving Our Past. Historic Preservation Association, at www.hpa.org/aboutpa.html (accessed June 9, 2000).

Hobsbawm, Eric
1983a Introduction: Inventing Tradition. In *The Invention of Tradition,* edited by Eric Hobsbawm and Terrence Ranger, 1–14. Cambridge University Press, New York.
1983b Mass-Producing Tradition: Europe, 1870–1914. In *The Invention of Tradition,* edited by Eric Hobsbawm and Terrence Ranger, 263–307. Cambridge University Press, New York.

Horton, James
1998 Confronting Slavery and Revealing the "Lost Cause." *CRM* 21(4):14–20.
2000 Freedom Fighters: African Americans, Slavery, and the Coming Age of the Civil War. Paper presented at the National Park Service Symposium on Strengthening Interpretation of the Civil War Era. Ford's Theater National Historic Site, Washington, D.C., May 9.

Howe, Stephen
1999 Speaking of '98: History, Politics and Memory in the Bicentenary of the 1798 United Irish Uprising. *History Workshop Journal* 47:222–39.

Hsu, Spencer S.
1998 Slavery "Abhorred," Gilmore Says: Words Anger Confederate Defenders; Event Upsets Rights Groups. *Washington Post,* April 10, C1, C7.

Hughes, Jim
2000 Tribes Fetes Sand Creek Designation Recognition of Massacre "Still Seems Like a Dream." *Denver Post,* November 12, A1.

Hughes, Langston, Milton Meltzer, and Eric Lincoln
1973 *A Pictoral History of the Negro in America.* 5th ed. Crown Publishers, New York.

Irish-American [newspaper, New York City]
1863 Corcoran's Irish Legion. August 1.

Jefferson County Court Records (on file, Jefferson County Court House, Charleston, West Virginia)

1901 Alexander Murphy vs. J. D. Billmyer, Sheriff, Administrator of Kate Field, dcsd, Circuit Court of Jefferson County, Chancery Book K:27, November, 192–94.

1902a Alexander Murphy vs. Kate Field's Administrator and Others, Circuit Court of Jefferson County, Chancery Book K:247.

1902b Alexander Murphy vs. Kate Field et al., Circuit Court of Jefferson County, Chancery Book K:307.

Jefferson County Deed Book (on file, Jefferson County Court House, Charleston, West Virginia).

1895 Vol. 91 (July 23):473–74.

Jet Magazine

1995 Monument to the First Black Killed at Harpers Ferry Raid Draws Criticism. September 18, 22–23.

Jimenez, A.

1998 Don Juan de Onate and the Founding of New Mexico: Possible Gains and Losses from Centennial Celebrations. *Colonial Latin American Historical Review* 7(2):109–28.

Johnson, Mary

1995 Heyward Shepherd Memorial and John Brown Fort Tablet, Harpers Ferry National Historical Park. On file, Harpers Ferry National Historical Park, Harpers Ferry, West Virginia.

1997 An "Ever Present Bone of Contention": The Heyward Shepherd Memorial. *West Virginia History* 56:1–26.

Johnson, Sam

1995 Prepared Statement of Congressman Sam Johnson before the Senate Committee on Rules and Administration Hearing on the Smithsonian Institution: Management Guidelines for the Future. Federal News Service: Federal Information System Corp., May 18.

Jones, R. A.

1996 Whitewashing Manzanar. *Los Angeles Times,* April 10, B2.

Jordan, Winthrop

1978 Unthinking Decision: Enslavement of Negroes in America to 1700. In *Interpreting Colonial America,* edited by Kirby Martin, 140–61. Harper & Row, New York.

Journal Messenger

1961 125,000 See Spectacular Reenactment of Manassas Battle on Henry Plateau: Crowds Brave 100 Degrees at Observance. July 27, 1.

Journal of American History

1995 "History and the Public: What Can We Handle?" A Round Table about History after the Enola Gay Controversy. 82(3):1029–114.

Joyner, Charles
1984 *Down by the Riverside.* University of Illinois Press, Urbana.

Kammen, Michael
1991 *Mystic Chords of Memory: The Transformation of Tradition in American Culture.* Knopf, New York.
1997 Public History and the Uses of Memory. *The Public Historian* 19(2):49–52.

Kane, Michael B.
1970 *Minorities in Textbooks: A Study of the Treatment in Social Studies Texts.* Quadrangle Books, Chicago.

Karsner, David
1934 *John Brown Terrible "Saint."* Dodd, Mead, New York.

Kaye, Harvey
1994 Review of *Mystic Chords of Memory:* The Transformation of Tradition in American Culture, by Michael Kammen. *American Quarterly* 46(2):257.

Keita, S. O. Y., and Rick A. Kittles
1997 The Persistence of Racial Thinking and the Myth of Racial Divergence. *American Anthropologist* 99(3):534–44.

Kilty, William
1799 *The Laws of Maryland. Volume I.* Printed by Frederick Green, Printer, Annapolis, Maryland.

Knott, J. O.
1936 The Re-Enactment at Manassas. Editorial. *Washington Post,* July 24. Newspaper clipping. On file, Manassas National Battlefield Park Archives, Manassas, Virginia.

Kohl, Philip L.
1998 Nationalism and Archaeology: On the Constructions of Nations and the Reconstructions of the Remote Past. *Annual Review of Anthropology* 27:223–46.

Kook, Rebecca
1998 The Shifting Status of African Americans in the American Collective Identity. *Journal of Black Studies* 29(2):154–78.

Kulikoff, Allan
1986 *Tobacco and Slaves: The Development of Southern Culture in the Chesapeake, 1680–1800.* University of North Carolina Press, Chapel Hill.

La Capra, Dominick
1998 *History and Memory after Auschwitz.* Cornell University Press, Ithaca, New York.

Larrabee, John
1997 Blacks Claim Share of Civil War Glory: The Growing Number of

Blacks in Reenactment Groups Recalls the Sacrifices of Thousands Who Fought and Died. *USA Today*, June 2, A3.

Larson, P. M.
1999 Reconsidering Trauma, Identity, and the African Diaspora: Enslavement and History Memory in 19th-Century Highland Madagascar. *William and Mary Quarterly* 56(2):335–62.

Lauerhass, Ludwig
1997 *The Shaw Memorial: A Celebration of an American Masterpiece.* Eastern National, Conshohocken, Pennsylvania.

Layman, B. J.
1970 Monument Ambiguity at Harpers Ferry. *Washington Post.* Newspaper clipping. On file, Harpers Ferry National Historical Park, Harpers Ferry, West Virginia.

League of the South
2000 The Right of Secession, at www.dixienet.org/position/seceed.htm (accessed June 9, 2000).

Leff, Mark
1995 Revisioning U.S. Political History. *American Historical Review* 100(3):829–53.

Leiberman, Leonard, and Fatimah Linda C. Jackson
1995 Race and Three Models of Human Origin. *American Anthropologist* 97(2):231–42.

Leone, Mark P.
1981 Archaeology's Relationship to the Present and the Past. In *Modern Material Culture: The Archaeology of Us,* edited by Richard A. Gould and Michael B. Schiffer, 5–14. Academic Press, New York.

Leone, Mark P., Parker B. Potter Jr., and Paul A. Shackel
1987 Toward a Critical Archaeology. *Current Anthropology* 28(3):283–302.

Letters (on file, Harpers Ferry National Historical Park, Harpers Ferry, West Virginia)
N.d. Field, Kate, to *Chicago Daily News,* Murphy family collection.
N.d. Walker, James, to Miss Pearl Tatum (Tatten), undated typescript, reel 117, flash 9.
1895 Chambers to Field, November 4.
1895 Cummins, C. T., to Kate Field, August 11.
1895 McCabe to Field, November 12.
1895 Stuckwain, Stuckwain, and Neeser to Field, November 4.
1922 Taylor, Lee R., to McDonald, November 16, reel 113, flash 4.
1932 McDonald, Henry T., to J. R. Clifford, Esq., March 17, HAFE microfilm, reel 123, flash 9.

1932 McDonald, Henry, to Walter White, March 25, HAFE microfilm, reel 123, flash 9.

1932 McDonald, Henry, to Walter White, April 25, HAFE microfilm, reel 123, flash 9.

1932 White, Walter, to Henry McDonald, March 23, HAFE microfilm, reel 123, flash 9.

1932 White, Walter, to Henry McDonald, April 16, HAFE microfilm, reel 123, flash 9.

1932 White, Walter, to Henry McDonald, May 2, HAFE microfilm, reel 123, flash 9.

1943 Andrews, Matthew Page, to Hon. Jennings Randolph, HAFE microfilm, reel 117, 1.

1943 Powell, Sally Lee, to Jennings Randolph, HAFE microfilm, reel 117.

Letters (Heyward Shepherd Binder, HFR 299, on file, Harpers Ferry National Historical Park, Harpers Ferry, West Virginia)

1980 Draft letter, reply to Lucille Bush, United Daughters of the Confederacy, February 1, 1980.

Letters (Heyward Shepherd Folder, on file, park historian, Harpers Ferry National Historical Park, Harpers Ferry, West Virginia)

1970 Prentice, Joseph R., to Ben———, August 28, A36.

1980 Campbell, Donald, to Mrs. James Johns, division president, United Daughters of the Confederacy, July 15.

1981 Headen, Herbert H., West Virginia State Conference of Branches of the National Association for the Advancement of Colored People, to James G. Watt, secretary, U.S. Department of the Interior, October 5.

1994 Cummings, Eliot, to Donald Campbell, January 13.

1994 Cummings, Eliot, to Roger Kennedy, September 23.

1994 Grabows, Gene Haney, to Donald Campbell, March 17.

1994 Sollers-Hoffmaster, Virginia, to Donald Campbell, June 15.

1995 Cummings, Elliot G., to Jesse Helms, January 30.

1995 Fafarman, Lawrence, to Bruce Noble, September 20.

1995 Helms, Jesse, to Marilyn Merrill, April 3.

1995 Palmer, Margaret S., to Bruce Noble, November 8.

1995 Pitcaithley, Dwight, to Elliot Cummings, July 17.

Letters (McDonald/Sutler Collection, vol. 1, on file, Harpers Ferry National Historical Park, Harpers Ferry, West Virginia)

1931 Sutler, Boyd B., to Henry T. McDonald, October 4.

Letters (McDonald Collection, on file, Harpers Ferry National Historical Park, Harpers Ferry, West Virginia)

1931 Andrews, Matthew Page, to Henry T. McDonald, McDonald Collection, box 4, folder 3, October 12.

1931 Hill, Charles E., to Henry McDonald, McDonald Collection, box 4, folder 3, November 15.

1931 McDonald, Henry T., to *Afro-American,* McDonald Collection, box 4, folder 3, October 6.

1931 McDonald, Henry T., to Matthew Page Andrews, McDonald Collection, box 4, folder 3, October 15.

1931 McDonald, Henry T., to Matthew Page Andrews, McDonald Collection, box 4, folder 3, October 19.

1931 McDonald, Henry, to Carl Murphy, McDonald Collection, box 4, folder 3, November 13.

1931 McDonald, Henry T., to Walter White, McDonald Collection, box 4, folder 3, October 8.

1931 McDonald, Henry, to Walter White, McDonald Collection, box 4, folder 3, October 19.

1931 Murphy, Carl, to Henry McDonald, McDonald Collection, box 4, folder 3, November 12.

1931 Tatum, Pearl, to Henry McDonald, McDonald Collection, box 4, folder 3, September 22.

1931 White, Walter, to Henry T. McDonald, McDonald Collection, box 4, folder 3, October 6.

1931 Winters, O. Wilson, to Henry T. McDonald, McDonald Collection, box 4, folder 3, October 16.

1931 Winters, O. Wilson, to Pearl Tatum, McDonald Collection, box 4, folder 3, October 16.

1932 Barber, Max J., to Henry T. McDonald, McDonald Collection, box 5, folder 5, February 21.

1932 McDonald, Henry, to J. Max Barber, McDonald Collection, box 5, folder 5, February 23.

Letters (Storer College Binder, on file, Harpers Ferry National Historical Park, Harpers Ferry, West Virginia)

1922 Campbell, George H., to Henry T. McDonald, June 23.

1922 Carr, Julian S., to Daniel Willard (president, Baltimore & Ohio Railroad), May 12.

1922 Proposed inscription, Heyward Shepherd Memorial, June 2.

1922 Recorder (Henry McDonald) to Willard, June 2.

1922 Willard, Daniel, to Henry McDonald, June 27.

1943 McDonald, Henry T., to Dr. Ford, November 11, 1–2.

Levinson, Sanford

1998 *Written in Stone: Public Monuments in Changing Societies.* Duke University Press, Durham, North Carolina.

Libby, Jean
1979 *Black Voices from Harpers Ferry: Osborne Anderson and the John Brown Raid.* Libby, Palo Alto, California.

Lifton, Robert J., and G. Mitchell
1995 *Hiroshima in America: Fifty Years of Denial.* G. P. Putnam's Sons, New York.

Linenthal, Edward T.
1993 *Sacred Ground: Americans and Their Battlefields.* University of Illinois Press, Urbana.

Linenthal, Edward, and Tom Engelhardt
1996 *History Wars: The Enola Gay and other Battles for the American Past.* Henry Holt, New York.

Linton, Ralph
1943 Nativistic Movements. *American Anthropologist* 45(2):230–40.

Lipsitz, George
1998 *The Possessive Investment in Whiteness: From Identity Politics.* Temple University Press, Philadelphia.

Little, Barbara J.
1994 People with History: An Update on Historical Archaeology in the United States. *Journal of Archaeological Method and Theory* 1(1):5–40.

Loewen, James
1999 *Lies across America: What Our Historic Sites Get Wrong.* New Press, New York.

Logan, Charles Rusty
1996 "Something So Dim It Must Be Holy": Civil War Commemorative Sculpture in Arkansas, 1865–1934. National Register of Historic Places, Washington, D.C.

Love, Alice A.
1995 Latest Round in War of the Statue Pits Warner against GOP Women. *Roll Call,* October 5, 3.

Lowenthal, David
1985 *The Past Is a Foreign Country.* Cambridge University Press, Cambridge.
1996 *Possessed by the Past: The Heritage Crusade and the Spoils of History.* Free Press, New York.
1997 History and Memory. *The Public Historian* 19(2):31–39.

Lyon, James S.
1882 *War Sketches. From Cedar Mountain to Bull Run.* Buffalo, New York.

Mackintosh, Barry
1985 *The Historic Sites Survey and National Landmarks Program: A History.* History Division, National Park Service, Department of the Interior, Washington, D.C.

Magee, Rex B.

1960 Letter, Rex B. Magee to Robert J. Radcliff, March 24. In First Manassas (a Prospectus), a Commemorative Reenactment of a Great Moment in History, a Ceremony Officially Opening the Civil War Centennial Years 1961–1965, 17. On file, Manassas National Battlefield Park, Manassas, Virginia.

Malin, James

1942 *John Brown and the Legend of Fifty-Six.* American Philosophical Society, Philadelphia.

Manassas Battlefield Confederate Park

1923 The Manassas Battlefield Confederate Park. On the Battlefield Manassas (Bull Run): A Fitting Federal Tribute, an Unsurpassed Confederate Symbol, an Endowed Educational Center, a National Asset. On file, Manassas National Battlefield Park, item no. 1911, acc. 52.

Manassas Journal

1911 The Great Peace Jubilee: President Taft Closes Last Chapter with Hearty Approval—Brings Peace Message. July 28, 1, 7.

1921 Crowd Gathers at Henry House for Park Inaugural Ceremony. July 22, 1.

1936a Reenactment of First Manassas Battle, July 21. July 16, 1.

1936b There Stands Jackson. July 16.

Markovits, Andrei S., and Simon Reich

1997 *The German Predicament: Memory and Power in the New Europe.* Cornell University Press, Ithaca, New York.

Martin, Erika, Mia Parsons, and Paul Shackel

1997 Commemorating a Rural African-American Family at a National Battlefield Park. *International Journal of Historical Archaeology* 1(2):157–77.

Martinsburg Journal

1964 No title. November 12, 8.

1976 UDC Delegates Plan for Safe Keeping of Monument. August 3, 7.

Mason Report

1860 Testimony of John D. Starry. *Select Committee of the Senate Appointed to Inquire into the Late Invasion and Seizure of the Public Property at Harpers Ferry.* Senate Report 278, 36th Cong., 1st sess., 1859–1860, 23–36.

Masters, Edgar Lee

1922 *Children of the Market Place.* Macmillan, New York.

1926 *Lee: A Dramatic Poem.* Macmillan, New York.

Mauser, Kate
2000 Changes in the Offing for Civil War Sites. Perspectives Online, at www.theaha.org/perspectives/issues/2000/0003/0003new1.cfm (accessed June 9, 2000).

McConnell, Stuart
1992 *Glorious Contentment: The Grand Army of the Republic, 1865–1900.* University of North Carolina Press, Chapel Hill.

McDonald, Henry T.
1931 Remarks at the Unveiling of the Heyward Shepherd Marker, October 10, 1931. McDonald Collection. On file, Harpers Ferry National Historical Park, Harpers Ferry, West Virginia.

McFeely, William
1997 The Impact of African-American Soldiers on the Civil War. Paper presented at Hope and Glory: Centennial Celebration of the Augustus Saint-Gaudens Monument to Robert Gould Shaw and the Fifty-Fourth Massachusetts Regiment, Boston, May 29.

McPherson, James M.
1969 Foreword to *A Brave Black Regiment: History of the Fifty-Fourth Regiment of Massachusetts Volunteer Infantry 1863–1865.* Arno Press and the New York Times, New York.
1982 *Ordeal By Fire: The Civil War and Reconstruction.* Alfred A. Knopf, New York.
1988 *Battle Cry of Freedom: The Civil War Era.* Oxford University Press, New York.

Melton, R. H.
2001 Va. Scraps Tribute to Confederacy: Gilmore Salutes Includes Unionists. *Washington Post,* March 21, A1, A19.

Meltzer, Milton, and Patricia Holland (eds.)
1982 *Lydia Maria Child: Selected Letters, 1817–1880.* University of Massachusetts Press, Amherst.

Meyer, Eugene L.
1995 As Civil War Monument Returns, So Does Controversy. *Washington Post,* July 10, C1, C2.

Minutes of the Civil War Centennial Commission
1960a Records of the Civil War Centennial Commission. January 5, 1960. Box 22, R.G. 79. National Archives, Washington, D.C.
1960b Records of the Civil War Centennial Commission. June. Box 20, R.G. 79, National Archives, Washington, D.C.
1961 Records of the Civil War Centennial Commission. December. Box 21, R.G. 79, National Archives, Washington, D.C.

Morgan, Edmund
1975 *American Slavery: American Freedom.* W. W. Norton, New York.
Morton, Samuel G.
1839 *Crania Americana.* Dobson, Philadelphia.
Morton, Susan
1939 Seventy-Eight Years Ago: Bull Run Battlefield: Some Intimate Sketches of the Sites Closely Associated with the Battle of Bull Run, with Sidelights on Places and People, from Original and Authoritative Sources. J. T. Richards, Bull Run, Virginia.
Mukhopadhyay, Carol C., and Yolanda T. Moses
1997 Reestablishing "Race" in Anthropological Discourse. *American Anthropologist* 99(3):517–33.
Murphy, Mrs. Will
1961 Personal communication, June 19.
Murry, Freeman H. M.
1916 *Emancipation and the Freed in American Sculpture: A Study in Interpretation.* Freeman Murry, Washington, D.C.
Nash, Gary
1974 *Red, White, and Black: The Peoples of Early America.* Prentice Hall, Englewood Cliffs, New Jersey.
Nash, Gary B., Charlotte Crabtree, and Ross E. Dunn
1998 *History on Trial: Culture Wars and the Teaching of the Past.* Knopf, New York.
National Register of Historic Places
1996 "Something So Dim It Must Be Holy": Civil War Commemorative Sculpture in Arkansas, 1865–1934. National Register of Historic Places, Washington, D.C.
National Tribune
1890 Valuable History Matters. June 12.
Neustadt, Richard, and Ernst May
1986 *Thinking in Time: The Uses of History for Decision-Makers.* Free Press, New York.
Newsweek (magazine)
1963 Gettysburg: "The Task Remaining." July 15, 18.
New York Times (newspaper, New York City)
1961 No title. January 9, 1. Newspaper clipping. On file, Manassas National Battlefield Park Archives, Manassas, Virginia.
1962 No title. September 22, 1, 50. Newspaper clipping. On file, Manassas National Battlefield Park Archives, Manassas, Virginia.
Nobile, Philip
1995 *Judgement at the Smithsonian.* Marlowe & Company, New York.

Nora, Pierre
1999 *Realms of Memory: Rethinking the French Past.* Translated by Arthur Goldhammer. Columbia University Press, New York.

Norkunas, Martha K.
1993 *The Politics of Memory: Tourism, History, and Ethnicity in Monterey, California.* State University of New York Press, Albany.

Nunn, William C.
1956 *Escape from Reconstruction.* Texas Christian University Press, Fort Worth.

Oates, Stephen B.
1970 *To Purge This Land with Blood: A Biography of John Brown.* Harper & Row, New York.

O'Donnell, Mike
1986 *At Manassas: Reunions, Reenactments, Maneuvers.* Rapidan Press, Mechanicsville, Virginia.

Omi, Michael, and Howard Winant
1994 *Racial Formation in the United States.* Routledge, New York.

Onesty, Catherine
1961 First Battle of Manassas—First Great Battle. *Alexandria Gazette,* May 23, 14–17.

Patriot (pseudonym)
1936 The Re-Enactment at Manassas. Editorial. *Washington Post,* July 24. Newspaper clipping. On file, Manassas National Battlefield Park Archives, Manassas, Virginia.

Patterson, John
1989 From Battle Ground to Pleasure Ground: Gettysburg as a Historic Site. In *History Museums in the United States: A Critical Assessment,* edited by Warren Leone and Roy Rozenzweig, 128–57. University of Illinois Press, Chicago.

Peri, Y.
1999 The Media and Collective Memory of Yitzhak Rabin's Remembrance. *Journal of Communication* 49(3):106–24.

Peterson, Merrill
1994 Lincoln in American Memory. Oxford University Press, New York.

Pitcaithley, Dwight
1996 Personal communication, National Park Service chief historian, June 21.

Pittsburgh Courier (Pittsburgh, Pennsylvania)
1931 Heyward Shepherd Memorial. October 24.

Pollard, Edward A.
1866 *The Lost Cause: A New Southern History of the War of the Confederates.* E. B. Treat, New York.

Poppenheim, Mary, et al.

1938 *The History of the Daughters of the Confederacy.* Garrett and Massie, Richmond, Virginia.

Potts, L.

2000 Onate Gets His Day. *Albuquerque Tribune,* March 7, A1.

Powell, Colin

1997 General Colin Powell on the 100th Anniversary of the Shaw Monument. *The Museum of Afro American History* (newsletter), September, 1–2.

Public Ceremony

1997 Hope and Glory: Centennial Celebration of the Augustus Saint-Gaudens Monument to Robert Gould Shaw and the Fifty-Fourth Massachusetts Regiment. Boston, May 31.

Public Law

1997 Public Law 105–29. 105th Congress, July 24.

Quarles, Benjamin

1974 *Allies for Freedom; Blacks and John Brown.* Oxford University Press, New York.

Rabinow, Paul

1992 For Hire: Resolutely Late Modern. In *Recapturing Anthropology,* edited by Richard Fox, 59–72. School of American Research Press, Santa Fe, New Mexico.

Rainey, Reuban M.

1983 The Memory of War: Reflections on Battlefield Preservation. In *The Yearbook of Landscape Architecture,* edited by Richard L. Austin, Thomas Kane, Robert Z. Melnick, and Suzanne Turner, 69–89. Van Nostrand Reinhold, New York.

Reardon, Carol

1997 *Pickett's Charge in History and Memory.* University of North Carolina Press, Chapel Hill.

Redpath, James

1860 *The Public Life of Captain John Brown.* Thayer and Eldridge, Boston.

Reingold, Beth, and Richard S. Wike

1998 Confederate Symbols, Southern Identity, and Racial Attitudes: The Case of the Georgia State Flag. *Social Science Quarterly* 79(3):568–80.

Richmond News Leader

1936 Thousands See Manassas Rites: Synthetic War Is Played on Manassas Battlefield. July 21. Newspaper clipping. On file, Manassas National Battlefield Park Archives, Manassas, Virginia.

Roberts, Diane

1998 The New Dixie Manifesto; Coming to Your Neighborhood: The

Secret War to Bring Back the Old South. *Utne Reader,* January–February, 67–69, 101–3.

Robinson, Richard
1996 Personal communication with Erika Martin, April 5.
1998 Personal communication with Erika Martin, September 12.

Rogers, P.
1997 W.W. II Internment Camp Survivors Upset by Lack of Progress on Memorial. *San Jose Mercury News,* March 10, A1.

Rolle, Andrew F.
1965 *The Lost Cause: The Confederate Exodus to Mexico.* University of Oklahoma Press, Norman.

Rolston, Bill
1999 Are the Irish Black? *Race and Class* 41(1/2):95–102.

Roseberry, William
1992 Multiculturalism and the Challenge of Anthropology. *Social Research* 59(4):841–58.

Rosenberg, Scott
1999 Monuments, Holidays, and Remembering Moshoeshoe: The Emergence of National Identity in Lesotho, 1902–1966. *Africa Today* 46(1):48–72.

Ross, C.
1991 Return to Manzanar. *Americana* 19(1):55–58.

Round, George Carr
1911 The Manassas Jubilee: Aftermath. Four pages printed. On file, Manassas National Battlefield Park, Manassas, Virginia.
1917 Is the United States Too Poor to Own Its Own Monuments? Brochure. On file, Manassas National Battlefield Park, Manassas, Virginia.
1918 Letter, George Carr Round to Senator Cross, July 21. On file, Manassas National Battlefield Park, Manassas Virginia, 1303–15.

Ruchames, Louis (ed.)
1959 *A John Brown Reader.* Aleland-Schuman, New York.

Ruffins, Fath Davis
1991 Mythos, Memory, and History: African American Preservation Efforts, 1820–1990. In *Museums and Communities: The Politics of Public Culture,* edited by Ivan Karp, Christine Mullen Kreamer, and Steven D. Lavine, 506–611. Smithsonian Institution Press, Washington, D.C.

Sacharnoski, Jennifer
1998 Historian Active in Fight to Protect Civil War Sites. *The News* (Frederick, Maryland), June 11, A7.

Saint-Gaudens, Homer
1913 *The Reminiscences of Augustus Saint-Gaudens.* 2 vols. The Century Company, New York.

Sanborn, Franklin B.
1885 *Life and Letters of John Brown: Liberator of Kansas, and Martyr of Virginia.* Roberts Brothers, Boston.

Sandage, Scott A.
1993 A Marble House Divided: The Lincoln Memorial, the Civil Rights Movement, and the Politics of Memory, 1939–1963. *Journal of American History* 80(1):135–67.

Sandri, Kenneth
1994 *Architectural Fabric Investigation and Documentation of the Robinson House.* Manassas National Battlefield Park, National Capital Region, Williamsport Preservation Training Center, Williamsport, Maryland.

Savage, Kirk
1994 The Politics of Memory: Black Emancipation and the Civil War Monument. In *Commemorations: The Politics of National Identity,* edited by John R. Gillis, 127–49. Princeton University Press, Princeton, New Jersey.
1997a The Monument to Robert Gould Shaw and the Fifty-Fourth Massachusetts Regiment. Paper presented at Hope and Glory: Centennial Celebration of the Augustus Saint-Gaudens Monument to Robert Gould Shaw and the Fifty-Fourth Massachusetts Regiment. Boston, May 29.
1997b *Standing Soldier, Kneeling Slaves: Race, War, and Monument in Nineteenth-Century America.* Princeton University Press, Princeton, New Jersey.

Savery, Thomas
N.d. Savery Collection. Letter. Microfilm, A&M 399. Hagley Museum, Wilmington, Delaware.

Scham, Sandra A.
1998 Mediating Nationalism and Archaeology: A Matter of Trust? *American Anthropologist* 100(2):301–8.

Schultz, Duane
1990 *Month of the Freezing Moon: The Sand Creek Massacre, November 1864.* St. Martin's Press, New York.

Scott, Douglas D.
2003. Oral Tradition and Archaeology: Conflict and Concordance Examples from Two Indian War Sites. In *Remembering Landscapes of Conflict,* edited by Paul A. Shackel. *Historical Archaeology* 37(3):55–65.

Shackel, Paul A.
1995 Terrible Saint: Changing Meanings of the John Brown Fort. *Historical Archaeology* 29(4):11–25.

1996 *Culture Change and the New Technology: An Archaeology of the Early American Industrial Era.* Plenum, New York.

2000 *Archaeology and Created Memory: Public History in a National Park.* Kluwer Academic/Plenum, New York.

Shanks, Michael, and Christopher Tilley

1987 *Re-Constructing Archaeology.* Cambridge University Press, Cambridge.

Shepherdstown Register

1931 October 15. Newspaper clipping. Heyward Shepherd Binder, Harpers Ferry National Historical Park, Harpers Ferry, West Virginia.

Simmons, Marc

1991 *The Last Conquistador: Juan de Onate and the Settling of the Southwest.* University of Oklahoma Press, Norman.

Smedley, Audrey

1993 *Race in North America: Origin and Evolution of Worldview.* Westview Press, Boulder, Colorado.

1998 "Race" and the Construction of Human Identity. *American Anthropologist* 100(3):690–702.

Southern Party

2000a Constitution of the Southern Party, at www/southernparty.org/constitu.htm (accessed June 9, 2000).

2000b Our View on Independence, at www/southernparty.org/positions/independence.htm (accessed June 9, 2000).

2000c Why a Southern Party, at www/southernparty.org/why-a-sp.htm (accessed June 9, 2000).

Spirit of Jefferson [newspaper, Charles Town, West Virginia] On file, Harpers Ferry National Historical Park, Harpers Ferry, West Virginia

1888 No title. August 14, 1.

1889 No title. September 17, 3.

1890 No title. October 21, 2.

1894 No title. June 1, 2.

1895a No title. August 27, 2.

1895b No title. October 1, 2.

1895c No title. October 8, 2.

1902 No title. February 18, 3.

1903 No title. August 18, 2.

1976 UDC Members Discuss Monument Location, Park Supt. Conway. August 5.

1995 The Monument to Heyward Shepherd. July 27.

Stanton, Robert

1998 NPS Founder's Day Memo to All Employees from Director Robert

Stanton. Memorandum, on file, Department of the Interior, National Park Service, Washington, D.C.

Stephenson, Alexander
1870 *Constitutional View of the Late War between the States: Its Cause, Character, Conduct and Results Presented in a Series of Colloquies at Lake Liberty Hill.* National Publishing Company, Philadelphia.

Sturman, Shelley
1997 August Saint-Gaudens' Memorial to Robert Gould Shaw and the Massachusetts Fifty-Fourth Regiment. Brochure. National Gallery of Art. September 21–December 14, 1997.

Sunday Star
1961 Editor's Commentary. July 23, D4.

Taft, Lorado
1969 *The History of American Sculpture.* [Orig. published 1924.] Arno Press, New York.

Teski, Marea C., and Jacob J. Climo
1995 Introduction. In *The Labyrinth of Memory: Ethnographic Journeys,* edited by Marea C. Teski and Jacob J. Climo, 1–10. Bergin & Garvey, Westport, Connecticut.

Thomas, David
1926 *Arkansas in War and Reconstruction, 1861–1874.* United Daughters of the Confederacy, Arkansas Division, Little Rock.

Thomas, David Hurst
2000 *Skull Wars: Kennewick Man, Archaeology, and the Battle for Native American Identity.* Basic Books, New York.

Thompson, Benjamin F.
1903 *An Authentic History of the Douglass Monument.* Rochester Herald Press, Rochester, New York.

Thompson, Robert Farris
1989 The Song That Named the Land: The Visionary Presence of African-American Art. In *Black Art Ancestral Legacy: The African Impulse in African-American Art,* edited by Alvin Wardlaw, 97–132. Dallas Museum of Art, Dallas.

Trigger, Bruce
1989 *A History of Archaeological Thought.* Cambridge University Press, Cambridge.

Trouillot, Michel-Rolph
1995 *Silencing the Past: Power and Production of History.* Beacon Press, Boston.

Tucker, H. St. George
1936 Opening Invocation. Manuscript M 38 M. On file, Manassas National Battlefield Park, Manassas, Virginia.

Tucker, Neely
2001 A Wheelchair Gains a Place at FDR Memorial. *Washington Post*, April 5, C1, C8.

Turner, Ronald Ray
1993 *An Annotated Census for Prince William County, Virginia 1850.* Prince William County, Manassas, Virginia.

United Daughters of the Confederacy—National Chapter (UDC)
1920 *Minutes of The Twenty-seventh Annual Convention of The United Daughters of The Confederacy*, Asheville, North Carolina, November 9–13, 38–40.
1921 Report of the Faithful Slave Memorial Committee, *Minutes of the Twenty-Eighth Annual Convention of the United Daughters of the Confederacy*, St. Louis, Missouri, November 8–12, 56, 207–10.
1922 Report of the Faithful Slave Memorial Committee, *Minutes of the Twenty-Ninth Annual Convention of the United Daughters of the Confederacy*, Birmingham, Alabama, November 14–18, 216–18.
1924 Report of the Faithful Slave Memorial Committee, *Minutes of the Thirty-First Annual Convention of the United Daughters of the Confederacy*, Savannah, Georgia, November 18–22, 226–28.
1925 Report of the Faithful Slave Memorial Committee, *Minutes of the Thirty-Second Annual Convention of the United Daughters of the Confederacy*, Hot Springs, Arkansas, November 17–21, 225–29.
1931 Report of the Faithful Slave Memorial Committee, *Minutes of the Thirty-Eighth Annual Convention of the United Daughters of the Confederacy*, Jacksonville, Florida, November 17–21, 58–61.

United Daughters of the Confederacy—West Virginia State Chapter (UDC-WV)
1923 Report of Division Historian (Orra Tomlinson), *Minutes of the Twenty-Fifth Annual Convention of the West Virginia Division of the United Daughters of the Confederacy*, Martinsburg, West Virginia, September 18–19, 20.

U.S. Civil War Centennial Commission
1968 *The Civil War Centennial: A Report to Congress.* U.S. Civil War Centennial Commission, Washington, D.C.

U.S. War Department
1880, 1885 *War of the Rebellion: A Compilation of the Official Records of the Union and Confederate Armies.* Series I, vols. 2 and 12. U.S. War Department, Washington, D.C.

Unrau, Harlan D.
1996 *The Evacuation and Relocation of Persons of Japanese Ancestry during World War II: A Historical Study of the Manzanar War Relocation Center.* 2 vols. U.S. Department of the Interior, National Park Service, Washington, D.C.

Updike, Fritz
1961 An American Heritage: Bull Run Re-Enactment Shows Spirit American Needs Today. Unknown newspaper article from scrapbook. On file, Manassas National Battlefield Park, Manassas, Virginia.

Villard, Oswald Garrison
1910 *John Brown, 1800–1859: A Biography Fifty Years After.* Houghton Mifflin, New York.

Virginia Civil War Centennial Commission
1965 Final Report 1865. Records of the Civil War Centennial Commission. R.G. 79, box 91. National Archives, Washington, D.C.

Virginia Free Press
1859a No title. October 20, 2.
1859b No title. October 27, 2.
1867 No title. May 23, 2.
1879 No title. November 29, 2.
1881 No title. June 18, 2.
1884a No title. October 16, 2.
1884b No title. November 13, 2.
1887a No title. January 6, 3.
1887b No title. October 29, 2.
1887c No title. November 3, 2.
1888a No title. January 16, 2.
1888b No title. December 4, 2.
1892 No title. September 7, 2.
1893 No title. July 19, 2.
1894 No title. August 15, 2.
1895 No title. August 7, 2.
1896 No title. January 22, 2.
1899 No title. October 25, 2.
1902 No title. July 31, 2.

Visweswaran, Kamala
1998 Race and the Culture of Anthropology. *American Anthropologist* 100(1):70–83.

Vitanza, Thomas
1999 Personal communication with Paul Shackel, June 26.

Volz, J. Leonard
1961 Critique—Reenactment of the Battle of First Manassas. Draft memorandum from J. Leonard Volz, regional chief of visitor protection, to regional director. On file, Manassas National Battlefield Park, Manassas, Virginia, August.

Von Holst, Hermann
1888 *John Brown.* Cupples and Hurd, Boston.
Wallace, Anthony F. C.
1956 Revitalization Movements. *American Anthropologist* 58(2):264–81.
Wallace, Michael
1981 Visiting the Past: History Museums in the United States. *Radical History Review* 25(1981):63–96.
1998 The Battle of the Enola Gay. In *Hiroshima's Shadow,* edited by Kai Bird and Lawrence Lifschultz, 317–37. The Pamphleteer's Press, Stony Creek, Connecticut.
Warren, Robert Penn
1929 *John Brown: The Making of a Martyr.* Payson and Clarke, New York.
Washington Evening Star
1936 35,000 Watch Confederates Conquer Yanks at Manassas. July 21. Newspaper clipping. On file, Manassas National Battlefield Park Archives, Manassas, Virginia.
Washington Post
1936 "Sham" Battle of Bull Run to Be July 21; U.S. Soldiers to Enact Famous Fight; Field to Be Dedicated; Thousand Men on Each Side Will Depict Conflict. July 6. Newspaper clipping. On file, Manassas National Battlefield Park Archives, Manassas, Virginia.
1965 Unknown title. April 10, 3. Newspaper clipping. On file, Manassas National Battlefield Park Archives, Manassas, Virginia.
1997a Poll Shows Majority Support Confederate History Month in Va. May 19, B3.
1997b Va. Cross Burning Reported. May 3, B5.
1999 A Debatable Picture of the Confederacy: Tenn. Museum Says Many Blacks Fought for South; Scholars Call Claim Bogus. December 27, A16.
Washington Tribune
1932 No title. May 27, HAFE microfilm, reel 123, flash 1.
Webb, Richard
1861 *The Life and Letters of Captain John Brown, Who Was Executed at Charles Town, Virginia, 2 December 1859, for an Armed Attack upon American Slavery.* Smith Elder, London.
White, Jean M.
1961 50,000 at Manassas Brave 101-Degree Heat. Unknown newspaper article from scrapbook. On file, Manassas National Battlefield Park, Manassas, Virginia.
White, Rodney A.
1989 The Monument in the Box: The Journal's Weekend Magazine. *Martinsburg Journal* 12(23), June 10, 4, 11.

Whitfield, Stephen
1987 Sacred in History and in the Art: The Shaw Memorial. *New England Quarterly* 60(1):3.
Widner, Ralph W., Jr.
1982 *Confederate Monuments: Enduring Symbols of the South and the War between the States.* Andromedia, Washington, D.C.
Will, George F.
1997 Ladies in the Rotunda. *Washington Post,* February 23, C7.
Williams, George W.
1969 *A History of the Negro Troops in the War of the Rebellion, 1861–1865.* [Orig. published 1888.] Negro University Press, New York.
Williamson, Joel
1984 *The Crucible of Race: Black-White Relations in the American South since Emancipation.* Oxford University Press, New York.
Wilshire, Francis F.
1948 Interview with McKinley Robinson, February 21 and 27 and March 12, 1948. On file, Manassas National Battlefield Park, Manassas, Virginia.
1960 Letter, Francis F. Wilshire to James J. Geary, March 27, 1960. In First Manassas (a Prospectus), a Commemorative Reenactment of a Great Moment in History, a Ceremony Officially Opening the Civil War Centennial Years 1961–1965, 14–15. On file, Manassas National Battlefield Park, Manassas, Virginia.
Wilson, Charles Reagan
1980 *Baptized in Blood: The Religion of the Lost Cause, 1865–1920.* University of Georgia Press, Athens.
Wilson, Hill Preeble
1913 *John Brown Soldier of Fortune: A Critique.* Hill P. Wilson, Lawrence, Kansas.
Winchester Star [newspaper, Winchester, Virginia]
1995 Our Opinion. Harpers Ferry: Why the Fuss about Heyward Shepherd? August 24, E1.
Wolf, Eric
1990 Distinguished Lecture: Facing Power—Old Insights, New Questions. *American Anthropologist* 92(3):596–96.
Wolfe, Medora Mason
1961 First Manassas Corp. Scores Victory in Reenactment of First Battle of Bull Run. *Alexandria Gazette,* July 24. Newspaper article from scrapbook. On file, Manassas National Battlefield Park, Manassas, Virginia.

Woodward, C. Vann

1952 John Brown's Private War. In *America in Crisis,* edited by Daniel Aaron, 109–30. Alfred A. Knopf, New York.

1993 *The Burden of Southern History.* 3rd ed. Louisiana State University Press, Baton Rouge.

Workman, Courtney

2001 "The Woman Movement": Memorial to Women's Rights Leaders and the Perceived Images of the Women's Movement. In *Myth, Memory and the Making of the American Landscape,* edited by Paul A. Shackel, 47–66. University Press of Florida, Gainesville.

Zenzen, Joan M.

1995 Battling for Manassas: The Fifty-Year Preservation Struggle at Manassas National Battlefield Park. History Associates, Inc., Rockville, Maryland. On file, Manassas National Battlefield Park, Manassas, Virginia.

1998 *Battling for Manassas: The Fifty-Year Struggle at Manassas National Battlefield Park.* Pennsylvania State University Press, University Park.

INDEX

ABOUT THE AUTHOR

Paul Shackel is a professor of anthropology at the University of Maryland. He received his Ph.D. from the State University of New York at Buffalo in 1987 and has been teaching at the University of Maryland since 1997. Previously, he was employed as an archaeologist at Harpers Ferry National Historical Park.

Shackel also serves as director of the Center for Heritage Resource Studies in the Department of Anthropology, University of Maryland. The Center provides leadership and encourages research in applied activities that focus on the relationship between the uses of the past, local cultural expression, and the natural environment.

Shackel is interested in the ways material items are used by individuals and groups in order to create social relations and group identity. Material culture is a powerful tool that can express gender, ethnicity, class, and power relations. Taking an anthropological and historical perspective of material culture allows him to pursue questions on how the value and meaning of goods may change over time in order to define and redefine individual and group relations. Shackel is interested in what nationally significant sites mean to the American public and how they help create and maintain a national identity. Material culture plays a significant role in revealing controversial issues of our country's development, such as labor, racism, and slavery.

Some of Shackel's recent books include *Myth, Memory and the Making of The American Landscape* (University Press of Florida, 2001); *Archaeology and Public Memory: Harpers Ferry after the Civil War* (Kluwer/Plenum, 2000); *Annapolis Pasts: Contributions from Archaeology in Annapolis* (with Paul Mullins and Mark S. Warner; University of Tennessee Press, 1998); *Culture Change and the New Technology: An Archaeology of the Early American Industrial Era* (Plenum, 1996); *Historical Archaeology of the Chesapeake* (with Barbara J. Little) (Smithsonian Institution Press, 1994); and *Personal Discipline and Material Culture: An Archaeology of Annapolis, Maryland, 1695–1870* (University of Tennessee Press, 1993).